THE HOUSE THAT
MADIGAN BUILT

THE HOUSE THAT MADIGAN BUILT

THE RECORD RUN OF
ILLINOIS' VELVET HAMMER

RAY LONG

Foreword by
Charles N. Wheeler III

**UNIVERSITY OF
ILLINOIS PRESS**
Urbana, Chicago, and Springfield

Library of Congress Cataloging-in-Publication Data
Names: Long, Ray, author.
Title: The house that Madigan built : the record
    run of Illinois' Velvet Hammer / Ray Long.
Other titles: Record run of Illinois' Velvet Hammer
Description: Urbana : University of Illinois Press,
    [2022] | Includes bibliographical references and
    index.
Identifiers: LCCN 2021042920 (print) | LCCN
    2021042921 (ebook) | ISBN 9780252044472
    (cloth) | ISBN 9780252053481 (ebook)
Subjects: LCSH: Madigan, Michael J. | Illinois.
    General Assembly. House of Representatives—
    Speakers—Biography. | Legislators—Illinois—
    Biography. | Chicago (Ill.)—Politics and
    government—1951- | Chicago (Ill.)—Biography.
Classification: LCC F546.4.M28 L66 2022 (print) |
    LCC F546.4.M28 (ebook) | DDC 973.7092 [B]—
    dc23/eng/20211006
LC record available at https://lccn.loc.gov/
    2021042920
LC ebook record available at https://lccn.loc.gov/
    2021042921

To my parents, Scott and Elizabeth Long, and my sister, Marilyn Mayberry, whose support and love have inspired me from the day I was born.

And a special dedication and thanks to my life partner, Peggy Boyer Long. We fell in love in the Capitol pressroom. A former statehouse reporter and magazine editor, she shared invaluable insights as this book took shape.

CONTENTS

Foreword   Charles N. Wheeler III   ix

Preface   xvii

Introduction: The Long Reign   1

PART I: THE LEGEND

1   Remap Victory   15

2   White Sox Miracle   29

3   Operation Cobra   41

PART II: POWER PLAYS AND POLITICAL FLOPS

4   Historic Impeachment   55

5   Partisan Math   73

6   The Art of Persuasion   84

7   Pension Failure   97

PART III: A CAREER POLITICAL LEADER

8   A Patronage Army   121

9   Madigan and Madigan   136

10   The Politics of Money   147

PART IV: CRACKS IN THE SYSTEM

11 Turning Point   163

12 Ups and Downs   180

13 Shams?   188

14 Marty's Campaign   202

PART V: THE FALL

15 Himself   213

16 Public Official A   220

Epilogue   231

Acknowledgments   239

Notes   243

Index   275

Photographs follow page 111

FOREWORD

CHARLES N. WHEELER III

If Richard J. Daley of Chicago was the "American Pharaoh," so titled by the authors of a 2000 biography of "Da Mare," his most notable protégé, Michael J. Madigan, has been characterized as another notable in the history of ancient Egypt. "Mike is like the Sphinx: he sits and listens and looks and never changes expression; you don't quite know where he's coming from," former Illinois Senate President Philip J. Rock told an oral history interviewer in 2009.

Now Madigan, the longest-serving legislative leader in U.S. history, has seen his long reign come to an end, ironically fifty years to the day he first took the oath as a state representative in 1971 and thirty-eight years since he first assumed the Illinois House speakership he had held for all but two years since. Supporters and detractors—and there are many in each group—generally agree that few lawmakers can match Madigan's work ethic, intense focus, and political acumen. "He plays three-dimensional chess while everybody else is playing checkers" was a frequent comment, and he was typically long regarded as inscrutable as the famed monument from antiquity.

In the following pages, readers will get an up-close look at some of the highlights and low points of the former speaker's long tenure, provided by veteran *Chicago Tribune* investigative reporter and onetime Springfield bureau chief Ray Long, who has covered Madigan for some forty years. But I go back even further with Madigan, to 1969 and his very first time in public office as a delegate to the Sixth Illinois Constitutional Convention, which I covered as a rookie reporter for the *Chicago Sun-Times*. So from my half-century vantage point, I hope to offer readers a bit of perspective to pave the way for the fascinating vignettes that follow.

A frequent complaint/compliment about Madigan was that he has no policy agenda, nothing that can label him as liberal or conservative, fiscal hawk or reckless spender—just an obsession with power, with wanting a Democratic-controlled House with him as its speaker. And until January 2021, he was very good at it—Democrats have enjoyed a House majority for thirty-six of thirty-eight straight years, a run made possible in part because Madigan and Co. drew the maps in 1981, 2001, and 2011. He left his Democratic successors in good shape to draw the districts for the 2022 elections. What's most impressive, though, is that Madigan won House majorities in four out of the five elections held under the 1991 redistricting plan, a Republican gerrymander. True, demographic changes helped thwart the GOP aims, yet Republicans held the Senate for the entire ten-year period.

While Madigan is gone from the top job, he gifted new House Speaker Emanuel "Chris" Welch of Hillside with a 73–45 supermajority. But I submit there's more to the story than just another would-be autocrat, that indeed there are several threads that run throughout Madigan's decades in the speakership that help explain his overriding interest in keeping the Illinois House in Democratic hands.

True, he had no public policy agenda that he tried to advance, unlike some other leaders, a point that reporters have chided him on in the past. His response? Being tied to specific positions on individual issues would handicap his flexibility to respond to the challenge of the moment: What is the path forward that would best elect Democratic House candidates? He did not pursue grander ambitions—say, a run for U.S. Senate or for governor; he was not one to indulge in wishful thinking, even before the relentless Republican character assassination of the last two decades. Rock's unsuccessful bid for the party's 1984 U.S. Senate nomination would give one food for thought; despite solid credentials, the Senate president came in fourth, more than 250,000 votes behind winner Paul Simon and trailing two less-qualified candidates, state Comptroller Roland Burris and attorney Alex Seith.

Nor has Madigan sought the chairmanship of the Cook County Democratic Party, the post held by his legendary mentor, Richard the First, from

1953 until his death in 1976. Chicago has fifty wards and Cook County has thirty townships, Madigan explained to a reporter years ago. All have local Democratic organizations, all of which have fund-raising banquets, golf outings, and assorted other events that the chairman might be expected to attend, few of which would appeal to Madigan. But didn't he chair the state Democratic Party for years? Correct, but about the only public event he usually showed up for in that role was Democratic Day at the Illinois State Fair.

So what motivates Madigan? Keeping a Democratic majority has allowed him to succeed in two key areas: protecting the city of Chicago and its institutions from suburban barbarians at its gates, and safeguarding the Illinois General Assembly's constitutional role as a coequal branch of government.

Consider a few examples of his success in defending the structure of his beloved city: Probably most notably, when Harold Washington was elected as Chicago's first Black mayor in 1983, he faced a City Council dominated by powerful opposition aldermen determined to thwart his every initiative, led by Edward Vrdolyak of the Tenth Ward and Edward M. Burke of the Fourteenth. In the ensuing "Council Wars," Washington had only twenty-one of the fifty aldermen with him, as the two Eddies and their cohorts dictated the agenda. As part of the plan, the anti-Washington forces' legislative allies introduced measures that would strip power from the mayor and shift it to the City Council. But Speaker Madigan slammed the door; the bills never saw the light of day. As he explained to reporters at the time, his Thirteenth Ward alderman, John S. Madrzyk, would vote with the white ethnics in the Chicago City Council, but he would not tolerate bringing "Beirut by the Lake" to Springfield.

Less colorful but just as important to Chicago and Cook County was Madigan's adamant refusal in 1991—in tandem with Senate President Rock—to agree to the property tax caps that newly elected Republican Governor Jim Edgar wanted to impose on all local taxing bodies statewide in order to deliver on one of his main campaign pledges. The stalemate also included the fight over whether to make the temporary tax hike permanent, as described more fully in chapter 3.

The standoff between the rookie GOP governor and the veteran Democratic leaders pushed the legislature into nineteen days of overtime before a compromise was reached. Edgar got his tax caps but only in Chicago's five "collar counties," excluding home-rule cities. Madigan and Rock temporarily protected Chicago, Cook County, and its scores of other local governments, villages and schools, parks and libraries, even mosquito abatement districts, from state-mandated limits on how much they could ask property owners to pony up.

The speaker also consistently rebuffed suburban Republican efforts to strip control of O'Hare and Midway airports from the city and lodge it with a regional authority, ostensibly to provide more efficient operation. More jaded observers figured the suburbanites were more interested in the airports' jobs and contracts than in their operations; whatever their intent, though, Madigan thwarted them at every turn. As an aside underscoring the speaker's all-consuming interest in his troops' electoral fate, some Northwest Side Chicago Democrats would routinely vote for the Republican efforts with Madigan's blessing. A bill losing by a few votes is just as dead as a bill getting swamped; those "no" votes would endear the lawmakers to constituents' complaining about O'Hare noise. And granting these lawmakers the flexibility ultimately made the speaker's majority bloc of Democrats stronger.

Madigan's other recurring concern has been keeping well-defined boundaries between the executive branch and the legislative branch, as a succession of governors have tried in the speaker's eyes to encroach on General Assembly powers. The best example might be the 2009 impeachment of former Democratic Governor Rod Blagojevich for assorted offenses. The most eye-catching, of course, was Blagojevich's attempt to sell the U.S. Senate seat being vacated by President-elect Barack Obama. More despicable, I submit, was his effort to shake down the executive of a children's hospital that was owed state reimbursement for pediatric care. But five of the thirteen counts in the House impeachment resolution detailed Blagojevich's encroachment on legislative authority. One instance—his refusal to accept a joint legislative panel's rejection of his attempt to expand health-care programs without lawmakers' approval, which the resolution described as "utter disregard of the doctrine of separation of powers."

A few years later, Madigan and Senate President John Cullerton joined together to sue Governor Pat Quinn, a fellow Democrat, when the populist crusader cut legislative salaries out of the budget in an effort to force lawmakers to approve cost-saving changes in state pension systems. The leaders contended that Quinn's veto violated the separation-of-powers doctrine, and the court agreed, restoring lawmakers' paychecks.

Madigan also waged an ongoing battle against what he considered governors' abuse of the amendatory veto (AV), a constitutional provision that allows the chief executive to rewrite legislation and return it to lawmakers for their approval. In fact, as a Con-Con delegate, Madigan voted to include the AV in the new charter, which he later reflected was likely his biggest mistake at the convention. The struggle goes back decades, to what the speaker saw as former Republican Governor Jim Thompson's penchant for playing legislator. So amendatory veto messages that Madigan deemed beyond mere tweaks were rejected. Some folks suggested a political power struggle over the substance of the bills, but not infrequently what Thompson proposed in an amendatory veto would surface later and follow the regular path to enactment. The speaker objected to the process as gubernatorial usurpation of the General Assembly's role in lawmaking, and for some years House rules have called for all AVs to be cleared by the rules committee as not overstepping the governor's bounds before they can be considered on the floor. Even so, Madigan routinely worked with Thompson on a host of major issues, most famously keeping the White Sox in Chicago, as you'll see in chapter 2.

While Madigan's quest for House control often has been aided by favorable maps, the speaker also actively promotes candidates with campaign staff and fund-raising help and then, once elected, affords them opportunities to burnish their records for the next campaign. For example, in the late 1990s Madigan played an outsized role in legislative efforts to regulate mega hog farms, industrial-size pork-producing factories. A reasonable question might be, Why would a guy from Sixty-Fourth and Keeler get involved in the nitty-gritty of livestock management? Because the issue was important in legislative races in western Illinois, Madigan pushed for local regulation of the industry, in line with Democratic candidates' platforms.

Nor was Madigan hesitant to go against some of the same special interests that helped fill his campaign war chest, as long as the move would aid House Democrats on the campaign trail. As a case in point, a 2005 law that limited non-economic damages, so-called pain and suffering, in medical malpractice suits to $500,000 in cases against doctors and $1 million against hospitals. The trial lawyers—among Madigan's largest and most reliable contributors—vehemently opposed the measure, which the speaker shepherded through the House and ultimately into law. Why had he apparently betrayed significant supporters? The explanation was simple. The medical society, the hospitals, and other cap proponents had waged a successful public relations campaign that convinced downstaters, particularly in Southern Illinois, that they were about to lose healthcare providers because of rising malpractice insurance premiums. So an "aye" vote was good politics for Democrats representing those areas. One might suspect Madigan also was counting on the Illinois Supreme Court to declare the new law unconstitutional, as it had with two prior efforts to limit damage awards. And so it was in 2010, when the justices held that the law impermissibly infringed on a jury's right to determine damages, in violation of the separation-of-powers doctrine.

Similarly, Madigan outraged teachers and public workers in 2013 when he engineered passage of a measure to cut their retirement benefits. Here, too, one wonders whether Madigan figured the courts would strike the new law, ruling that it violated the constitutional guarantee of pension benefits. After all, he was there for the extended convention debate attending its addition to the new charter. Still, the speaker insisted the proposal would pass muster, only to be contravened two years later by a unanimous high court opinion tossing the law. But adopting the ill-fated measure bought his members a couple of years' relief from the strident voices calling for pension cuts.

One could even see Madigan's departure in that same vein—passing the torch to a new generation, reflecting the changes in a younger and more diverse caucus than Madigan first led some four decades ago. After nineteen of the seventy-three incoming Democrats publicly vowed not to support Madigan for speaker, some pundits speculated a protracted leadership battle, perhaps rivaling the ninety-three-ballot marathon in 1975, before Madigan ultimately would prevail. Others foresaw what actually transpired: Still a shrewd vote counter, he chose not to try to coerce his members to repudiate their public stance against him, which would likely be tantamount to political suicide. Instead, he chose to relinquish the post he had held for so long.

Wrapping up, the cartoon image that Republican operatives present of the former speaker—a combination of Darth Vader and Lord Voldemort, the worst thing to happen to Illinois since Lincoln's assassination—really doesn't pass a fact check, in this writer's opinion. Recall former Republican Governor Bruce Rauner's lament that he wasn't in charge, that Madigan has called the shots? "We've been a state controlled by one person, one person, for 35 years," Rauner said in late 2017. "And until that changes, we don't have a good future."

Political scientists and historians might dispute Rauner's assessment. No House speaker—not even Madigan—can "control" the state, where the Senate and a competent governor would play a role. And thirty-five years prior to Rauner's complaint, 1982, the House speaker was actually Republican George Ryan and the governor was Republican Jim Thompson. Moreover, the state had twenty-one more years of Republicans in the governor's mansion before Blagojevich arrived in 2003.

A fitting final witness would be former Senator James "Pate" Philip, the Wood Dale Republican and Senate president from 1993 to 2003. During a chance meeting a few years ago at the wake for Jim Harry, the Senate secretary during Philip's presidency, I asked Philip whether he agreed with the governor that Madigan controlled everything, including himself. No, Pate said, he got along well with Madigan, whom he described as a man of his word. It was hard to get Madigan to give his word, Philip added, but once he did, you could count on it. An interesting observation, I thought, coming a few months after Rauner came under fire for lying to conservative lawmakers and even to Chicago Cardinal Blase Cupich by promising them he would veto an abortion rights bill and then signing it into law.

Keeping one's word might be the First Commandment of politics, one that to my knowledge Madigan has always honored. So on balance, I submit Michael J. Madigan leaves a record as speaker of near-unrivaled political skill in service of two overarching goals—protecting Chicago and its institutions, and safeguarding the legislative branch of Illinois government against executive branch encroachment. Along the way, he oversaw changes that would have been unthinkable to a twenty-eight-year-old Madigan embarking on a legislative career—legalized gambling, recreational marijuana, concealed carry, abolition of the death penalty, gay marriage, to name a few. Bottom line, in my opinion, Madigan has been a positive force for the state of Illinois. Whether you agree is your decision, of course, but after reading the in-depth chapters that follow, you'll be much better informed to make that call.

PREFACE

This book represents my attempt to give readers a chance to size up the unprecedented career of former Illinois House Speaker Michael J. Madigan, the longest-serving leader of any state or federal legislative body. Madigan has had more impact on Illinois than any other politician in the last half century. For better or worse, he put his thumbprint on virtually every issue big and small. The following pages offer a look at Madigan's public role. It's not a biography of his entire life, though the influences of people like his mentor, Mayor Richard J. Daley, are explained when they help to better understand Madigan. Knee-jerk Madigan haters will think this book goes easy on him; Madigan lovers will think it hits him too hard. That is what happens when a journalist attempts an objective character study that shows how the longtime speaker handled the events and issues before him. So it goes.

My goal is to offer a true, accurate, and fair depiction of some of Madigan's biggest moments. There are chapters that will amaze or anger you, including a play-by-play of the White Sox Miracle. There are chapters that let you geek out on policy, such as taxes and pensions. But they will give you the on-the-scene detail of a secret tax hike plan called Operation Cobra and a major political calculation Madigan made on a pension reform he championed. There are chapters on how Madigan handled patronage and impeachment. And there are chapters that give readers a peek into how a big-city boss runs an old-fashioned, aggressive, ward-style political operation and the overzealous allegiance of those around him. This book also provides an overview of what knocked Madigan off stride and, eventually, out of the speakership he held for all but two years from 1983 to early 2021. Most people in or around state government have a Madigan story they will think should be in here, but I've tried to sift through my files and firsthand memories to pull out the most telling tales dating from the time I first covered him forty-plus years ago, the times he was on top, the times he was under fire.

Many of the stories are culled from my own work since I started covering the Illinois state Capitol in 1981, the first year Madigan became a legislative leader, the first of two terms when he was Minority Leader Madigan. For most of those four decades, I covered all or part of each session as a reporter based in the statehouse pressroom. In the competitive journalism of politics and government in Chicago and Illinois, no one reporter captured the total picture. I've broken my share of stories about Madigan, but the truth is that many reporters across the state have contributed to the trove of tales that help define him. I worked on numerous stories over the years with great reporting partners, such as Rick Pearson, my predecessor at the statehouse and the *Tribune*'s stellar political writer since 1998, and Christi Parsons, my longtime *Tribune* bureau mate in Springfield, who went on to become president of the White House Correspondents Association and is now with CNN. This book takes note of many reporters and news organizations, including competitors, who told stories that the speaker did not want reported. For without reporters willing to dig out facts, we wouldn't know half of what's in this book. The secretive Speaker Madigan was not one to volunteer a lot of information, especially in his latter days at the helm of the House. It is with the spirit of shining a light onto major public officials that I've noted the authors of many scoops along the way. Madigan and scores of major figures of his era shaped the political landscape. Reporters wrote about the good and bad, the balls and strikes, the power plays and political flops.

Throughout my career at five different news outlets—*The Telegraph* of Alton, the Peoria *Journal Star*, the *Chicago Sun-Times*, the Associated Press (AP), and the *Chicago Tribune*, where I've spent nearly a quarter of a century—I always managed to work my way back to the statehouse, what I viewed as the "Greatest Beat on Planet Earth." Washington reporters rightfully can lay claim to that title intermittently, depending on the year, the crises facing the nation, or, of course, the president's good or bad behavior. Statehouse reporters in Albany, Austin, Annapolis, Boston, Indianapolis, Sacramento, and Tallahassee can make a fair argument for the title in their own times of turbulence. Chicago City Hall also is a monster beat, among the toughest of the competitive hotspots in the entire country and one I've covered myself. But the Illinois statehouse is a never-ending mosh pit of sophisticated, complex, and raucous politics. Big-city, suburban, and rural values collide every day with an unusually strong desire to put greed and partisanship over positive progress for all. Since the 1970s, four Illinois governors have gone to federal prison—one for crimes after leaving office and the others for misdeeds while in office. One state senator from Illinois—the self-proclaimed "skinny kid with a funny name" from the South Side of Chicago—went straight from the Illinois General Assembly to the U.S. Senate and then quickly moved into the White House. This is the world of Michael J. Madigan, who held the speakership for thirty-six years, a period never before seen and one that may never be seen again.

Over the years, Madigan carried a presence that no lawmaker could match, gaining respect with each legislative victory, each bill he reshaped to fit his needs, each politician who tried to take him on and lost. But his winning ways too often overlooked the people inside and outside his own organization who got run over along the way, too often by the staffers he put in charge of carrying out his government and politics, too often out of the public eye. His old-style patronage ways, developed under the elder Mayor Daley, brought the speaker periodic scrutiny, including as part of the Commonwealth Edison bribery scandal that eventually cost him the speakership.

Madigan's first year as a legislative leader was the same spring session that I began as a full-time intern, so green I could barely be called a cub reporter. I was assigned to the statehouse bureau of *The Telegraph* of Alton. The pressroom was loaded with legends led by the Peoria *Journal Star*'s Bill O'Connell, whose sidekick was the self-proclaimed sorcerer's apprentice, Loren Wassell. They shared a room with Dennis McMurray, the Alton *Telegraph* bureau chief, who was my boss, and Tom Schafer, who ran the Gannett bureau. Down the hall was the *St. Louis Post-Dispatch*'s Bill Lambrecht, the *Chicago Tribune*'s Daniel Egler and Mitch Locin, the AP's Bob Springer, the *Belleville News-Democrat*'s Barb Hipsman, Lee Enterprises' intensely driven Mike Lawrence—all part of a couple of dozen TV, radio, and print reporters looking to scoop each other every day. This pressroom did it all, hard-hitting investigations and daily scoops that could match the finest work in the country. It was a marvelous place to learn. At the *Chicago Sun-Times*, there was the hard-charging G. Robert Hillman and budget guru Charles N. Wheeler III, the statehouse press corps president. Wheeler had covered every step of Madigan's rise since 1969, when he arrived as a delegate for the state's Sixth Constitutional Convention and won his first House race in 1970. Wheeler, who eventually became director of the graduate-level Public Affairs Reporting Program at the University of Illinois Springfield, chronicled the full Madigan run as a reporter and political analyst. It is an honor that he wrote the foreword to this book with an eye toward the arc of the speaker's tenure.

Keeping watch over the state Capitol is formidable—even more difficult when overloaded with one-of-a-kind characters whose ideologies and attitudes clash every day under the glistening chandeliers of the House and Senate chambers. Along with the ever-calculating Madigan, leading actors in the political theater of 1981 became household names in Illinois, such as the bigger-than-life Republican Governor Jim Thompson and the deep-voiced, cigar-chomping GOP deal cutter George Ryan, speaker of the last "Big House" of 177 lawmakers. Throw in a politically mischievous absence, courtesy of outgoing Democratic Senator Harold Washington, who was headed to Congress before he would rise to mayor of Chicago. Add a touch of mayhem as Thompson led a minority party of Senate Republicans that temporarily denied the gavel in the Senate to President Phil Rock, an Oak Park Democrat. Perhaps it is fitting that the disruptive Senate leadership fight was resolved on—what else?—a party-line decision written by the Democratic majority in the Illinois Supreme Court. It's no wonder the rollicking spring session I first covered culminated with partisan fisticuffs in the Illinois Senate. Two years later, Madigan began his record reign as speaker.

THE LONG REIGN

"It's not easy."
—Speaker Michael Madigan, Illinois
  House floor, June 1, 2019

What does the speaker think? At the Illinois state Capitol, the question loomed over every major issue. The question came in over the phones, got whispered in the hallways, popped up at committee hearings, and rolled out in press conferences. It's a simple query, of course, one that is expected to be asked in statehouses all across America. In Illinois, though, the answer carried far greater weight. For in Illinois politics, the House speaker's moves at the end of the twentieth century and the beginning of the twenty-first provided a road map for how Illinois got to where it is today.

Have you talked to the speaker about your legislation? Can you get your bill through the House? What does he want? These questions dominated internal debate in Springfield, be it on guns, pensions, education, gay rights, or taxes, before a vote was contemplated, let alone taken. The same questions were asked time after time—by Democrats and Republicans, ranking lawmakers and rookies, lobbyists, labor and business leaders, reporters and editors, generations of governors, and, yes, mayors of Chicago.

All wanted to know the positions of the secretive man who did more to shape Illinois politics, government, and laws than anyone in the last half century: House Speaker Michael Joseph Madigan, chairman of the

Democratic Party of Illinois, committeeman of Chicago's Thirteenth Ward, lifelong resident of the city's Southwest Side. Wielding the gavel for all but two years from 1983 to early 2021, making him the nation's longest-serving speaker, Madigan built the House where he ruled. But in a larger sense, he built the house where Illinoisans lived. What the speaker thought became more than an academic question. The answer gave the best clues for politicians who wondered which ideas would succeed or suffocate.

Lori Lightfoot nodded to that dynamic even before she took the oath of office as Chicago's mayor in 2019. She provided a modern template for how to cope in a world dominated by Madigan. Despite railing against machine-style politics on her way to a historic landslide victory, Mayor-Elect Lightfoot immediately traveled to Springfield to give Madigan his due. After meeting with rookie Democratic Governor J. B. Pritzker, she went to the speaker's Capitol suite and then addressed the House.

When she emerged from Madigan's office, Lightfoot offered no apologies to her far-left critics, long tired of the speaker's Springfield reign. She gave a carefully worded comment to reporters eager to hear what went down between the incoming Democratic mayor—the Black, openly gay, progressive, former federal prosecutor—and the all-powerful speaker, a straight, white Democrat schooled in Irish, ward-style politics a half century earlier by Mayor Richard J. Daley, the party boss who perfected the Chicago machine. "The speaker occupies an important space in state government," Lightfoot said. "We're not going to be aligned on every issue, but he's an important person to the city of Chicago."[1] Understated, to be sure, Lightfoot's neutral remarks acknowledged the clear political and practical realities: loved, revered, hated, or feared, Madigan commanded an outsized role.

Lightfoot knew that Madigan could help determine the success of the new mayor in fighting crime and violence, bolstering public education, building better roads, expanding mass transit, landing a casino, and delivering the social services that Chicago needed to prosper. Long a protector of Chicago's interests, Madigan, when conferring with Lightfoot, only further fueled discussions about what the speaker's thoughts and plans might be—a new chapter of speculation in the most popular parlor game in Springfield.

It all played into the Madigan Mystique—which existed somewhere between real and perceived power. Whether one viewed Madigan as a genius, a jerk, or both, he managed consistently to mesmerize his admirers and frustrate his foes. Madigan's political opponents found themselves beaten down so often by his persistent but subtle force that he became known early on as "The Velvet Hammer." He underscored the nickname when he first lifted the wooden gavel as speaker in 1983 and called the House to order. Instead of the hammer-like slams that his Republican predecessor George Ryan often used to quiet the chamber, Madigan held the barrel-shaped end of the gavel and tapped the handle lightly on the podium. To the astonishment of lawmakers, the House went silent. Madigan grinned. "This is a new era," he said.[2]

Madigan's career could be a tragedy worthy of the classics. He rode old-school politics to the mountaintop and lived at the height of power for decades. He ran Springfield as if it were his own personal kingdom, the Capitol a palace where he commanded so much authority that lobbyists groveled and his own rank-and-file Democrats too often crawled. He expected House Democrats to vote for him for speaker and support his House rules. Voting against Madigan could mean losing out on being the chair of a committee—and the extra ten thousand dollars that went with the post. In 2017 Madigan handed out gift bags with engraved clocks to mark his record run as the nation's longest-serving speaker, but he pointedly stiffed the one House Democrat who voted "present" rather than support Madigan's speakership for another term.

Madigan sought capitulation on budgets, legislation, prominent projects, and discreet deals—all in the name of building a reputation of strength and consolidating one of the most formidable political operations in the nation. He put winning above ideology. He demanded fanatical loyalty and got it. He outworked, outmaneuvered, and outlasted whoever got in his way. All of these qualities enabled him to rise in the pantheon of Illinois politics, but confidence in his control, faith in his old-school methodology, a preternatural pull toward patronage-style politics, and a blind spot for friends ultimately brought him down. After years of doing whatever he wanted with a sly, unmatched hubris—an attitude picked up by imperious minions who abused the authority he delegated—the speaker's long reign crumbled from within.

Michael J. Madigan long wanted to be a powerful leader, much in the form of his mentor, the first Mayor Daley. And Madigan fulfilled that goal a thousand times over, the student expanding on his mentor's playbook throughout all branches of state and local government, from judges to county officeholders to statewide officials. "The person that finds themselves as a leader in the legislature is pretty much in the position to shape exactly how they wish to perform their job. They can be strong or they can be weak. Active or passive. In my case, I decided years ago that I wanted to be a strong legislative leader, an active legislative leader," Madigan once mused. "I would hope that, acting from a position of strength, that I do good things, not bad things. I would hope."[3]

Over the years, Madigan has been viewed as conservative, moderate, and liberal—depending on the time and the topic. A social conservative early on, which fit with his Catholic upbringing, the speaker opened up as the members in his caucus pushed him to lead a chamber that voted for same-sex marriage, an expansion of abortion rights, and a ban on the death penalty. Once representing a heavily white enclave on the Southwest Side, he still racked up big wins when the population tilted Hispanic. He fought to scale back public pension benefits for public employees, but then labor rallied around him when he rebuffed aggressive efforts to roll back union rights. He shunned labels. "I always classified myself as a Democrat," Madigan said following the 2016 Democratic National Convention. "I don't use an adjective when I describe my political party. I'm a Democrat. I've been a Democrat for a long time. I've seen, experienced, lived through significant changes in the American Democratic Party."[4]

Madigan worked meticulously through a series of cold calculations as he read every bill, often looking to tweak a line here and there with the goal of strengthening his grip. He lorded over a vaunted political machine filled with payrollers and Thirteenth Ward precinct workers willing to travel the state to help Democratic candidates win. He raised political cash at a clip that made his competitors envious. And he poured money into races wherever he thought he could topple a foe.

Extremely deliberative, Madigan usually knew how to make a course correction when he misread political winds. He lost the Illinois speakership in the 1994 nationwide Republican tide that empowered U.S. Representative Newt Gingrich to take over the House in Washington. But Madigan built a political team that—despite running in districts gerrymandered to favor Republicans—took back the Illinois House two years later. He once took a political potshot at a rising Democratic star named Barack Obama by deriding him as "The Messiah."[5] But then Madigan gave Obama's presidential campaign a lift by moving up the Illinois primary to help Obama's race for the Democratic nomination. He would later propose $100 million for Obama's presidential center on Chicago's South Side, host him in the House chamber for a presidential address, and call for putting a giant painting of Obama in the House opposite the portrait of Abraham Lincoln. Madigan sparred repeatedly with Democratic Governor Rod Blagojevich and then backed him for reelection in 2006. But the speaker launched impeachment proceedings two years later when the FBI took Blagojevich away in handcuffs. In 2018 Madigan acted quickly to quell calls for him to step down from his state and political posts because of the way he handled accusations of sexual harassment and abusive behavior among his top aides: he jettisoned the offenders, including a longtime chief of staff, rather than keep them in his inner circle, showing once again that knowing when to act is a huge reason he had stayed around so long. Yet political concerns among a diverse caucus that had more women than men lingered over the speaker.

In person Madigan thrived on an intimidating ice-blue glare. Though in early years he unleashed thunderous floor speeches, he delivered fewer high-energy speeches later in his career. His words became more deliberate and determined, depending more on a recitation of facts in floor speeches than sound and fury. He counted on votes in the precincts and on the House floor more than on the number of syllables he spoke. Less well known is that he often acted with the dry wit or aloofness of a shorter version of a Clint Eastwood movie character. He came off in news reports, talk shows, and sound bites as a cross between "Dirty Harry" and the old man in *Gran Torino*. But on the floor of the Illinois House, particularly in his later years, his demeanor became more measured. He wore a dark, well-fitted suit and tie that set him apart from the rank and file. His disciplined work ethic reflected his health regimen, including the apple he sliced for lunch, cutting it up with such precision that visitors wondered whether it represented a metaphor for their future.

He spoke with a near-perfect exactitude—clearly and slowly—as if the teachers of St. Adrian and St. Ignatius schools still listened to his public statements. He graduated from the University of Notre Dame and Loyola University Law School, followed his father into Democratic politics, became part of the Daley machine, won his first House race when Republican Richard Nixon was president, and went on to dominate Illinois politics.

When he rose on the House floor, lawmakers on both sides of the political divide went silent. For Republicans, who couldn't get through the closed doors of his Democratic caucus, his comments may have been the first and last time they heard him explain what he was doing—or doing to them. What he and his lieutenants didn't always explain is what was buried hundreds of pages inside a bill. The language sometimes looked so vague that the average person—or even a trained budget analyst—might be left in the dark. Getting a fuller explanation from the speaker was tough. And getting an audience with him was usually tougher.

Odd as it seemed for a big state like Illinois, where governors have enormous power and a sizable bully pulpit, Madigan stayed in control for decades. He didn't sit in the big chair, running the day-to-day ship of state that deals with everything from the deaths of children overseen by the state's child welfare agency, to towns destroyed by tornadoes, to a pandemic that shuts the state down. Those are administrative tasks. Technically, and more accurately for purists, the governor sits on top of the flow chart and in a different branch of government, but Madigan upended the balance of power. Even casual observers came to understand that he had a lengthy reach. He could block any bill he wanted, and he rarely struggled to pass what he wished in his own chamber. He could force Republicans to take bad votes and exploit the roll calls in the next election. He could play the long game, sometimes as far as a decade ahead, as he drew the lines on legislative boundaries that ensured Democrats kept control of the House he built. He would make that message clear when he handed a new governor a list of previous chief executives who came and went on his watch.[6] A frustrated Republican Governor Bruce Rauner, who repeatedly tried and failed to outmaneuver Madigan, blurted out during his unsuccessful 2018 reelection campaign, "I'm not in charge. I'm trying to get to be in charge."[7]

No one in Springfield wondered what Rauner meant. Only five months earlier, Madigan had outlasted the one-term Rauner after a devastating 736-day budget standoff that drew national attention. Madigan picked off fifteen Republicans to join his Democrats in passing a budget and raising income taxes to help pay down a growing $15 billion backlog of overdue bills, replenish underfunded universities, and restore a tattered statewide social services safety net. The speaker then held on to override the veto of an exasperated Rauner days later.[8]

When Madigan made big moves, lobbyists leaning on the rotunda's brass railing nodded knowingly, spellbound in delight or disgust at how much the speaker could do. They learned to accept the unusual way the Illinois political world worked under Madigan as the speaker. His stock answer to describe himself? "Peculiar."[9]

For decades, any scrap of information about Madigan's thinking might have become an hours-long debate over how the speaker's stance could mean victory or catastrophe for one party over another, this special interest over that one. Ultimately, though, their conversations almost always turned to how the speaker would come up with the winning strategy—for himself. The inevitable conclusion that whatever happened was exactly "what Madigan wanted" drove his many critics crazy. Especially Republicans.

Over the years, Madigan made secrecy his most consistent trait. He kept his thoughts largely to himself—save for a tight circle of loyalists who spent decades earning walk-in privileges to his statehouse suite or the trusted allies invited to his corner table at places like Saputo's, an old-school Italian joint where he would eat a sparse fish dinner. He rarely gave up his full game plan, tipped his hand, or revealed more than the basics—if he bothered to speak at all. The bigger the secret, the bigger the surprise.

With governors, Madigan spent time sizing up their strengths and weaknesses, looking for ways to advance his politics, accommodate his caucus, and keep his campaign contributors engaged. If House Democrats benefited, he could throw up legislative roadblocks to governors of either party. He could make government action support his politics and politics support his hold on government. When Republicans held the Senate and the governorship in the 1990s, Madigan's allies in City Hall, labor, and the legal community looked to him as the "stopper," the one person who could block conservative and anti-Chicago agendas, a virtual veto power of his own.

In the 1980s Madigan made time stand still to help Republican Governor James Thompson twist arms on the House floor to win votes for a new White Sox stadium on Chicago's South Side. He battled Thompson over a push for higher taxes but then surprised him by slamming through a smaller, temporary tax hike with all Democratic votes in less than six hours. In the 1990s Madigan fought multiple skirmishes over taxes, budgets, and gambling with Republican Governor Jim Edgar but then teamed up with him to pass a tax overhaul in the House—only to be stymied in the Republican-led Senate.

As Illinois Democratic Party chair, Madigan unleashed a brutal 1998 campaign ad that tied the infamous licenses-for-bribes scandal under then Secretary of State George Ryan to a fiery van crash that killed six children. But when Ryan won the governorship in that race, Madigan and his fellow legislative leaders joined the Republican chief executive on a major public works program complete with overly generous pork-barrel spending, casino legislation, airport expansion, and a series of other high-profile initiatives.

As governors came and went, Madigan demonstrated when to fight, when to deal, and when to cut ties. Ryan's departure from the Executive Mansion brought Illinois the strangest and most ill-equipped governor of modern times: the self-aggrandizing, undisciplined, and unfocused Chicago Democrat Rod Blagojevich. Madigan supported Blagojevich on a series of programs, such as expanded health care for kids, early childhood education, and a two-year holiday on public pension payments. He also cochaired Blagojevich's 2006 reelection campaign even as the feds kept peppering the governor's friends and state agencies with subpoenas. But when the FBI arrested Blagojevich on December 9, 2008, Madigan would launch hearings that led to the governor's impeachment.[10]

The removal of Blagojevich ushered in Lt. Gov. Pat Quinn as governor. Quinn built a career by throwing bombs at establishment politicians. Still, Madigan and Quinn found themselves needing each other. But for Madigan that marriage of convenience clearly went only so far. Quinn needed Madigan's support to win a full term in 2010. Madigan needed Quinn to hold on to the governorship so that he could sign legislation that would redraw boundaries of legislative districts to help Democrats build bigger majorities. They also needed each other to pass and sign a temporary income tax increase in the postelection, lame-duck session—one that drew scorn for years because only Democrats supported it.

Four years later, Quinn lost his race against Republican Bruce Rauner, and the intraparty Democratic fights looked tame compared to the partisan ideological warfare that would take place. Rauner unleashed a four-year, full-scale effort to portray Madigan as the center of all evil in state government. Instead of trying to find reasonable compromise with Madigan and other Democrats as his Republican predecessors had done, Rauner spent millions of dollars lashing out in uncompromising television commercials that portrayed Madigan as corrupt and that Madigan called "defamation."[11] The relentless TV ads put a stain on the speaker that became harder to rub off over the years. Like a number of Illinois politicians, Madigan made money through a law firm specializing in fighting big property tax bills. As speaker, he automatically attracted clients. Rauner ripped the cozy relationship between Madigan and Cook County Assessor Joe Berrios, the respective chairs of the Illinois and Cook County Democratic parties. In their side gigs, Madigan's property tax law firm, where he once acknowledged he could make $1 million in a "good year," would have success before Berrios, the county assessor who also had previously served on the county's tax appeals board for years. Berrios, in turn, would have success lobbying the legislature. Rauner also argued that the alliance between Madigan and big labor was too strong, but Rauner had caused it to be exponentially stronger by pushing a series of antilabor stances that had no chance of success in the Democratic-controlled Illinois General Assembly.

In November 2018, Democrat J. B. Pritzker beat Rauner. And Madigan? The speaker won the largest number of House Democrats he had ever controlled—a 74–44 supermajority. The GOP, hurt also by the drag of midterm elections under Republican President Donald Trump, lost seats in both the Illinois legislature and the state's delegation in the U.S. Congress. At the next gathering in Springfield, Madigan reveled in the victories inside his closed-door House Democratic caucus. Along with House Democratic victories, the Illinois Senate Democrats picked up seats, and the Democratic statewide ticket swept every office. The Madigan-led Democratic Party of Illinois thumped its chest, releasing a statement saying the "election results definitively proved that the Rauner Republican playbook of attempting to make the entire 2018 election a referendum on Speaker Madigan, to distract from Republicans' record, is a failure."[12]

Pritzker played a different hand. He mostly refrained from making critical comments about Madigan while campaigning. After he won, Pritzker turned out to be agreeable in virtually every way that Rauner was disagreeable. With their large Democratic majorities, Madigan and Cullerton sent Pritzker a massive expansion of casino gambling, including the long-sought palace for Chicago, sports betting, and recreational marijuana. They struck deals for a $40 billion operating budget and a $45 billion construction plan—a pork-barrel bonanza that let rank-and-file members spread millions of dollars around their districts. Madigan, as always, raked in more than most.[13]

"In the end, people came together, recognized that there are differences in the General Assembly, but there are differences that can be reconciled," Madigan told colleagues as they wrapped up the spring 2019 session. "It's not easy. Sometimes it's pretty difficult. Sometimes it's painful. But if everybody comes to work with the goal of being reasonable and showing accomplishments, we have shown this Session it can be done." Madigan called the first few months of 2019 under Pritzker "an extraordinarily productive session of the General Assembly. Simply historic."[14]

History, though, is not just about the past. A little more than two weeks before lawmakers adjourned, the FBI quietly raided the homes of three longtime Madigan associates—a former aide ousted in a sexual harassment scandal; a former alderman in a neighboring ward; and a former Commonwealth Edison contract lobbyist, Michael McClain, a former Democratic representative and one of the speaker's closest confidants. By the 2019 fall session, Madigan had to play defense. Under questioning from reporters, he denied being a target of any investigation. Before year's end, the *Tribune* reported that federal authorities had tapped McClain's phone and had begun asking questions about Madigan and his allies.[15]

In the summer of 2020, prosecutors put the spotlight directly on Madigan. They charged Commonwealth Edison (ComEd) with a "years-long bribery scheme" tied to giving jobs, contracts, and payments to a roster of Madigan's political allies in hopes of winning favorable treatment on the utility's big legislative agenda. ComEd agreed to pay a $200 million fine and vowed to cooperate in a deferred prosecution agreement. Madigan was not charged and emphatically denied wrongdoing, but prosecutors implicated the speaker and gave him an unwanted designation: "Public Official A."[16]

The fallout left him politically vulnerable. Republicans piled the ComEd scandal onto anti-Madigan narratives in races up and down the ballot. With the erratic Trump topping the Republican ticket in November 2020, Madigan had reason to hope for major success in blue-state Illinois. Instead, Madigan lost a seat in the House. An Illinois Supreme Court justice he backed lost too. Voters defeated Pritzker's proposal—which Madigan supported—to amend the state constitution so people with the biggest incomes would pay higher taxes. Top Democrats blamed Madigan, and calls for him to step down from both his party chairmanship and his speakership accelerated.

Prosecutors then delivered more uncomfortable postelection news: McClain, the speaker's longtime friend, was indicted with a former top ComEd executive and two other lobbyists. Despite the serious questions swirling around him, Madigan still remained positioned to take the long view. Getting Pritzker in the governor's chair ensured that a Democrat would be in place to sign a new legislative map, the most critical component of determining which party would control the General Assembly for the next decade. But instead of seeing Madigan as the invincible powerhouse no one dared to take on for decades, a bloc of nineteen mostly female House Democrats viewed him as a political liability and refused to support him. Madigan allowed other lawmakers to see if they could round up enough votes to lead the House. And then the unthinkable happened: He lost the speakership. Democratic Representative Emanuel "Chris" Welch of Hillside, a Madigan ally, put together the votes and became the first Black speaker in Illinois history. The once-unbeatable Madigan voted for Welch, congratulated him, and issued a statement wishing him well.[17]

Almost forty years to the day that he first became a legislative leader, Michael J. Madigan ended his record reign. He had always played to win, but this time he lost the gavel. Times had changed, his ability to adapt had faded, and his power had slipped away. Despite trying to hang on, Madigan had completed his journey as the top man in his caucus, one that began as the fiery minority leader of 1981 who went on to build the Illinois House in his image.

PART I

THE LEGEND

1

REMAP VICTORY

"I think, Mr. Speaker, that you have
committed an unforgivable act of human
disrespect."
—House Minority Leader Michael
Madigan, D-Chicago, to House Speaker
George Ryan, R-Kankakee, June 23, 1981

To Michael J. Madigan, there are few political figures who stand as tall as
Richard J. Daley, the last of the nation's all-controlling big-city Democratic
bosses. There likewise were few, if any, legislative issues more important
to Madigan than redistricting, the brutally partisan process of redraw-
ing the legislative boundary lines every ten years. Redistricting provided
Madigan with a path to power, a road map for taking over state government and becoming the state's most influential politician. Many moments
during Madigan's long career placed him at a political crossroads, but
few would be more symbolic than June 23, 1981. He was minority leader,
potentially destined to be nothing more. Daley had been dead less than
five years, and the future success of Madigan and his Democratic allies
was not guaranteed. On that sweltering summer day, though, Madigan's
past and his future met head-on. Nobody could predict that Madigan's
future would be propelled as much by luck as by skill.

Richard J. Daley's memory would be feted with the unveiling of a statue
at a Capitol ceremony. Though Daley once held office as a state senator in Springfield, his statue served as a paean to the way he exercised
his clout as mayor of Chicago and leader of Cook County's Democratic

Party. Yet for all he meant to Madigan, Daley also represented the past. A crucial redistricting fight unfolding in the House that same afternoon represented Madigan's future—one that was as uncertain as the lines that would be drawn on legislative maps.

Inside the ornate House chamber, where giant paintings of Abraham Lincoln and Stephen Douglas warily watched the debates below, Republican Speaker George Ryan ruled with gruff gusto. In control of the flow of legislation, Ryan made a move that would resonate with Madigan like little else could. Instead of halting House floor debate between noon and 3:00 p.m. that day so that all who wished could attend the unveiling of the Daley statue, Ryan held a debate over two redistricting bills—one dictating the boundary lines for the Illinois members of the U.S. House and one for the Illinois House and Senate. Together, these were two of the most politically sensitive pieces of legislation that year and part of a tumultuous period in Illinois history. This was not just an ordinary, tense redistricting. This one would end with more widespread political pain than usual, and this day stood to go a long way toward determining which party would suffer most.

The reason the stakes would be so high in this particular redistricting battle was because the House would eliminate 59 of 177 seats, reducing the size of the "Big House" to 118 seats for the 1982 election. The downsizing would be accompanied by the end of Illinois' unique, cumulative voting system, which allowed three representatives to be elected from each House district—with a maximum of two from the majority party and one from the minority party. In Chicago, of course, there would be two Democrats and one Republican in most districts. Chicago Democrats, as one would expect, had a few ringers among the Republican lawmakers. Republican areas of the state elected their own suspect Democrats as well. That system was done away with when a maverick named Pat Quinn pushed through the cutback amendment in 1980. The citizen initiative he championed called for reducing the House by a third and electing one representative per district rather than three. Quinn, who would serve as governor thirty years later, capitalized on the public's anger over lawmakers passing an eight-thousand-dollar annual pay hike—from twenty thousand to twenty-eight thousand dollars—in the 1978 lame-duck fall veto session. Voters ratified the cutback in 1980, setting up the redistricting fight in the House in 1981.

Four decades later, it is still debated in political circles whether reducing the size of the House was good or bad for Illinois. Those who yearn for the former system say it forced more bipartisanship because each district included a minority representative. Few predicted how the change would consolidate power among the four legislative leaders. But fewer still could predict the change would mean the Democratic minority leader would become the longest-serving leader of any state legislature in the country. In fact, most lawmakers don't think beyond the next election, but all knew this two-year session under Ryan would be the last Big House. They realized their political lives could be cut short based on which legislative map was adopted. Nerves were frayed.

The ambitious Madigan needed to rally his Democratic troops. Ryan's Republican-majority map for the Illinois House and Senate would come up for a vote, and Madigan needed to block it. The Ryan map proposed new district boundaries that would favor Republican majorities. No doubt Daley would have understood that Madigan had a job to do.

To appreciate the high degree of tension, consider the chaos that had erupted on the House floor only days before. On voice votes, Ryan slammed both the congressional and state legislative maps through the preliminary stage known as "second reading," a time when amendments are considered, and advanced them to passage stage. Democrats demanded roll call votes and didn't get them. They wanted to be recognized to speak and they weren't. But what triggered full-scale bedlam is that Ryan's leadership team, with GOP Representative Art Telcser of Chicago wielding the gavel, didn't give Democrats the chance to fight for amendments they wanted. Democrats pounded fists and screamed that Ryan and his Republican lieutenants abused the power of the gavel. Agitated Democrats stormed the speaker's podium, yelling their way into a story that made national news. A raging Democratic Representative John Matijevich of North Chicago shouted at a security guard seeking to remove him: "I'm elected here. Don't tell me to leave. You leave before I do."[1] Republican Representative Dwight Friedrich of Centralia attempted to block TV coverage of the bedlam. He and Representative Joseph Ebbesen of DeKalb dashed up to the House balcony as fellow Republicans on the floor yelled at WCIA-TV cameraman Mike Gawel to stop filming the House fracas from his post in the gallery. The lawmakers contended he did not have permission to film—a quirky rule that required camera operators to seek an okay from the person wielding the gavel before filming. The Associated Press reported, "Friedrich was seen moving and pushing the camera and at one point, Gawel fell over. Gawel then took the camera and left the chamber. WCIA's reporter Lindsay Gedge later said the camera was not running when Friedrich confronted Gawel." Friedrich, of course, said he did not try to toss the cameraman, saying, "Your eyes must be bad."[2] *Sun-Times* reporter Charles N. Wheeler III, then the president of the statehouse press corps, recalled Friedrich threatened to throw the cameraman over the railing. "It was wild," said Wheeler, who hustled out to Friedrich's desk on the House floor to calm him down.[3]

Reporters are banned from the actual House floor, but Wheeler rushed out to Friedrich's desk with a pack of young journalism interns in tow ready to report on the exchange. G. Robert Hillman, the *Sun-Times'* bureau chief, spotted Wheeler and Friedrich, dashed up between the two of them, and began rolling his shoulders against Wheeler as he called out, "Charlie! Charlie!" The mild-mannered Wheeler was only explaining calmly and firmly to Friedrich—whom Wheeler knew from covering the 1970 constitutional convention, at which Friedrich was a delegate—that pushing the TV crew out of its perch in the House balcony was way out of bounds. After several manic minutes, Ryan eventually made his way from his seat on the House floor, climbed onto the podium, banged the gavel, and, speaking in his deep baritone, called for order in the chamber and for the news crew to return. "Just calm down and sit down," Ryan told the House. "When you get to order, I'll talk to you. Now, sit down. When you bring yourselves under control, we'll talk."[4]

Madigan broke for a private Democratic caucus. But he returned to see armed guards from the secretary of state standing next to the speaker's podium. Ryan agreed to move them, but Republicans didn't back away from the legislative maneuver. A top Democrat, Representative Jim McPike of Alton, would later tell colleagues on the House floor that the *Washington Post* ran the headline "Armed Police Calm Legislators in Illinois House." He then read the story describing the political melee and compared the denial of rights for Illinois Democrats to unconstitutional actions in foreign countries.[5] Madigan called Ryan's moves to advance his Republican redistricting legislation "reminiscent of tactics used by the Nazis in Germany and by dictatorial regimes all over the world." Madigan said Ryan should resign, a suggestion the Republican leader of the House did not embrace.[6]

Madigan wouldn't let it drop the next day, charging that the Republican chicanery "makes us all look like a pack of idiots." The minority leader vowed to get back at Republicans for supporting "acts of tyranny." Warning of his own prolific "legislative abilities and capabilities," Madigan pointedly reminded his political foes that he knew the ins and outs of the House rules. "I know this process, I know when I can win. I know when I can lose," Madigan said.[7]

Specifically lashing out at Ryan, Telcser, and Governor James R. Thompson, Madigan delivered the sternest of warnings:

> I know this system[,] and there will be a day of reckoning for every person in a power position who decides to abuse their position of power and to trample over the rights of any Member of this House. So, you can sit here comfortably today but just remember, your time is coming. Just wait and wait, and it will arrive and you will regret what you've done because we are all here as individuals and as human beings. And as a human being we have rights. We have a right to address a Bill. We have a right to a record vote. And by God, when you fail to look upon others as human beings, you're making a mistake and you will regret it.[8]

When Madigan and Ryan finally squared off on June 23 to vote on the passage stage of the state and federal redistricting bills, the bitterness in the chamber was palpable. First up was Ryan's proposal to reshape the district lines for Illinois' delegation in the U.S. House. Illinois had to shrink the size of the congressional delegation from twenty-four to twenty-two because population in other states had grown faster. The Ryan plan would shift the partisan breakdown from fourteen Republicans and ten Democrats by reducing the number of Democrats to eight. The GOP map forced matchups between such incumbent Chicago Democrats as U.S. Representatives Frank Annunzio and Dan Rostenkowski—more than a decade before the once-mighty U.S. House Ways and Means chairman went to prison for corruption. Fully playing out his role as the top Democrat in the House, Madigan condemned the GOP's cartography. "It is a purely and highly partisan bill drafted by the Republican staff for the Republican Party in the House of Representatives," Madigan said. "It maximizes the election of Republican members to the United States Congress without due consideration for Democratic constituencies located throughout the state. . . . It will, in effect, dilute the representation given to Democratic voters throughout this state and, in a sense, will disenfranchise those Democratic voters who are living throughout the state of Illinois."[9]

The proposal also drew opposition from a line-up of future luminaries in the General Assembly: Democratic Representatives Barbara Flynn Currie, who later would become the first woman to serve as House majority leader; Emil Jones, a future Senate president; and John Cullerton, a future Senate president—all of Chicago—and Mike McClain of Quincy, a future powerhouse lobbyist. The fear of establishment Democrats—both Black and white—was that the Republican map would shift the balance of power from the state's congressional delegation, which already favored Republicans, and create an even further tilt to the ideological right. Similar arguments came from a Republican, Susan Catania of Chicago, a white liberal House lawmaker with an overwhelmingly Black constituency. She decried the Ryan congressional map for weakening the city's Democratic power structure in Congress. "I don't think it will help my city, which I love very deeply, to take away the representation of the party that has worked a little harder for my city," said Catania, one of five Republicans voting against the Ryan map.[10]

Ryan held a slim 91–86 Republican majority, but many lawmakers were ready to play footsie with the other party if the right deal came their way. To make up for losing votes from Catania and other Republicans, Ryan reached out to Black Democrats.[11] He promised to keep three Black congressional seats, a move that drew support from the Rev. Jesse Jackson's Operation PUSH and votes from such Chicago lawmakers as Representative Art Turner, who one day would join Speaker Madigan's leadership team, and Representative Carol Moseley Braun, a future U.S. senator. Representative Emil Jones, though, argued that Blacks voting for the Ryan map were being "hoodwinked" and were shortsighted because the proposal would cut Democratic representation in Washington overall. In the end, Ryan's fragile coalition on the congressional map received eighty-nine votes, the bare minimum majority needed to pass in the Big House.[12]

Hoping for a second win, Ryan moved immediately to vote on his Republican-leaning map for the Illinois House and Senate. Ryan argued that his map gave Chicago 31 seats, downstate 44 seats, and suburban Cook and its five collar counties the final 43 seats. He said 15 seats were majority Black, and three favored Hispanics. He called the map fair. But Madigan immediately pounced. He said the Ryan map would give Republicans 63 safe seats—districts with boundaries drawn so favorably that GOP lawmakers virtually could not lose them in future elections—even when national turnout swung overwhelmingly in favor of Democrats. Sixty-three seats would be three more than a majority of 60 in the new 118-seat House. "It's a partisan, political effort, partisan power grab," Madigan said, "and it should be thoroughly rejected." Madigan, at that moment, did not mention the Daley statue presentation that the House would miss because of the lengthy debate over two redistricting bills, but McClain did. "Why are you holding us captive here?" McClain protested. His question was futile, as Ryan pressed forward.[13]

On the state legislative map, Speaker Ryan used a different strategy for the redistricting proposal that also would favor Republicans. Though he had passed his congressional map by winning over some African American lawmakers, Ryan would need a different coalition. Braun shifted back onto Madigan's side after breaking with Democrats and siding with Ryan's Republicans on the congressional map. Turner would stick with Ryan, though Turner acknowledged it began to look like a "suicide mission" because the roll call was tight.[14]

To shore up his votes, Ryan sought to lure some Democrats into approving the GOP map by drawing downstate districts that would be safe seats for these Democrats. The theory? That a lawmaker could not resist voting for self-preservation, that not even party loyalty could best a lawmaker's chance to vote for an all but guaranteed legislative district for the next decade. Nothing is assured in politics, of course, but a sweetly drawn district is about as good as it gets.

Even so, Ryan's strategy didn't sway bedrock Democrats. Representative Dick Mautino, a Spring Valley lawmaker who also served as the Democratic chairman of Bureau County, marveled at the Republican map's personal appeal, but he would not put his own interests above the party. He voted against the Ryan map even though it would have been easy for him to win in the district that Republicans presented him. "It's very difficult for a Democratic County Chairman to drool over a Republican presented map," Mautino said. "This is Christmas in June for some of us that are from those downstate areas. But I don't think that I could do my neighbors and friends and constituents in Bureau County any good if I allowed this map to have my 'yes' vote on it."[15]

When House Clerk Tony Leone finished ticking off names on a roll call, a few lawmakers who had initially taken a pass started popping up from their seats and casting votes for Ryan's map. The number on the big electronic tally boards slowly grew to eighty-eight—one short of passage. Finally, the entire room turned to Representative Gary Hannig, a Democrat from Macoupin County, an area so steeped in labor history that Mother Jones is buried alongside coal miners whose rights she long fought to protect. Watching from the wooden press box at the front of the Democratic side of the chamber, reporters saw Hannig speaking tentatively and admiringly about the district the Republicans had drawn for him. His young career in Springfield had led to notoriety. Hannig opposed the Equal Rights Amendment (ERA) and was accused in 1980 of considering a bribe offered in connection with his ERA vote—a point he vehemently denied.[16] But none of that would matter on this day, because the future of Ryan's map was in Hannig's hands, and his words added suspense to the moment. Would he break with Democrats? Would he side with Republicans to preserve his own chances of reelection? "I see it as a winnable map in my particular district," Hannig said. "It's a map that would at least give a Democrat downstate a chance. It's a map that I think that I could at least have a chance."[17]

Reporters scribbled furiously. But just as it sounded as though he might jump to Ryan's side, Hannig fell in line with Democrats. "As I look over the House floor for the last two or three years and think back of the friends that I've made here, I think that at some point I have to draw the line and vote with the party that has brought me here over the last two years," Hannig said. He then declared how he would vote: "No."[18]

That was it. The bill needed eighty-nine votes to pass. It received only eighty-eight. The Republican map that Ryan wanted, the safe districts he offered Democrats in order to lure their votes, the chance to beat Madigan at the most important political game of the year—well, that map had failed. Ryan lost. Madigan won. Gary Hannig had done what so many successful pols in Illinois learned to do: He danced with the one that brung him.

Victory in hand, Madigan left no doubt who had brought him to the dance. He told Ryan:

> I'm sure all of us have different views of Mr. Daley in retrospect, but there are many Democrats and I'm sure many Republicans who thought of Mr. Daley with the utmost respect, reverence and love. And there were very, very many of us who desired very much to attend that event to observe the unveiling of that statue. You had led us to believe that the House, like the Senate, would recess in order to view that ceremony. For some reason, I'm sure it's involved with the legislative strategy concerning the last two Bills, you choose to revoke your earlier statement and to deny to many of us who have very fond memories of Mayor Daley the opportunity to attend that ceremony. My opinion, Mr. Speaker, [is that] you and I are engaged in a legislative conflict, and the rules of conduct in that legislative

conflict generally permit quite a few things to be done, me to you and you to me. But I think in this instance you've gone well beyond the bounds of civil conduct. This [redistricting] Bill could have been called right now, at this time [after the Daley statue ceremony]. It could have been called yesterday. It could have been called later today. But for your own selfish reasons, as has been the hallmark of your administration as the Speaker of this House, you choose to deny to those who wanted to attend that ceremony the opportunity to be there. I think, Mr. Speaker, that you have committed an unforgivable act of human disrespect.[19]

Ryan, a pharmacist by trade, who rose from the Kankakee County Board, enjoyed the backing of his local Republican machine, a mini version of the Chicago Democratic operations with polar opposite political leanings. The conservative Republican would spend a decade climbing the leadership ladder in the House, capping it in 1981 with his rise to speaker. Rarely one to take criticism well, Ryan showed no willingness to give ground to Madigan. In response, Ryan fell back on a rejoinder that so often accompanies legislative debates and political hijinks: He tried to make it sound as though he were taking the high road.

First, Ryan noted that he had prepared remarks to give during the Daley statue unveiling and intended to take a break so that all could go. But he then suggested that the importance and lengthiness of the redistricting debate forced him to keep the chamber in session during the Daley event. "At any time that I have to adjourn the business of the House to do a social function, I don't feel that I owe any apologies to you or to anybody else," Ryan said. "We were elected here. We were sent here to do the business of the House, and at the time that I called the Bills, Mr. Madigan, we had one hour and 30 minutes to debate those Bills. There was plenty of time, but we didn't finish, as you can tell now. It's 3:30 [p.m.] And so it's one of those unfortunate things, but I will not apologize to you or to anybody else in this House for conducting the business that we were elected to do while we are here."[20]

The Senate didn't let the House have all of the fun in the redistricting game. Even though the upper chamber is known for more decorum than the House, senators erupted into a fistfight when they took up redistricting. Frustrated by the Democratic majority's attempts to outdo him, suburban Republican Senator Mark Rhoads of Western Springs pointed his finger during proceedings on the Senate floor and called Democratic Senate President Phil Rock a "son of a bitch."[21] The Rhoads outburst stunned everyone. For Illinois, it was roughly the equivalent of when—years later in 2009—Republican U.S. Representative Joe Wilson of South Carolina would shout "You lie" from his House seat during a national address by Democratic President Barack Obama.[22] Because Rhoads's rage was aimed at Rock, an Oak Park politician viewed by many as the walking embodiment of a true statesman, the sudden verbal attack prompted physical retaliation. Pint-sized Democratic Senator Sam Vadalabene, a sixty-seven-year-old former bar owner from Edwardsville, leaped from his seat as Rhoads shouted and landed a haymaker on the thirty-five-year-old Republican's jaw. Rock, whose Democrats held a tight 30–29 majority, passed his own Democratic map in the Senate, but it went nowhere in Ryan's House. In the end, no map could pass both chambers.

The deadlock over the state House and Senate map put into play an unusual provision of the Illinois Constitution. A special panel is set up with an equal number of Democrats and Republicans appointed from each chamber. The goal is for this bipartisan group to forge a compromise. If they can't agree, the Illinois Supreme Court submits two names—not of the same political party. They are put into a hat—likely a replica of Lincoln's stovepipe—or a crystal bowl. A name is then drawn by the secretary of state, and that newly named person is placed on the panel as a tiebreaker who works with his party to fashion what would become a highly partisan map.

Democrat Dawn Clark Netsch, the former state senator and comptroller who served as a delegate to the constitutional convention that drew up the tiebreaker solution, once called the procedure "almost embarrassing." Netsch said it is not only "unique," but "a better word might be 'peculiar.' It's certainly not the ideal way for an important political and governmental decision to be made."[23] Authors of the state constitution were determined to replace the 1870 charter's solution to a mapmaking impasse—an at-large, statewide election for all 177 House seats, as happened in 1964 with a ballot so extraordinarily long it was dubbed the "Bedsheet Ballot." The authors of the new constitution, which included Madigan, reasoned that the mere threat of having a tiebreaker pulled from a hat—a winner-take-all approach to drawing partisan lines—would be enough to scare the two sides into reaching a compromise rather than risk losing the luck of the draw and watching the other party approve favorable maps. That strategy worked in 1971, when the two sides reached a compromise. But it was not to be in 1981.

Early on, both sides wanted a deal in the commission. Republicans may have felt they could withstand going to the tiebreaker, that they could recover even if the Democrats won the draw. But Democrats were ready to cut a deal, according to Alan Greiman, who served with Madigan and later became a judge. "We felt we had a lot more to lose than the Republicans," Greiman told the *Tribune* a few years after the showdown. "If the Democrats had lost . . . we'd have been out of power for 12 generations."[24]

But that didn't happen. The Democrats won the draw. Republican Secretary of State Jim Edgar pulled from the stovepipe the name of Democratic former Governor Sam Shapiro instead of Republican former Governor Richard Ogilvie. Shapiro would be the tiebreaker for Democrats, a monumental break for Madigan that propelled him directly into the speakership. With Madigan acting as the chief author, the new map guaranteed that Democrats would be in charge of the House and Senate for at least a decade. Chicago would win a bigger percentage of seats than they had before the cutback, and Republicans predicted the leadership would be Chicago-centric. Democrats lost only sixteen of the fifty-nine House seats that disappeared; Republican numbers declined by forty-three. The congressional maps aren't subject to the winner-take-all tiebreaker; so their issues are resolved in the courts. The state maps can go to court too. The state and federal maps that year would be tweaked to improve African American and Hispanic representation and redesign a House downstate district to address objections that it was 6 miles wide and 125 miles long. Madigan made sure Republican legal arguments to throw out the overall state and federal Democratic maps were "obliterated."[25]

More significant for Madigan, his record-setting tenure as speaker would begin when the new legislature was sworn in—in January 1983. Even when Republicans won the tiebreaker to control the next map drawn for the 1990s, Madigan managed to hold the speakership in four of the next five races. He lost control of the Illinois House only in 1994 during Governor Jim Edgar's big reelection win, which was coupled with the nationwide Republican fervor that put Newt Gingrich into the speakership of the U.S. House. Senate Republicans under President James "Pate" Philip of Wood Dale, the DuPage County GOP chair, held the upper chamber the full ten years. But Madigan took advantage of an increasing number of Democrats in the suburbs and regained control of the Illinois House in the 1996 election, a political year when President Bill Clinton headed the ticket and won reelection.

When the 2001 redistricting year kicked off in the House, Madigan delivered a message to the uninitiated: "For those of you who are new to that, fasten your seat belts."[26] Democrats won the random-chance drawing and focused on lumping Republican incumbents into districts where they'd have to run against each other. Democrats would take both houses, where they've remained in charge ever since. In 2011 there was no need for a commission or a tiebreaker, because Democrats held both chambers and Democratic Governor Pat Quinn signed their map.

Following that 2011 redistricting, Madigan's mapmaking skills drew national attention. A *Politico* writer flatly proclaimed that Madigan had "punched his ticket to the partisan hall of fame" when he constructed the congressional map in 2011. *Politico* placed Madigan in the "pantheon of state power brokers whose efforts rippled well beyond their state capital and helped reshape Congress, for better or for worse. Madigan's masterstroke, and its expected effect, ranks him with other storied pols whose mapmaking exploits have become the stuff of political legend."[27] The new boundaries turned the partisan breakdown upside down—initially from eleven Republicans and eight Democrats in 2011 to twelve Democrats and six Republicans in 2013—a boost that would eventually help Nancy Pelosi grip the gavel in the U.S. House for a second round as speaker—and hang on to a slim majority when Joe Biden became president.[28]

When a 2014 citizen initiative sought to take redistricting away from lawmakers and give it to an independent panel, Madigan opposed putting the proposed constitutional amendment before voters. Michael Kasper, Madigan's longtime Democratic Party lawyer, the speaker's former House legal counsel, and a prominent lobbyist, went to court. Leading the group of plaintiffs challenging the citizen initiative was John Hooker, a longtime ComEd lobbyist. Cook County Circuit Court Judge Mary Mikva upheld the challenge, and the initiative effort stalled. Backers of establishing a commission tried again to put a citizen initiative on the ballot in 2016. Hooker's group, called the People's Map, challenged again. That gave Madigan a fig leaf to stand behind, allowing the speaker and the Madigan-led state Democratic Party to say they weren't technically involved in the suit.[29] This second citizen initiative case went to the Illinois Supreme Court, where the Democratic majority, led by Justice Thomas Kilbride, long backed politically by Madigan, threw out the initiative on a 4–3 party-line vote in August 2016. Madigan got what he wanted. But the ruling came with a sharp dissent from Republican Justice Robert Thomas, a former kicker for the Chicago Bears: "The Illinois constitution is meant to prevent tyranny, not to enshrine it."[30]

Only six months earlier, President Obama had traveled to Springfield and, during a speech to his former Illinois House and Senate colleagues, proposed rethinking how redistricting is handled at the congressional level. He called for the changes from the speaker's podium in the Illinois House chambers—a rich irony given that Madigan was a grand master of drawing highly partisan district boundaries for state and federal lawmakers. Illinois Democrats who drew the lines for 2012 districts pitted more than two dozen Republican state lawmakers against one another. Still not satisfied, Democrats also carved out potential primary and general election challengers to their incumbents in the state legislative races while also helping Democrats make inroads in Congress.[31]

Obama acknowledged that both parties seek a partisan edge when they control how lines are drawn:

Nobody's got clean hands on this thing.

The fact is, today technology allows parties in power to precision-draw constituencies so that the opposition's supporters are packed into as few districts as possible. That's why our districts are shaped like earmuffs or spaghetti. (Laughter.) It's also how one party can get more seats even when it gets fewer votes.

And while this gerrymandering may insulate some incumbents from a serious challenge from the other party, it also means that the main thing those incumbents are worried about are challengers from the most extreme voices in their own party. That's what's happened in Congress. You wonder why Congress doesn't work? The House of Representatives there, there may be a handful—less than 10 percent—of districts that are even competitive at this point. So if you're a Republican, all you're worried about is what somebody to your right is saying about you, because you know you're not going to lose a general election. Same is true for a lot of Democrats. So our debates move away from the middle, where most Americans are, towards the far ends of the spectrum, and that polarizes us further.

Now, this is something we have the power to fix, and once the next census rolls around and we have the most-up-to-date picture of America's population, we should change the way our districts are drawn. In America, politicians should not pick their voters; voters should pick their politicians. (Applause.) And this needs to be done across the nation, not just in a select few states. It should be done everywhere.[32]

Illinois, of course, did not leap into gear to address this reform. In 2019 the U.S. Supreme Court then went easy on the partisan cartographers. On a 5–4 vote, the high court ruled that federal courts cannot determine whether maps are too partisan, giving what critics feared was a freer hand to state legislatures. Writing for the majority, Chief Justice John Roberts stated, "Federal judges have no license to reallocate political power between the two major political parties, with no plausible grant of authority in the Constitution and no legal standards to limit and direct their decisions."[33] Justice Elena Kagan dissented, saying the majority ruling meant that "state officials' intent to entrench their party in power is perfectly 'permissible,' even when it is the predominant factor in drawing district lines. But that is wrong."[34]

By 2020 Madigan's mapmaking skills from the prior redistricting process had given him his biggest majority ever in the Illinois House, and Democrats led the Illinois congressional delegation 13–5 over Republicans. Government reformers sought again in Springfield to alter the redistricting process in the spring of 2020. They wanted more fairness and transparency through an independent commission, but coronavirus delayed the legislative session and effectively ended that attempt to reform the system. It was an odd yet fortuitous break for the status quo. By 2021, CHANGE Illinois, a nonpartisan reform group, had shifted strategy and focused on making the remapping of districts more open and responsive to the public, but that effort ultimately didn't get traction with the Democratic supermajorities.[35]

Those Democratic supermajorities are largely due to Madigan's strategy over the decades—as well as his luck, of course. He took advantage of the luck of the draw in the 1981 redistricting that helped elevate him to speaker. In fact, Representative McClain declared, "It was the luck of the Irish."[36]

Maybe it was. Richard J. Daley would have heartily approved. But for all of the talk about Madigan's luck—which definitely didn't hurt—he became a predominant legislative tactician who knew when and how to make the most of his political prowess.

2

WHITE SOX MIRACLE

"By my watch, it was 11:59."
—Speaker Michael Madigan, very early on
July 1, 1988

Mark it down. Speaker Madigan's political prowess even was judged to
have reached near-biblical proportions on June 30, 1988. That's the day
Mike Madigan, Chicago White Sox fan, made time stand still. For years,
White Sox owners Jerry Reinsdorf and Eddie Einhorn had been threaten-
ing to pull the South Side team out of Chicago. They talked about moving
to Addison in DuPage County, not a favorite destination for hard-core
Sox fans, and they talked about a variety of other places.[1] But one of the
biggest efforts to move the Sox came from St. Petersburg, Florida. Despite
an abundance of spring training sites, Florida had yet to coax a team into
calling the Sunshine State home for the regular baseball season. Sensing
an opportunity as Illinois politicians warred over costs, payment methods,
and locations for a new stadium, Florida lawmakers thought they had
outmaneuvered the Land of Lincoln.

In early June, Florida officials approved an attractive package of incen-
tives—potentially tens of millions of public dollars—to entice the Sox into
moving to St. Petersburg. Illinoisans, of course, were wary of using public
financing for a stadium. But now, with a serious competing offer on the
table, Illinois politicians faced their own legislative session deadline to act.
The Sox needed Illinois to approve a new stadium plan before midnight
on June 30 or they'd be saying good-bye to Chicago. The reason June
30 was the deadline was simple: on July 1 the number of votes necessary

to pass most legislation to take effect immediately upon the governor's signature, including the Sox bill, would rise from a simple majority, of 30 of 59 lawmakers in the Senate and 60 of 118 lawmakers in the House, to a supermajority, three-fifths vote, of 36 in the Senate and 71 in the House. No one believed there was any chance a Sox stadium bill could pass if a supermajority were needed. Added to the mix was the confounding reality that Springfield's politicians—like many throughout the country—are classic procrastinators. They don't move on tough political votes until they have a deadline that forces them to make a decision. Sometimes waiting is a legislative strategy to put pressure on the fence-sitters. Sometimes it's just easier to do nothing rather than take a stand. But losing the Sox? That's one vote fans in Chicago would remember. And just as they are unafraid to let Sox players know when they make bad plays, the Chicago fans would be happy to boo the politicians—at the ballot box.

By June, St. Petersburg's leaders had reason to be hopeful. Illinois newspapers wrote of the slim hopes that Chicago could hang onto the White Sox. Numerous supporters had declared the stadium proposal dead. The politics of the day complicated the issue. Republican Governor Jim Thompson had sought an income tax increase since the beginning of his fourth term in 1987, and Madigan stood in the way. "Madigan killed it," Thompson said. But Madigan disagreed. "Madigan did not kill the tax increase," the speaker said of himself. "The people of Illinois killed the tax increase because the people of Illinois did not want the tax increase."[2] Many lawmakers from both parties thought it was bad optics to pass a stadium bill without boosting taxes to help schools and human services. Further, the idea of using any form of public financing for a baseball field didn't go down well with many lawmakers, particularly downstaters who won kudos from constituents for panning any program that helped Chicago. They did not see any reason for the government to be in the business of helping a professional sports team finance a stadium—even though Thompson and lawmakers tied payments heavily to hotel taxes paid mostly by out-of-town visitors. There were fears that the state—and thus regular taxpayers—would end up on the hook in a big way no matter how tightly the legislation was drafted to protect them. The Sox stadium bill caused the deep-seated geographic rivalry between downstate and Chicago to grow more divisive. But many, including Thompson, saw the Sox as too symbolic to let go. Chicago is a two-team baseball town, North Siders and South Siders—one National League, one American League.

Carl Sandburg dubbed Chicago the "City of Big Shoulders," but letting one team slip away would be a loss of civic pride, a loss of swagger and bragging rights that come with being one of only three cities with two major league ball clubs.

If the politicians struck out, they would be remembered for letting the Sox get away. Anticipating a Sox defeat, reporters in the statehouse pressroom began polishing up stories as deadlines neared. They all but sounded the death knell for Sox baseball in Chicago. Well into the night, newspaper reporters writing for their first edition deadlines and TV anchors on the 10:00 p.m. news were telling viewers that there was no joy in Mudville, but few knew that Senate President Phil Rock, Thompson, and Madigan had gamed out one more play.

Taking command, Rock, an Oak Park Democrat, suddenly gave an opening to the first conference committee report on Senate Bill 2202. Desperation was in the air. "It's the last of the ninth, we hope the bases are loaded," said Senator Tim Degnan, whose district encompassed the ancient, feeble, and beloved Comiskey Park. Degnan, a close ally of Cook County State's Attorney Richard M. Daley, the future mayor, and a product of the Eleventh Ward neighborhood where Hizzoner Richard J. Daley once roamed, knew the stakes. "They are about to turn the lights off in Comiskey Park," said Degnan, who had held out little hope of passage only hours earlier. He defended the financing, saying the hotel taxes and other public funds would prop up the $150 million stadium. He ticked off estimates that economic activity generated by baseball teams ranged from $130 million to $160 million a year. "For ninety years, Chicago has been a two-team town," he told colleagues. And he implored them to consider that cities a fraction of the size of Chicago were building or planning new sports stadiums: "I ask you how Chicago and Illinois will look to the tourists, the residents and the fans if we allow less . . . a city less in size, less in spirit and less in sports tradition—to steal our White Sox."[3]

Looking for help from his own Republican Party, Thompson had appealed to Senate Minority Leader Pate Philip, the DuPage County powerhouse, to give the governor a hand in rounding up votes. "I came up to the Capitol about 4 o'clock," Thompson said, "and I was coming up the steps when I saw my guys. . . . They all had long faces. I said, 'What's the matter?' They said the bill was dead. I got mad and said, 'No, it's not.'" He went straight to Philip's office: "I said, 'Pate, I don't care whether you're a Sox fan or not. It's now personal,'" Thompson said. "'We're one of the few cities to have two major league teams, and we're not losing one. . . . You have to help me. It's personal.' And Pate said, 'OK.'"[4] Senator Jack Schaffer of Crystal Lake, one of fourteen Republican senators who wound up voting for the Sox stadium, talked to Thompson: "He told us, 'Do it for Illinois. Do it for me.'"[5]

Thompson's reputation as a dealmaker was on the line. Well past 11:00 p.m., the Senate was just beginning its debate. But one by one, Republicans started putting up votes. Senator Adeline Geo-Karis, a Republican from Zion, told colleagues, "I like baseball. I'd like to see the White Sox stay here even though its owners were running back and forth to St. Petersburg, and I like St. Petersburg, but I don't think the White Sox belong in St. Petersburg."[6]

Suburban Democratic Senator Richard Kelly of Oak Forest acknowledged that he had been prepared to vote against the bill only a few hours earlier. "But I've had a conscience problem, and I know that I'm not the only one that's had that conscience problem," Kelly said. "I . . . I'm going to vote for this 'cause I believe in it, that we should make every effort to keep the White Sox in Chicago. I know I'm going to have a better conscience when I leave this General Assembly to know that I was on . . . on the Yes vote for keeping the White Sox here."[7]

When Degnan gave his closing pitch, he warned colleagues that the competition for the Sox is real: "I believe we're both racing the clock and St. Petersburg at this juncture. So I would hope that we have in this Chamber a combination of thirty Sox fans, Chicago boosters or Illinois fans."[8] His hope came true. The bill got thirty votes—the bare minimum.

Adrenaline was pumping. Reporters raced to recraft their stories with no surety of the outcome. Some had prepared one story for a Sox victory, another for a Sox loss. Stories filed for early editions gave little hope of keeping the White Sox. As the clock in Springfield ticked toward midnight, spirits rose in St. Pete.

It was 11:40 p.m. There were only twenty minutes left. Thompson tore across the Capitol rotunda, raced through the giant wooden doors of the House, and started going desk to desk. Madigan hurried through his list of House lawmakers who still might be persuaded. He broke toward Democrats. Thompson moved toward Republicans, Democrats, and anybody who would listen. "Both of us, Mike and I, scurried around, grabbing people, cajoling people, arguing with people, promising people," Thompson said.[9]

Thompson's lieutenant governor, George Ryan, the former House speaker, even stepped in to help. Thompson aides shouted out the names of lawmakers who might switch sides. "I had sent spotters over to the House floor to tell me where the possible votes were," Thompson recalled. "They were standing over the chairs of these guys pointing, and I went from one to another. Mike Madigan was working the Democratic side of the aisle, and then I switched and worked the Democratic side of the aisle."[10]

With the midnight deadline approaching fast, radio reporter Charlie McBarron went live on the air from the press box on the House floor. The intensity of the moment kept building as he walked his audience through a remarkable play-by-play narrative of the unfolding debate for Chicago's WMAQ-AM. Up in the House balcony, television reporters from Chicago, Florida, and other Illinois stations were following the action step-by-step. The wooden press boxes on each side of the speaker's podium started filling up even as other reporters raced back down marble staircases to the pressroom a half floor below. They called their editors, hunched over computers, and began banging out new developments, picking off quotes while listening to squawk boxes pumping the live debate into the pressroom. McBarron told his listeners that the volume in the House grew from a dull roar to deafening. It got to be so loud that he could not hear what radio producers were telling him over the phone as he broadcast for the next twenty minutes to Chicago and St. Petersburg audiences. "I had to assume I was live on the air," McBarron recounted.[11]

Representative Peg Breslin, a Democrat from Ottawa who often presided long days over the chamber, had the gavel in her hand as the White Sox measure arose in the House. Unlike the speaker, Breslin opposed the legislation—as did many of her downstate colleagues. Representative John Dunn, a Decatur Democrat, shouted a warning that helping the Sox could cost as much as $14 million a year in city and state aid. According to transcripts of Dunn's remarks, he declared: "I say to the taxpayers of the State of Illinois, don't take this, rise up and revolt, it's time to tell State Government to get [its] priorities in order. What in the name of heaven are we doing at this hour with every top ranking politician in this state standing out on the floor of this chamber with a Senate that just passed this Bill, and we can't take care of the children, we can't take care of the poor, we can't take care of the sick, we can't take care of the mentally ill [—] let's shut this place down and go home and forget the White Sox, vote 'no.'"[12]

Around that moment, Democratic Majority Leader Jim McPike of Alton, a U.S. Naval Academy graduate and former navy pilot with an intense glare, took the gavel from Breslin and called on Madigan to address the full House. The chamber went silent. Madigan tried to calm fears. He said the funding provisions reflected legislation that had been approved two years earlier. He dismissed what he called "quite a bit of hysteria" from opponents while also acknowledging risks.[13] "But there is an upside," Madigan said, adding, "Let's keep the Sox in Chicago."[14]

A rare Chicago Republican, Representative Roger McAuliffe implored fellow lawmakers to vote for the Sox legislation: "It would be an outrage if we allowed the state of Florida to come up to Illinois and kidnap one of our baseball teams."[15]

And then came Democratic Representative John Daley, another son of Richard J. Daley, who would one day move to the Senate and on to become finance chairman of the Cook County Board. In comments short but to the point, Daley acknowledged the privilege of having a Bridgeport-based legislative district that represented the White Sox neighborhood. Like most Daleys, he had a habit of not saying his main point directly but coming close enough for most people to know what he meant. Hoping to appeal across the partisan divide, Daley pointed out how Republicans had received help from Democrats when they needed it for a legislative relief package for Arlington International Racecourse. But with time ticking down, the voting boards gave little hope.[16]

"The pressure is really mounting here," McBarron said, telling listeners that one lawmaker whom Thompson was lobbying flat-out shook his head no. "Things are getting very rowdy here in the chamber. Governor Thompson looking very glum right now. We're at fifty-four votes. Six more votes have to be found to pass this legislation. If it doesn't get sixty votes, many people believe this will be it for the White Sox in Chicago."[17]

Sounding like a seasoned sports announcer breaking down the intricacies of the biggest game in town, McBarron said only five minutes were left until the midnight deadline. He said Thompson kept talking to House Republicans as others shouted, "'Let's go, let's go, let's bring the gavel down.' But the governor is just plodding along. He's searching out lawmakers who voted no. He's trying to talk them into going along with this. Things are getting very, very agitated here. Everybody is standing up. The governor gesturing. He's got his palm open."[18]

Thompson stood in the back of the Republican side of the chamber in front of one lawmaker as he pointed across the House to another, suggesting that getting one person's vote would convince another to go along. "He needs six votes here. Time is running out," McBarron said. "I'd say there's about four minutes left—four minutes left—for this legislation to pass. Everyone now on their feet here in the House chamber. The tension continues to mount."[19]

Some lawmakers started singing a White Sox favorite used when an opponent is down and out: "Na, na, na, na! Hey, hey-ay! Goooood-bye." Even some Democrats chimed in. "If the fat lady sings for the Sox tonight here in the House chamber, that's undoubtedly the song she'll be singing," McBarron said.[20]

But McPike would not rap the gavel to conclude the voting. He refrained from announcing passage or failure of the bill, choosing to give the equivalent of a final warning. "Have all voted who wish?" McPike asked. "Have all voted who wish? Have all voted who wish? Take the record, Mr. Clerk."[21]

Taking the record froze the roll call with only fifty-four of the sixty votes needed for the stadium. Was it over? Not in Illinois. McPike had not yet slammed the gavel to end the debate.

Fully focused, McPike called out the name of Hoffman Estates Republican Representative Terry Parke, who changed his vote from no to aye. The same thing happened with another suburban lawmaker, this time Democratic Representative Lou Lang of Skokie. They represented the fifty-fifth and fifty-sixth votes.[22]

"Governor Thompson really, really doing all he can, figuratively twisting arms on the Republican side," McBarron told his audience. "Now he's over on the Democratic side. He really, really wants this to happen. He's going all out. The governor now bent over speaking to a lawmaker on the Democratic side, emphatically gesturing to her and now to the tote board, where 56 votes show. The vote fifty-six [aye] to fifty-nine [no]. Four more Sox votes have to be found, and they have to be found quickly. We're about two minutes away from midnight."[23]

As Thompson frantically worked the House floor in rolled-up shirt sleeves and suspenders, legislative opponents of the Sox deal started chanting a "5, 4, 3, 2, 1" countdown like a crowd waiting for the ball to drop at Times Square on New Year's Eve.[24] They wanted McPike to drop the gavel on the White Sox. On McBarron's broadcast, that all-too-familiar sharp electronic radio signal marked midnight with a loud beep. But nobody broke out champagne. In fact, the legislative floor action took a turn into the surreal.

Before the clock on the electronic tally board hit midnight, House Democrats jammed up the counter. They flipped on what's called the shot clock, which tracks how much time a lawmaker has to speak in debate.[25] The move meant the actual time no longer appeared. Instead, it looked like indecipherable characters jumping around with every tick of the clock. Nobody could tell what time was on the tally board. "I'm not sure what clock these folks are using," McBarron said, adding, "They're asking lawmakers now if they wish to change their vote. Very unusual, but this is an unusual time. Time is just about running out."[26] Still four votes down, Thompson picked up his already frenzied pace. "Some of the members of the leadership team are running around now passing out information from the governor to other lawmakers," McBarron said. "It seems that some sort of deals or discussions are being cut right now. We are very close to midnight here."

A true pro in the moment, McBarron detailed only what he knew and didn't know, keeping his narration pitch-perfect and reemphasizing how the time in the House appeared deceiving. "I don't know exactly what clock the House is using," McBarron restated, "but we are very close to the time that this vote is going to have to be called off."[27]

From the speaker's podium, McPike turned to Representative Jim Rea, a downstate Democrat from Christopher. "Representative Rea, did you wish to change your vote? Representative Rea. Representative Rea. Representative Rea changes his vote from 'no' to 'aye.'" Rea's vote brought the tally to fifty-seven for the Sox. McPike quickly announced that another vote had flipped: Democratic Representative Don Saltsman, a burly firefighter from Peoria who had been holding out. Thompson had tag-teamed Saltsman against Representative Fred Tuerk, a Republican, also from Peoria. The two pointed back and forth at each other while standing at their seats on opposite sides of the chamber. Both downstaters wanted to make sure the other was going to vote for the stadium before either switched their vote from no to aye. Each wanted the other to commit first. Saltsman's vote brought the tally to fifty-eight.[28]

There was no question it was past midnight—in the real world, that is. Florida broadcasters started anticipating a victory. One Tampa–St. Pete television reporter even shouted to viewers, "That's it. That's it. The Sox are going to Florida."[29]

McPike, scanning the green and red votes on the tote board as he looked for help, called out the name of one of his neighboring lawmakers,

Representative Sam Wolf, a Democrat from Granite City, where families grow up rooting for the Cardinals baseball team across the Mississippi River in St. Louis. Perhaps thinking Wolf would go along, McPike declared that Wolf had changed his vote from no to aye. That would have pushed the vote to fifty-nine—one away from victory. But Wolf balked, telling McPike, "I don't believe I changed my vote." With pressure building, McPike pulled Wolf's green aye vote off the board. The tally fell back to fifty-eight, not a good time for a setback.

McPike, now practically acting like quarterback with no time left on the clock, spied Tuerk and said he "changes his vote from 'no' to 'aye.' Is that correct?" Tuerk, despite time ticking down, sought to savor his moment: "Who says? Hey, at least give me the opportunity to say that." McPike yielded, and Tuerk said the obvious: "I'll change my vote to 'aye.'"[30]

Pandemonium broke out: fifty-nine. Just one vote away.

Every eye turned to Thompson, who went into an animated conversation with Representative James Stange, a Republican from Oak Brook. McPike called on Stange to speak: "I change my vote from 'no' to 'aye.'"[31]

That was it. Sixty!

Locked in on his mission, McPike moved swiftly to announce the legislation passed on a 60–55 vote: "Senate Bill 2202, having received the constitutional majority at the hour of 11:59, is hereby declared passed."[32]

That declaration of 11:59 p.m.—a minute before the midnight deadline, drew thunderous catcalls from opponents. Dunn, the Decatur Democrat, hurled a stack of paper into the air. "Arm-twisting," Dunn said later. "That's what it boiled down to."[33] Reporters in the press boxes dashed up to the well of the speaker's podium and grabbed copies of the roll call from the House clerk, who immediately leaned on the print button. As they started to run back to the pressroom, a few of the reporters noticed the roll call also had a curious time stamp: 12:03 a.m. July 1.

Celebrating like a conquering hero, Thompson strode through the House chambers shaking hands. He practically levitated across the House floor and into a scrum of reporters waiting in a hallway behind the speaker's podium. Broadcaster Carol Fowler, the statehouse reporter for CBS stations in Urbana and Peoria, challenged Thompson, saying the vote had been taken after midnight. "Was not," Thompson said. "Was too," Fowler countered. "Was not," Thompson said. "Was too," Fowler said. "Was not," Thompson said. "The speaker said it passed at 11:59." And there it was. The House of Madigan had made time stand still.

"It's a political resurrection from the dead," Thompson declared, confessing he'd worried about the outcome. "Now we should build a stadium."[34]

Still sweating the details, Madigan staffers learned about the time stamp, and suddenly new copies appeared with the 12:03 a.m. covered up with white correction fluid. That meant there was no time listed on the roll call at a moment when the exact time meant more than on almost any vote. But the staff that scrambled failed to redact the date. Their new roll calls still said July 1. Some folks tried a quick fix by handwriting 11:59 with pen.[35] To this day, the faded roll call in the secretary of state's archives shows 12:03 a.m. July 1.

In the end, none of that mattered. Immediately after the vote, Madigan said, "I don't think there is a judge in the nation, especially in Illinois, who would challenge this. By my watch, it was 11:59 p.m. I didn't know this would pass. The Republicans told me they had seven votes when we went in, but the governor and I and all the members took risks and passed this bill to keep the White Sox in Chicago."[36]

The pressroom reporters hit their final deadlines, and the story of the midnight miracle made national headlines. Political reporter Rick Pearson, then writing for Gannett's Rockford *Register-Star* before his decades-long run at the *Tribune*, beat the *USA Today* deadline and got banner headline treatment. Florida broadcasters who had watched only the actual time—versus Springfield time—at first believed they had a new team.

But the Floridians learned all too quickly that Illinois lawmakers run on their own clock. And what did Charlie McBarron tell his listeners? "The fat lady has not sung on the Sox yet."[37]

Thompson said he made a "personal plea" to lawmakers. "I think every representative and every senator I've talked to has either lost something or been threatened with the loss of something, and the first person they ever call for help is me. So I walked on the floors of both houses to remind them," Thompson said.[38] Years later he said, "I did some fast talking." And he acknowledged making some trades to get votes but "no big stuff." Thompson recalled that one lawmaker needed a roof on a home for veterans, and that was easy: "I said, 'You're sitting here telling me the veterans are roofless? I wouldn't let that happen.'"[39] But Thompson did concede he initially backed off that deal—just to make the lawmaker come back and ask for the roof again the next year.[40]

When Thompson worked the Democratic side of the aisle, he had stopped at the desk of Representative Wyvetter Younge of East St. Louis, whose legislative district is across the Mississippi from St. Louis and loaded with Cardinals fans. "I said, Wyvetter, why are you voting red on this bill?' She said, 'Oh, governor, did you want me to vote green?' I said, 'Yes,' She said, 'OK,' and she pressed the green button." But it was all happening fast. She didn't think of asking to get something in return for her vote until she showed up at Thompson's office the next day. "I said, 'Well, we'll talk about it, Wyvetter.'"[41]

The speaker—with three dozen of his Democrats ready to support the White Sox bill before the legislation came up for a vote—reportedly coaxed at least three more Democrats to jump on the bandwagon on that final night, but the legend still grows.[42] As the bill neared a vote in the House, Madigan rushed back into his office to find a list of lawmakers who might be convinced to vote for the legislation. He searched quickly in the dark so that he wouldn't wake one of his younger daughters, who was sleeping in the room. "Of all the time I've known Michael Madigan, that's the only time I've seen him run," recalled Steve Brown, the speaker's spokesman for thirty-seven years.[43] Democrats ended up putting forty-three votes on the bill, and Republicans added seventeen.[44]

Stange, who supplied the sixtieth vote, said Thompson virtually promised to support him for secretary of state. Thompson said he informed the lawmaker that he had a different candidate in mind but got Stange's vote anyway. House Minority Leader Lee Daniels, an Elmhurst Republican, remembered it a little differently, saying Thompson answered Stange's request with "'Why not? That's all I said. I didn't promise anything.'"[45]

"Between Madigan and I," Thompson said, "we got the 60 votes. And after I finished working the Republican side, I went over to the Democratic side to work that too, with Madigan. So that was . . . quite an unusual sight for the legislature, to see the [Republican] governor and the Democratic speaker working the Democratic members on that side of the House. It was a wild night."[46]

In a St. Petersburg courtroom following the Sox vote, Pinellas County Circuit Judge David Seth Walker spoke of the religious significance of the White Sox vote in Springfield. "At exactly 11:59 p.m., Central Daylight-Saving Time, the sun stood still, and time stopped," Walker said. "The first recorded instance of this miracle is found in the Judeo-Christian holy book. The second instance of this miracle is now recorded in the minutes of the Illinois House of Representatives."[47]

Did Madigan cheat? You be the judge. It's a discussion for would-be politicians and political science students. Madigan knew the rules, and he knew how to bend them, including time itself. Thompson garnered most of the headlines, but he wouldn't have gotten those three extra minutes without Madigan as speaker. The courts, of course, backed them up, holding that the time declared by the presiding officer is the official time a bill passes. The midnight miracle ranks as one of the most dramatic maneuvers of the Madigan-Thompson era, but the speaker was just getting started.

3

OPERATION COBRA

"Banzaiiiii!"
—Speaker Michael Madigan, May 17, 1989

The biggest raw power play I ever saw Speaker Madigan pull off came on an income tax increase late in the 1989 spring session, a year after saving the White Sox. The Madigan team code-named the surprise tax hike Operation Cobra. With secret planning and swiftness, Madigan introduced a temporary boost in rates and passed it in less than six hours with the bare minimum sixty votes—all Democratic votes. GOP Governor Thompson, who in three straight spring sessions had been calling for a 40 percent permanent income tax hike that Madigan opposed, found himself caught off guard as never before.

The pre-internet early warning came most prominently from two newspapers that hit the Capitol newsstand—the Peoria *Journal Star*, thanks to the well-sourced Bill O'Connell, the dean of the statehouse press corps, and the *Chicago Sun-Times*, courtesy of Charles N. Wheeler III, the paper's Capitol bureau chief, and Michael Sneed, that paper's columnist. The two papers put the scoops about Madigan's tax proposal on page 1 and started a buzz before most pols climbed out of bed. Many Capitol denizens heard the news first on public radio, where statehouse bureau chief Peggy Boyer had snagged the *Journal Star* and *Sun-Times* papers from the newsstand early and broadcast live what the papers reported. She called Thompson spokesman Jim Bray at home to see if he'd seen the papers and to get the governor's reaction. Bray grabbed a paper from his doorstep and quickly said he'd have to call her back.

Madigan's plan called for an 18.4 percent increase in the personal and corporate income tax rates over two years. That meant the rate at the time would rise from 2.5 percent on individuals to 2.96 percent. The corporate tax rate would see a corresponding increase, from 4 percent to 4.736 percent. Since his fourth term began in 1987, Thompson had called for bumping the personal income tax rate from 2.5 percent to 3.5 percent, levying a sales tax on services such as haircuts and auto repairs and increasing the gasoline tax.[1] But the Madigan plan had Thompson baffled.

The governor attracted a mob of reporters shouting questions as he dashed up the Capitol's grand staircase. The reporters scurried alongside with tape recorders rolling as they asked what he thought of the Madigan proposal. In the rarest of moments, the always-in-control Thompson looked shell-shocked, almost staggered, as if he'd gone a couple of rounds with downstate Jacksonville's heavyweight boxing champ, Ken Norton, the man who broke Muhammad Ali's jaw.

Thompson stopped momentarily once he reached the third floor of the rotunda to talk to the anxious reporters as they stuck microphones up to his face. The governor kept repeating that he wanted to find out "if it's true" what the *Journal Star* and the *Sun-Times* had written. He was still somewhat in disbelief. He charged unannounced into Madigan's office, located across a hallway behind the speaker's podium. Madigan did not leave Big Jim hanging. The speaker grabbed a copy of one of the papers headlining his plans and gave the governor a one-word answer: "Banzaiiiii!"[2]

The speaker had quietly surveyed his members and knew they stood with him. Confident of victory, he put the proposal in play and shoved it through his chamber while House Republicans remained stunned. After watching their GOP governor push for a permanent income tax since 1987 and Madigan almost robotically saying he was "not convinced of the need," House Republican leader Lee Daniels of Elmhurst could do little more than squawk.

Indeed, the Madigan power play of 1989 represented an approach to putting a temporary tax hike in place that was far different from what had happened in 1983, when Daniels himself helped break a deadlock over a previous Thompson push for a permanent tax increase. Thompson had led the public into believing the state finances were in good shape during the 1982 campaign, but he called for the tax hike to battle a recession once he was sworn into his third term in 1983, drawing caustic public criticism for changing his stance.

After summits between Thompson and the four legislative leaders that year, Daniels rolled out a plan with key House GOP caucus members, including Representative Jim Reilly, a political strategist from Jacksonville and a onetime Winchester schoolteacher who would later become Thompson's deputy governor and serve in top positions with Governor Jim Edgar as well. They offered an alternative temporary tax increase to counter Thompson's push for permanence. Thompson and the leaders finally endorsed an eighteen-month temporary income tax hike. It also increased the state sales tax rate from 4 percent to 5 percent starting in 1984. Other pieces of the plan included giving a bit of property tax relief and eliminating the final 2 percent sales tax on food and drugs. Madigan, in his first year as speaker, needed to persuade Democrats who were loyal to newly elected Mayor Harold Washington to go along. Thompson conceded that the Daniels plan was the only option left: "It's a question of this or nothing."[3] He signed it into law.

The backdrop of 1983 was different from that of 1989 in another way. Thompson had beaten Adlai Stevenson III by only 5,074 votes in the 1982 election—an election upheld when Democratic Illinois Supreme Court Justice Seymour Simon sided with three Republican justices to deny Stevenson a recount, much to Madigan's dismay and disappointment. Four years later, Thompson beat Stevenson overwhelmingly in a 1986 rematch to win the governor's unprecedented fourth term. Stevenson was hobbled when disciples of extremist Lyndon LaRouche won the lieutenant governor and secretary of state spots in the Democratic primary. Stevenson abandoned the Democratic nomination for governor and formed the Illinois Solidarity Party, but Thompson won by nearly four hundred thousand votes.

Once again Thompson had led voters during the 1986 campaign to believe that the state's finances were stable. And once again he unveiled a massive set of proposed tax hikes when he started his new term in 1987. Madigan said Thompson had lost credibility because he sent signals before both elections that Illinois' finances were rosy and then called for post-election tax hikes. The speaker put up a wall of resistance to Thompson's tax package for two full spring sessions and showed little sign of budging until he upended the statehouse in 1989 with his session-altering tax plan.

When he brought Operation Cobra to the House floor, Madigan displayed the full power of his speakership. He would not be raising money for spending increases throughout state government as Thompson wanted. The speaker explained that his proposal would raise money exclusively for two purposes: schools and local governments. "I have not changed my position regarding the governor's request for a 40 percent increase in the Illinois income tax," Madigan said. "I have said over the last two years, that Illinois does not need a 40 percent increase in the tax, that the Government of Illinois does not need to grow anymore."[4]

In his floor speech, Madigan pointed to an experience that some statehouse wits likened to the biblical Saul's conversion on the road to Damascus. Madigan recounted his rare visits to the Southern Illinois communities of Effingham and Mount Vernon at the request of lawmakers, meeting there with school officials and talking with such lawmakers as his close friend Representative E. J. "Zeke" Giorgi, the Rockford Democrat and father of the Illinois lottery. The discussions, Madigan said, "convinced me of the gravity of the situation concerning financing of local school districts in this state." He said the school problems came about because of local property assessment practices and the way the "nation has been ravaged by the current fiscal policies in Washington." The speaker also said the two-year increase—what he euphemistically called a "surcharge" on the income tax—would be temporary, so lawmakers would have a chance to review how the money was spent. "If after two years, we find that there is waste, if after two years, we find we made a mistake, then we simply don't renew the program," Madigan said. "If after two years, we make a decision that it's a good program, that it ought to be continued, then we vote it into effect again."[5]

The first of many Democrats to rise in support was Representative Al Ronan, a Chicago wheeler-dealer who would later become a lobbyist with a mile-long list of clients. "One of the things we're sent here for is to fund education, and we haven't done the job," Ronan said, adding, "We had the Reagan Revolution that said let's shift all the responsibility [to] the local level, but then nobody decided to help pay for it. And because of our inaction, we've raised local property taxes. This will help solve that problem."[6]

Daniels attempted to mount a Republican attack, zeroing in on the speaker's sudden embrace of an income tax increase after repeatedly opposing the governor's calls for higher taxes. "When I awoke this morning, it seemed to me like any other normal legislative day," Daniels said.

But when I entered the State House, it seemed to me that the usual clusters of kibitzers were charged with an unusual intensity. I couldn't help but overhear some of their conversations and I must say that I was slightly surprised and somewhat shocked. I was shocked because they were discussing Speaker Madigan's proposal for an Income tax increase. . . . Savor that idea for a moment with me. The speaker, the one Illinois politician who has tried to reshape his career into being "Mr. Anti-Income Tax Increase" [is] now sponsoring an income tax increase. It's like finding out, I might suggest, that Batman's nemesis, the Joker, is really a good guy. . . . How can we help but be skeptical by this thunderbolt?[7]

Daniels gamed out his options and chose an escape hatch. He said he would vote "present," meaning an abstention, and urged his caucus to join him. On the preliminary vote to adopt the amendment that attached Madigan's tax proposal onto a live bill, the roll call was sixty in favor, eleven against, and forty-four present. On the vote to pass the legislation and send it to the Senate, the roll call tallied sixty in favor, nineteen against, and thirty-six present. One bemused statehouse reporter noted that the huge pile of present votes from House Republicans revealed they were "scared voteless."

Madigan's plan was to raise more than $700 million and split it between Illinois cities and schools. For newly elected Mayor Richard M. Daley, the money was a gift to help get through a city budget coming in about $120 million short. The oddity of the figures in Madigan's proposal—2.96 percent for individuals and 4.736 percent for corporations—was linked to how much Daley needed to plug his budget hole. Madigan made the move twenty-three days after Daley took office in his first term as mayor. By the time Madigan jammed the income tax hike through the House, Daley had already announced his opposition to a local property tax hike. He wanted to keep voters happy given that his first term was for a special two-year period that meant he would face voters again in 1991. There was little doubt that the two forty-seven-year-old Irish politicians, with a well-documented history of political ups and downs since they served together in the state's Sixth Constitutional Convention, had found common ground. "I've spoken to Mayor Daley concerning this plan, and he said he thought it was a fine plan, especially because of its statewide application," Madigan said. Thompson said the Madigan plan "is bold, it's audacious, and it might even be diabolical."[8]

Local school leaders and education lobbyists for years had hounded the speaker for more money. Madigan timed the moment to strike with Operation Cobra when he knew he would get unquestioned support. To back up his plan, Madigan had staffers stuffing three thousand envelopes with letters to mayors, school superintendents, and county board chairs—all timed to hit mailboxes the day Madigan's plan would be announced in the papers.[9] Reporter fax machines, the swiftest way of getting word out en masse, poured out letters from thirty-nine groups that embraced Madigan's proposal—thanks again to the speaker team's well-orchestrated coordination of school advocates. *St. Louis Post-Dispatch* correspondent Kathleen Best, the paper's Capitol bureau chief, wrote that even Thompson "appeared dazzled" by Madigan's far-reaching effort. "It's clever, maybe too clever," Thompson said.[10]

In the Senate, as usual, pulling Democrats together to support the plan would not be easy. President Phil Rock of Oak Park struggled to get his small, 31–28 majority of Democrats on board. Rock had supported a permanent income tax increase but also backed the Madigan breakthrough. Rock needed thirty votes to pass the legislation, but too many of his jittery Democrats worried that supporting higher taxes would cause voters to throw them out of office. Fighting at every turn, Rock first pushed the bill through a Democratic-led Senate committee on a 7–5 vote. "This proposal is elegant in its simplicity," Rock testified. "It says we're going to raise the tax for a period of two years, and we're going to give the money to schools and local governments." Nonetheless, getting Rock's full caucus to go along gave the Senate president a Sisyphean task. Thompson played coy: "I would find it very hard to sign a bill that raised three-quarters of a billion dollars in state income taxes with not one penny for human services that came to me on a party-line . . . vote, with a bare majority, and it was temporary in nature. I think it is bad tax policy, bad politics."[11] With the June 30 deadline to act only three days away, Mayor Daley warned, "If we don't get more money from Springfield, we are going to have a big budget problem, and everybody knows that."[12]

Senate GOP leader James "Pate" Philip of Wood Dale said he was trying to draw up a plan to reduce the property tax burden—a particular concern in the wealthier suburbs—but had been having trouble getting traction. Madigan remained steadfast to his 18.4 percent plan. "We ought to focus on passing that bill and forget all of these other ideas," he said.[13]

Going into their last scheduled day of session, Rock worked with Madigan to put together an alternative, hoping it would be palatable enough to pass the Senate. The main elements called for a flat 20 percent increase in the income tax rate rather than the 18.4 percent sponsored by Madigan. That would increase income tax rates from 2.5 percent to 3 percent for individuals and 4 percent to 4.8 percent for corporations. Boosting the plan to an even-numbered 20 percent increase meant the Rock-Madigan proposal would provide enough new dollars to grant home owners a larger credit for property taxes on their income tax returns—giving Republicans a chance to save face and providing Chicago and other cities the money they needed. Thompson signaled minimal progress—"a step forward," he said—but he remained cagey on whether he would sign it.[14] All of the maneuvering set up the June 30 deadline day for a moment of truth.

In the House, Madigan stood before colleagues again and recalled how sixty Democrats had come together only weeks before: "Some said, 'Well, aren't you afraid that you're making a political mistake in advancing a tax increase with no Republican votes?' I said, 'No, I'm not afraid because I've got the courage of my conviction on this particular issue.' And I recall the advice that was given to me by my father many years ago, when he said, 'If you believe in something, stand up and say it and have the courage to stand behind the . . . position that you've adopted.'"[15] The newly revised tax proposal passed 72–45 with eight Republicans joining Democrats to support the bill. The trouble came once again in the Senate, where the Democratic caucus still could not put together thirty votes. Rock was stuck on twenty-nine. Suddenly, Republican Senator Ralph Dunn of DuQuoin, another former Con-Con delegate, whose sprawling district included schools that needed the money, pushed a green button on his desk to tally the thirtieth vote.

Lawmakers couldn't stop themselves once they got started. They also sent Thompson a six-cent-a-gallon gasoline tax increase and a dime-a-pack cigarette tax hike. They added a computer software tax that would help pay for improvements at libraries, the Lincoln Park and Brookfield zoos, and civic centers throughout the state. They also found time to approve legislation that bumped up pensions for Thompson and other top state officials. The package gave thousands of dollars in stipends for House and Senate leadership teams as well as dozens of committee chairs and minority spokespeople to be paid on top of their basic legislative salaries. Thompson signed all of those bills.[16]

In only his seventh spring legislative session as speaker, Madigan had seen Chicago Mayors Jane Byrne, Harold Washington, and Eugene Sawyer come and go. More important, though, the political value of holding on to the speakership became increasingly more evident. Madigan was the stopper of ideas he didn't like, and he could deliver what he wanted. He could strike at lightning speed. He could make everyone wait for his move. Both his friends and his political enemies would say the speakership in itself—not ideology, not issues, not specific bills—had become his end-all and be-all. His number one priority was keeping the speakership, the source of his growing power. All else came second.

Enter Republican Jim Edgar, a teetotaling politician who provided a change of style to the hard-partying but brilliant Thompson. Once Thompson announced he would not seek a fifth term, Edgar quickly revealed he wanted to step up from secretary of state and jumped into the 1990 campaign for governor. One of Edgar's key issues in his general election against Attorney General Neil Hartigan, the Democrat whom Madigan supported, was making Madigan's temporary income tax permanent. A former legislator from Charleston, Edgar figured Illinoisans were tired of getting told that state finances were in great shape during a campaign season and then being told that a tax increase was needed once the election was over. The argument provided Edgar, once a Thompson legislative aide, with one way to get out from under Thompson's long shadow. Edgar could build on his image as a straight-shooter and could show he was his own man. Thompson had appointed Edgar secretary of state when his predecessor, Democrat Alan Dixon, was elected in 1980 to the U.S. Senate. And Edgar made good on his decade in the job. He had championed tougher drunken driving laws and mandatory auto insurance—good-government issues that made the roads safer.

As a candidate for governor, Edgar said up front that he believed the responsible thing to do was to keep the money coming in from the Madigan temporary tax increase. But pushing to make the tax increase permanent was risky for Edgar, who bet that citizens would go along with keeping their taxes higher to support schools and government services. Hartigan took a populist vow to let the tax hike expire. His position was viewed in political circles as voter friendly but gutless—a refusal to take the heat when Edgar would. Ultimately, voters rewarded Edgar with a victory, setting the stage for a showdown with Madigan.

Edgar knew what Madigan was capable of doing. Even now, more than three decades after Operation Cobra, Edgar said Madigan's lightning-swift passage of the temporary income tax increase in 1989 was the "most amazing of all the legislative things I watched him do. Now people may not think it was good, but it was the most amazing. . . . It was just boom, boom, boom." And even up until shortly before Madigan stepped down, Edgar viewed him as the smartest politician in the Capitol since Thompson had left. "Madigan was more focused, more disciplined and in some ways could be more effective," Edgar said.[17] In 1991, though, the tax issue was just one matter before Madigan and the newly elected governor.

The speaker gave Edgar a cool reception as he took office, not even returning Edgar's telephone calls for months. Having dealt with Madigan as a rank-and-file legislator, as Thompson's legislative aide, and as secretary of state, Edgar had built a working relationship with him. But a Republican in the Executive Mansion meant Edgar would be in place to veto a redistricting map when Democrats who controlled the legislature would want to redraw favorable district boundaries for themselves and their party once again. A power struggle ensued as Madigan tried to get a feel for the rookie governor. They battled to a standoff as Edgar pushed for a permanent increase in the income tax and Madigan countered with a second, two-year extension. The fight turned into a test of wills. The duel took the General Assembly into overtime and led to the state's missing an employee payday for the first time since the Great Depression.[18] As it was playing out, Madigan dropped a rare hint to reporters about how his clash with Edgar could turn out: "This governor has said he's not going to raise taxes, that he wants to reduce state spending. He's going to get what he wants . . . and you will all write that the governor won."[19]

A little more than eighteen tension-filled days into overtime, Madigan's prediction came close to being on the mark. Eventually, a compromise came together that would make the education half of Madigan's initial surcharge permanent. The other half would be extended for another two years—and split between city and state governments rather than giving all of the money to the locals. Edgar had campaigned on enacting property tax caps on school districts and other local governments statewide, including on such home-rule units as the city of Chicago. Madigan and Rock balked, and the final compromise mandated caps only in the collar counties surrounding Cook County and exempted home-rule units. The caps limited annual property tax increases to 5 percent or the rate of inflation, whichever was less.[20]

Two years later, in the spring of 1993, the legislature and the governor made the second half of Madigan's original temporary income tax permanent. But the share of money to cities was reduced further over

Madigan's objections.[21] By then the legislative politics had shifted. The two chambers were no longer both controlled by Democrats. Redistricting had put Republicans in charge of the Senate under President Pate Philip, and his influence turned the suburbs into what the *Tribune* called the "state's predominant political force," putting the city into a defensive crouch. "It's a dramatic change," Madigan said. "I think you're going to see the legislature become more concerned with suburban needs because people have moved to the suburbs."[22]

Madigan Loses the Speakership

Madigan got a real dose of what dramatic change meant in the next election, November 1994. He lost the majority, the only time he was dislodged from the speakership in the middle of his decades-long reign. As they watched the vote totals coming in from around the state that night, Madigan's pack of loyalists said they had seen it coming and braced for the wipeout. They didn't have a firewall. Comptroller Dawn Clark Netsch, the astute lakefront liberal and former Con-Con delegate who taught law at Northwestern University, challenged Edgar in 1994 after winning in the March Democratic primary. Along with bashing her for being too soft on crime and a death penalty opponent, Edgar excoriated Netsch over her plan to raise the income tax by $2.5 billion and provide $1 billion to schools, $1 billion for property tax relief, and $500 million in income tax relief for low- and middle-class workers. Edgar focused on the tax-increase portion of Netsch's plan rather than tax relief and help for the working class. He unabashedly ripped into the Netsch proposal as a 42 percent income tax increase and cast doubt on the tax relief she offered. "I don't think she helped our cause," said Madigan, who had supported Cook County Board President Richard Phelan in the primary.[23]

Once Edgar won reelection in 1994, the tax debate turned a bit surreal. Less than two days after the polls closed, Republican Senate President Philip suggested that maybe a swap of sorts that provided true property tax relief was worth exploring. "If you would take 40 percent off the real estate tax, increase the income tax a little bit, the sales tax a little bit, maybe liquor tax a little bit, maybe cigarette tax a little bit and spread it around, it might be an interesting proposition," Philip said. Political postures can change rapidly in Springfield, but observers wondered whether Philip had watched as Edgar repeatedly pounded Netsch's tax-swap proposal during the campaign. "She stole that idea from me in the first place," Philip said.[24] Though glad the idea of a tax swap remained alive, Netsch laughed off Philip's suggestion that she had stolen the idea: "I've been advocating this going back long before the campaign began, and I'm not alone."

Edgar himself eventually turned into somewhat of a convert. He put together a task force headed by former University of Illinois President Stanley Ikenberry to come up with a better way to fund schools, and he embraced its proposal for voters to ratify an amendment to the Illinois Constitution that would require the state to pay half the cost of a basic level of school funding. The proposal, as described by the *Tribune*'s Rick Pearson, could have raised taxes by $2 billion while promising $1.5 billion in property tax relief by supplanting local school funds with state dollars. But the *Tribune* headline "Edgar Readies Tax Bombshell" didn't set well with the governor, particularly for the rollout of a potential legacy-building initiative.[25] Madigan's demotion to minority leader also didn't make Edgar's political path easier on the tax issue, though Republicans took over both houses. Edgar received a chilly reception from Philip and first-time speaker Daniels, who didn't want to risk losing the gavel to Madigan by running Republicans on the same ballot as the governor's tax proposal. Philip maintained it would take "an act of God" for Edgar's proposal to win approval in a Senate committee, let alone the full chamber. "Republicans aren't for tax increases. Nobody wants a large tax to be on the ballot. That's how simple it is," Philip said.[26]

It didn't help that Bob Kustra, Edgar's lieutenant governor, lost in the 1996 Republican primary for U.S. Senate to state Representative Al Salvi of Wauconda, a staunch antitax candidate who suddenly looked prescient for warning that Edgar and Kustra would propose a secret postprimary tax increase for schools. Edgar, though, still grumbled about the *Tribune* headline. He said Philip and Daniels didn't muscle up "because of the way . . . the *Tribune* reported it as a tax bombshell." In short, Edgar added, "I think it was more that they read the headline in the *Tribune* and got spooked."[27]

In a bow to the political adage of no permanent friends and no permanent enemies, Edgar and Madigan eventually found themselves working together. Madigan recaptured the speakership with a slim 60–58 majority in the 1996 general election, thanks to his near-fanatical focus on winning six south suburban seats and the turnout generated by Democratic

President Bill Clinton's run for reelection. Edgar said he received a call from the reinstated speaker:

> He said, "Governor, I just want you to know I'm going to work with you now." He said, "I learned my lesson." He said, "I fought Thompson. I fought you." He said, "I can't beat the governor. You've got the bully pulpit." He said, "I'm not going to win those battles. So unless there's something I really disagree with, I'll try to help you on whatever you want to do. . . ." He was good to his word on that. He was my best ally in trying to hold the line on spending. Madigan, he's pretty fiscally conservative. But, as he said, "my members aren't." He said, "You'll have to take the lead as governor. I'll support you."[28]

By the middle of the 1997 session, Madigan had embraced a new Edgar tax-swap effort. By mid-May the speaker said that more than forty of his House Democrats could support raising the income tax and lowering property taxes.[29] The Democrats in the House that Madigan had carefully rebuilt then put up fifty-five of sixty-two votes.[30] The Edgar package would have raised personal income tax rates 25 percent to give schools more money and property tax relief to home owners. The personal income tax under Edgar would have risen to 3.75 percent from 3 percent, but Philip labeled the legislation "totally unacceptable."[31] A Republican-led Senate committee killed the Edgar plan. And that was it. Edgar sought a full Senate vote, but Philip had blocked his own governor again. Madigan had tried but couldn't influence the Senate. "Mike Madigan is not the bad person that he's made out to be," Edgar said years later at an appearance at Southern Illinois University at Carbondale. "Is he difficult? Yes. Is he wrong? Yes. Often. But it's not all his fault. And, I found in my last years as governor . . . he was much more supportive of my efforts to balance the budget than my two Republican leaders were."[32]

After Operation Cobra, after the battles to make the temporary tax permanent, after Madigan's tax alliance with Edgar failed, the Illinois income tax rate would not budge during the terms of two more governors.

PART II

POWER PLAYS AND POLITICAL FLOPS

4

HISTORIC IMPEACHMENT

"Well, I've had an opportunity to get to
know Mr. Blagojevich over six years, and
so I was not surprised."
—Speaker Michael Madigan, December 15,
2008

By the time FBI agents arrested Governor Rod Blagojevich before dawn
on December 9, 2008, Speaker Madigan had gone to war with his fellow Democrat so many times that saying they were each other's political
nemesis was way past the point of cliché. Madigan, the master tactician,
virtually had given clinics on how to tame the erratic governor's worst
legislative impulses—blocking expensive business tax proposals, requiring
the governor to sign agreements to ensure he'd stick to his promises, scut-
tling proposed prison closures, and reining in large increases in proposed
spending. Blagojevich tried over and over to make Madigan bend, but the
governor found out that wasn't easy. Madigan, the student of government
intricacies, showed again and again he ruled in his House, where what
he said is what went down.

Blagojevich's inattention to details caused his aides to paint him as a
big-picture guy, but old-timers saw him as a faker, a style-over-substance
politician who preferred to hole up in his Chicago home or political
headquarters rather than work in the governor's offices in Chicago and
Springfield. No modern Illinois governor was so ill-prepared, so oblivi-
ous to the basic dynamics of governing. Stack up Blagojevich against the
previously indicted and convicted Illinois chief executives, and he wins

high marks for his devious level of corruption. Prosecutors alleged that days before he was first elected governor in November 2002, Blagojevich plotted with close confidants over how to enrich themselves from the spoils they could rake in by leveraging his office.[1] Yet his misdeeds, disinterest, and sheer malevolence fractured the state in ways the federal charges only touched upon. Not only did the House impeach him, but the Senate tossed him from office and disqualified him from ever again holding any public office of the state of Illinois. Previous scoundrels in Illinois history have portraits hanging in the Hall of Governors along one wing of the Capitol, but Illinois lawmakers banned spending public funds to paint Blagojevich's picture. They'd seen enough.

What Madigan and fellow lawmakers learned from Blagojevich's arrest in the heady weeks following Democratic U.S. Senator Barack Obama's election to the White House went far beyond their frustrations with a wayward governor. The marquee federal charge facing Blagojevich was that he tried to sell his power to appoint a U.S. senator to the Illinois seat vacated by the president-elect. They would learn how Blagojevich tried to shake down a horse-track owner for a one-hundred-thousand-dollar campaign donation in exchange for signing legislation that would help subsidize tracks with a share of profits from riverboat casinos. Perhaps most appalling, they would learn how the corrupt governor tried to squeeze a $25,000 donation from the head of Chicago's Children's Memorial Hospital before sending over a promised $8 million increase in state reimbursement rates for pediatric services. They also would learn, among other issues, that Blagojevich tried unsuccessfully to get *Tribune* editorial board members fired for writing critical opinions of him before he would entertain letting the company, then owners of the Chicago Cubs, have access to state financing for Wrigley Field. Robert Grant, special agent in charge of the FBI's Chicago office, explained how Illinois' political corruption ranked in America, saying, "If it isn't the most corrupt state in the United States, it's certainly one hell of a competitor." U.S. Attorney Patrick Fitzgerald, whose office already had put ex-Governor George Ryan behind bars, decried Blagojevich's activities as a "political corruption crime spree" and maintained the "breadth of corruption laid out in these charges is staggering."[2] But Fitzgerald didn't stop there. He dropped on reporters the "L" word that stands in Illinois for the highest of ethical standards: He said Blagojevich's activities "would make Lincoln roll over in his grave."[3]

Blagojevich received little sympathy in Springfield. Obama's historic victory had given most state lawmakers and much of the state of Illinois a moment of pride. One of their own—only four years removed from the Illinois state Senate—would move from the U.S. Senate to the presidency, the first African American leader of the most powerful country on earth. Blagojevich, jealous of Obama's meteoric rise, suddenly perpetuated Illinois' rancid reputation for political corruption. Late-night TV jokesters once again made the state a universal punch line. Ryan, Blagojevich's immediate predecessor, already sat in prison, and Blagojevich, who ran as a reformer, looked like he would soon have a cell of his own.

The clock started ticking on Madigan's legislative response even before Blagojevich had his mug shot taken in the powder blue jogging outfit he had worn to federal court the day of his arrest. In Chicago, Obama first spoke only of being "saddened and sobered" and unaware of what Blagojevich had done.[4] But the president-elect quickly would become the most prominent of Illinois' political luminaries demanding that Blagojevich resign. Madigan gave Blagojevich six days. But the governor didn't follow the playbook of Richard M. Nixon, the Republican Blagojevich had been enamored with as a young man. Nixon quit before impeachment could embarrass him further; Blagojevich wouldn't let go. So Madigan launched the first-ever impeachment probe of an Illinois governor. "We plan to proceed without delay," Madigan told reporters at the Capitol. "This action is reflective of probably a majority of people in the House, probably a majority of people in the state."[5]

Madigan appointed House Majority Leader Barbara Flynn Currie, a Chicago Democrat, to chair a bipartisan special investigative committee to hold hearings and make recommendations. Currie had consistently proven herself unflappable. She cochaired a 1997 House panel that concluded onetime Illinois Supreme Court Chief Justice James Heiple was "imperious" but not worthy of impeachment. As she took the reins of the Blagojevich panel, Currie vowed, "It's absolutely critical that we do this deliberately, that we don't rush to judgment, that we don't say, 'Because the public is clamoring for his head, we should take the head first and do the trial later.'"[6]

Blagojevich didn't bother to show up for the House hearings, sending powerhouse Chicago defense lawyers Ed Genson and Sam Adam Jr. instead. Genson maintained that the impeachment process left him "fighting shadows," but the Currie committee unveiled the equivalent of an overwhelming political indictment, voting 21–0 to recommend impeachment and removal.[7] Shortly thereafter, Genson would resign as Blagojevich's criminal attorney, telling reporters, "I never require a client to do what I say, but I do require them to at least listen to what I say. . . . I wish the governor good luck and godspeed."[8]

Still resonating since the day of his arrest were the recorded words that Blagojevich infamously used to describe how he relished cutting a deal for the Senate seat in order to make his own life better: "I've got this thing, and . . . it's f—ing golden, and I'm not giving it up for f—ing nothing."[9]

Blagojevich dreamed big, as the tapes and an FBI affidavit showed. He pondered trading the U.S. Senate appointment for heading the U.S. Department of Health and Human Services in Obama's administration, getting an ambassadorship to a foreign country, or heading a private group that would support the president politically. He wanted a salary of $250,000 to $300,000. And maybe something for his wife, Patricia, potentially a job for her while he finished his term as governor—a job where, he said, he felt stuck.[10]

In reality—a perspective that Blagojevich often lacked when weighing his own importance—none of those ideas was ever in the cards. Rahm Emanuel, who would give up his congressional seat to become Obama's chief of staff before becoming Chicago's mayor, delivered a message to Blagojevich emissary John Wyma, a lobbyist pal who used to work on the staff of the governor when he was in Congress. Emanuel said Obama would "value and appreciate" it if Blagojevich would use his appointment powers to make Valerie Jarrett the next U.S. senator from Illinois, according to Wyma's trial testimony.[11] Blagojevich fumed: "They're not willing to give me anything except appreciation. F— 'em."[12] Later, Jarrett would become one of Obama's closest White House advisers and confidants.

The idea of impeaching Blagojevich had already crossed Madigan's mind. Before Blagojevich was charged, thirteen people had been indicted or convicted in the spreading scandal. The list included Antoin "Tony" Rezko, who would be sentenced to ten and a half years in prison, and the governor's former chief fund-raiser, Christopher Kelly, who would commit suicide following a guilty plea on tax fraud counts linked to gambling activities in Las Vegas.[13]

Guilty pleas from other political operatives shed additional light on how Blagojevich and his team sought to trade state jobs, appointments, and contracts for contributing or raising campaign cash.[14] "We've reviewed impeachment for about a year," Madigan said, "and we never came to a judgment that impeachment was appropriate until the events of six days ago."[15]

The unpredictable Blagojevich worried Democrats and Republicans alike. Still governor but now out on bail, Blagojevich possessed the sole authority to make an appointment to the U.S. Senate vacancy. Republican Representative Tom Cross urged passage of legislation to take away Blagojevich's appointment power and set up a special election to replace Obama. "To avoid any appearance of impropriety, you've got to hold an election," said Cross, the House minority leader from Oswego.[16] But when lawmakers returned to Springfield to address the crisis, Madigan's plans to move forward on legislation for a special election didn't materialize. Much to the disappointment of Republicans thinking they could win the Obama seat because of the Democratic disarray, Madigan only offered the resolution to form the investigative committee looking at impeachment. The speaker did not offer legislation for a special election. On the House floor, Cross asked why. Madigan said his caucus was split over holding a special election, and he needed more time to reach a consensus. Cross pointedly warned that "every day that goes by . . . leaves this man with the ability to appoint the next U.S. senator."[17]

Blagojevich's support had cratered even before his arrest. In late October 2008, a *Tribune* poll found that only 13 percent of voters approved of the governor's job performance—the lowest rating ever recorded for an elected politician in nearly three decades of the paper's polls.[18] Federal recordings had caught Blagojevich raging about that lack of appreciation:

I f—— busted my ass and pissed people off and gave your grandmother a free f—— ride on a bus. OK? I gave your f—— baby a chance to have health care. I fought every one of those assholes, including every special interest out there, who can make my life easier and better, because they wanna raise taxes on you, and I won't. I, I fight them and keep them from doing it. And what do I get for that? Only 13 percent of you all out there think I'm doing a good job. So f— all of you.[19]

Madigan often waited for the right time before making a major move. The arrest and the sheer breadth of criminal allegations canceled any doubts. Asked whether Blagojevich's actions surprised him, Madigan was straightforward: "Well, I've had an opportunity to get to know Mr. Blagojevich over six years, and so I was not surprised."[20]

Over those six years, Democrats and Republicans had accumulated a giant pile of grievances against Blagojevich, ranging from his clumsy ward-style politics to his attempts to push programs that went against basic rules of governance, state and federal laws, and the Illinois Constitution. He charged that lawmakers spent "like a bunch of drunken sailors," called the state school board a "Soviet-style bureaucracy," and claimed he had the "testicular virility" to stand up to his estranged father-in-law, Alderman Richard Mell. The Thirty-Third Ward boss once charged that Blagojevich traded campaign contributions for jobs and appointments, but Mell backed down once threatened with a lawsuit.[21] Angered by *Tribune* reporters looking into Patti Blagojevich's cozy real estate deals with his political friends, the governor answered a couple of questions and walked away at an event in downstate Godfrey. A few seconds later, he leaped out of his black SUV, dashed over to me, and said his wife had a right to her own career. He called questions about her business "Neanderthal and sexist."[22]

Along the way, Blagojevich shrugged off legal roadblocks if he thought he had a popular idea, such as laudable goals of expanding health care or lowering the costs of prescription drugs. But because he didn't have legal authority, his moves ended up examined in the House impeachment hearings. In fact, five of the thirteen charges detailed in the House impeachment resolution were not criminal offenses but rather involved executive branch overreach into legislative matters.

In one headline-grabbing initiative, Blagojevich pushed to import prescription drugs for Illinoisans under a program called I-Save-Rx. What the impeachment committee recounted was that not only was it illegal to import the drugs, but the state also failed to adequately test or inspect them for quality, raising questions about the safety of the medicine. The Food and Drug Administration warned the state about breaking federal law and rejected a waiver request from Blagojevich, but he proceeded anyway. The Currie committee determined the "governor abused the power of his office."[23]

Blagojevich inquired overseas when the United States issued a warning about a shortage of vaccines for the flu season in October 2004. He and top aides negotiated to import flu vaccines from Europe, again without getting approval from the Food and Drug Administration (FDA). He was blocked from getting the medicine, but he tried anyway to pay $2.6 million to the drug maker. Democratic Comptroller Dan Hynes refused to pay the tab. Auditor General William Holland also testified the governor's office knew the proposed importation was unlawful and that the drugs would not be delivered.[24]

Blagojevich then touted a humanitarian solution: donate the drugs to earthquake-ravaged Pakistan, an idea that carried an altruistic spin until *Tribune* reporters John Chase, Kim Barker, and David Kidwell looked harder. They discovered the Pakistanis had destroyed the vaccines. They were past their expiration dates.[25]

After a brief honeymoon following Blagojevich's inauguration in 2003, Madigan and the governor feuded steadily, but 2004 brought their first major budget showdown, an impasse that lasted nearly eight weeks of overtime and almost caused Democrats to miss their national convention in Boston, where state Senator Obama's keynote address would propel him onto the world stage. Blagojevich and Democratic Senate President Emil Jones of Chicago pledged to push for more funding for schools and health care. Madigan repeatedly argued that Blagojevich wanted to borrow and spend more money than the state could afford. The speaker allied with the two Republican legislative leaders, Representative Tom Cross and Senator Frank Watson of Greenville, a group the speaker referred to as the "Coalition of the Willing." With Republican support needed to meet a three-fifths supermajority vote requirement to pass a budget when they missed their May 31 deadline, the two camps deadlocked. Trying to get Madigan to cave, Jones argued, "Someone has to be strong to the principles of our platform in the Democratic Party." But Representative Bob Molaro, a longtime Madigan loyalist from the speaker's Southwest Side sphere of influence, burnished the Madigan Mystique, saying no one could pressure the speaker: "He's like Superman. Not even kryptonite can affect him."[26]

The state budget battle finally did end. Obama had written passages of his now-famous convention speech in the cramped men's room at the back of the Illinois Senate chamber, close to his desk in case he needed to break away to cast a vote. Madigan and the two Republican legislative leaders forced Blagojevich to sign written memorandums of understanding designed to guarantee that the governor would keep his word to fund the projects he promised. Madigan said the memos addressed a "certain level of distrust."[27] They finished just in time to hear Obama speak in Boston.

Despite his steadfast wariness of Blagojevich, Madigan stood by him politically. A few weeks after Boston, the speaker didn't hesitate when asked between activities at the Illinois State Fair if he would back the

governor for reelection in 2006. "My plan would be to support Blagojevich," Madigan told me.[28] He would do one better.

Madigan and Jones—two Democratic leaders suspicious of each other
on a good day—signed up as cochairs of Blagojevich's reelection campaign. The political peace allowed them to work together rather than get
into another entrenched budget battle that could hurt them all. Madigan,
Jones, and Blagojevich soon agreed to an old trick: dip into the state pension funds to ease budget problems through Blagojevich's 2006 reelection campaign. Under the surface there was another political dynamic
unfolding. As Madigan sought at least a temporary political détente with
the governor, the speaker's daughter, Attorney General Lisa Madigan,
was investigating alleged hiring irregularities in the Blagojevich administration. Only four months before the 2006 general election, she made
public a letter from U.S. Attorney Patrick Fitzgerald saying she would
hand her team's work to his office in order to avoid interfering with his
own probe. He wrote he had identified "allegations of endemic hiring
fraud" in multiple state agencies under Blagojevich.[29]

The letter provided a rare public acknowledgment of their investigations. It also gave Lisa Madigan a marker on the table, establishing a
degree of political distance from a governor becoming more toxic by the
day. Numerous stories had exposed federal subpoenas tied to alleged illegal hiring and pay-to-play appointments to state boards. But Madigan's
letter came out right before the *Tribune* published a Sunday exclusive
that detailed a secret report by former Executive Inspector General Zaldwaynaka "Z." Scott. She said the governor's patronage office was the "real
machine driving hiring." Scott determined jobs went to political pals when
they were supposed to be free of political influence and that veterans'
preference laws were ignored at the Illinois Department of Employment
Security. "This effort reflects not merely an ignorance of the law, but
complete and utter contempt for the law," Scott wrote in the September
2004 report. Blagojevich defended his administration, saying, "As far as
I'm concerned, I'm as determined as anybody else to make sure there is
no wrongdoing in state government."[30]

Blagojevich weathered the growing scandals by burning through
roughly $27 million in campaign funds, thanks in part to his fund-raising
machine. He spent nearly three dollars to every one spent by Republican
challenger Judy Baar Topinka, the state treasurer.[31] Blagojevich saturated

the airwaves with hit pieces against Topinka that came with a devastating tagline: "What's she thinking?"[32]

Blagojevich's troubles and his attacks on Topinka left voters disenchanted, but he won even though a slim majority of voters thought it better to vote for another candidate. They gave Blagojevich only 49.79 percent of the vote, Topinka drew 39.26 percent, and the Green Party's Rich Whitney took a significant chunk at 10.36 percent, a share bolstered by a pox-on-all-your-houses voter rebellion against the major party candidates.[33]

Blagojevich's reelection came less than a month after fund-raiser Rezko was indicted for seeking kickbacks and campaign donations from firms wanting state business. Fitzgerald, the U.S. attorney, said Rezko participated in "pay to play politics on steroids."[34]

At the beginning of Blagojevich's second term, Madigan clashed with the governor immediately. Blagojevich pushed to increase school funding and health care with a major new $7 billion business tax known as a "gross receipts tax." The plan went nowhere fast. Businesses and lawmakers on both sides of the aisle argued that the taxes would push up prices for consumers. The Illinois Manufacturers' Association, headed by Gregory Baise, asked a question that played off Blagojevich's anti-Topinka commercial: "What was he thinking?"[35]

Tired of waiting for Blagojevich to offer specific legislation, Madigan stuffed the elements of the gross receipts concept into a nonbinding resolution and put it up for a vote. In a spectacular rejection, the House voted down the measure 107–0. Afterward, Blagojevich delivered a head-scratching reaction: "Today, I think, was basically an up."[36]

Exasperation with the governor finally boiled over on July 7, 2007, a Saturday near the conclusion of one more fruitless overtime special session that Blagojevich had called during budget deadlocks. Representative Mike Bost, a Murphysboro Republican, inquired during House debate about starting impeachment proceedings: "I don't say it lightly. I'm not joking. I'm dead serious." Madigan had estimated the sides were $3 billion apart in budgeting—a gap that can't be made up with nips and tucks even among friendly negotiators. "Ladies and gentlemen," Bost said, "we're trying to do the work of the people, and the chief executive officer, who has been elected by the voters of the state of Illinois, refuses to quit playing games and do what is right."[37] Bost, who would later go to Congress fueled by a rant about Madigan's restrictive House rules, would be chastised by colleagues for raising impeachment because it is such a grave step, but his frustrations over the lack of progress and wasted time reflected the mood on both sides of the partisan divide.[38]

One of the most gentlemanly legislators, Representative Joe Lyons, D-Chicago, also was fed up. He stood up at his desk on the House floor after a quick adjournment and called the governor a "madman." Lyons turned to reporters in the wooden press box and urged them to write that the governor was "insane." From there, Blagojevich, Jones, Madigan, and about sixty weary and angry lawmakers gathered in a closed-door ballroom at the governor's mansion to see budget negotiations for themselves. Blagojevich had accused Madigan that week of acting less like the chairman of the state Democratic Party and more like a George W. Bush Republican—a comparison that Madigan never liked to hear. As they stood near each other, Madigan called on Blagojevich to knock off the personal attacks. "I simply told him that I don't think it accomplishes anything to be attacking me personally, doesn't help what we're trying to do with the budget," Madigan explained later. Senator Mike Jacobs, an East Moline Democrat who recounted the clash, said Blagojevich did not shy away as he and Madigan stood side by side. "It was high theater," Jacobs said. Blagojevich played down the moment, spinning it as a "healthy, honest discussion."[39]

Even when the House and Senate sent Blagojevich a budget in mid-August, about eleven weeks into overtime, they still had major issues, such as transit funding, unresolved. In frustration, Representative Bill Black, the House Republican floor leader from Danville, summed it up: "This place is becoming the House of Horrors."[40]

It quickly did turn more contentious. The Democratic governor wielded his veto pen on the $59 billion budget with impunity. He slashed $463 million in pork-barrel projects and program spending and said he would use his discretionary power to shift around funds to cover costs of his health-care initiative. The cuts fell disproportionately on his biggest political foes—Madigan's House Democrats and Watson's Senate Republicans. Blagojevich also cut funds for Attorney General Lisa Madigan's office and for the Illinois Arts Council, chaired for decades by the speaker's wife, Shirley. Blagojevich approved pet projects for Jones's Senate Democrats and House Republicans led by Cross, whose off-and-on relationship with the governor dated to when they had served together in the House years before.[41]

Madigan felt double-crossed. Jones, who harbored long-festering resentment over what he viewed as Madigan's slights over the years, said Blagojevich's vetoes would not be overridden in the Senate. Madigan's House went ahead and overrode $424 million in an attempt to restore the cuts anyway, but Jones refused to take them up. Without an override from both houses, the vetoes remained intact.[42] Blagojevich was so giddy when he announced the plan to stick it to Madigan that, one person later said privately, the governor walked into his Capitol office, raised his arms like a referee in a football game, and declared a victory with one word: "Touchdown!"[43]

Blagojevich's plan to move forward with his health-care expansion through discretionary shifts in the budget instantly elicited constitutional questions. An obscure but important legislative panel called the Joint Committee on Administrative Rules determined he didn't have the authority to go ahead. But Blagojevich defied the panel, called its ruling "advisory," and moved forward. Currie's impeachment committee would determine Blagojevich had "no authority to make policy by fiat."[44]

The Special Investigative Committee's review of pay-to-play politics found other critical issues beyond the alarming federal charges. The panel reviewed a *Tribune* story aptly headlined "The Governor's $25,000 Club." The story found that three-quarters of the 235 individuals, companies, or interest groups who gave Blagojevich a campaign donation for exactly twenty-five thousand dollars got something—from lucrative state contracts, to coveted state board appointments, to favorable policy and regulatory actions.[45]

Cynthia Canary, then director of the Illinois Campaign for Political Reform, told the committee that "questionable, even alarming, fundraising practices were in evidence from the time that Mr. Blagojevich first set his eye on the governor's office." Taken together with pay-to-play testimony in federal court, the impeachment committee wrote in a footnote, it is hard to view the *Tribune's* findings as coincidental.[46]

Blagojevich did not sit idly while the Currie committee prepared to wrap up its hearings. He pulled off a shocker: He appointed Roland Burris a U.S. senator on December 30, 2008, prompting an outcry from Springfield to Washington.[47] Burris was the first Black elected statewide, winning the comptroller's office three times and the attorney general post once. But he had lost runs for governor, mayor of Chicago, and other public posts. He ran and lost to Blagojevich in a 2002 three-way primary that included Paul Vallas, a onetime CEO of the Chicago Public Schools. Burris's losing streak threatened to mark him as a perennial candidate, but he lunged at the chance to chisel "U.S. Senator" onto a tombstone where he already had carved most of his resume.

At first Obama backed U.S. Senate Democratic leaders who said Blagojevich's appointment "will ultimately not stand."[48] But Obama later pressed the Senate to settle the issue, because it started to become a distraction when the incoming president wanted politicians to dig in on his stimulus plan to boost the economy.[49]

Currie's committee needed to hear from Burris. Republican Representative Jim Durkin, a former prosecutor on the panel, raised questions about whether Burris had intertwined discussions about campaign donations for Blagojevich with talks about his appointment. Burris would amend his statements in affidavits, but he denied lying. The U.S. Senate Ethics Committee later determined that Burris's "misleading" and "shifting explanations" deserved a middling punishment called a "qualified admonition."[50]

The Burris appointment only served to intensify the Illinois House's Blagojevich impeachment hearings. After Currie's Special House Investigation Committee approved the scathing report on Blagojevich's conduct, the panel sent the impeachment case to the full House. It was at that point when Madigan acknowledged he had "regrets" about cochairing the governor's 2006 reelection campaign. Despite word of the developing Blagojevich scandal hitting the papers well before signing on as cochair, Madigan said, "We didn't know the intensity of the federal inquiry."[51]

One day later, on January 9, 2009, Madigan gaveled in the full House to consider the state's first impeachment of an Illinois governor, and lawmakers could barely contain themselves. They let loose six years' worth of pent-up anger at the freewheeling chief executive. Blagojevich was not in the House, but the vitriol over his chaotic term was unmistakable. "It's our duty to clean up the mess and to stop the freak show which has become Illinois government," said Representative Jack Franks, a Democrat from far north Marengo. Representative Susana Mendoza, a Chicago Democrat who would later become state comptroller, lashed out at Blagojevich for holding back state "funds for sick children to extort the president of the children's hospital. Repugnant is too kind a word to describe that action."[52]

When Currie spoke, she struck at the heart of Blagojevich's excuses that his remarks on secret federal recordings were nothing more than "talk." "But if that talk reflects the governor's view that the plums of government are his to distribute, not because they are in the public interest, but because doling them out to the right individuals will fill his campaign coffers or lead to jobs and salaries for himself and his wife, that to me is the definition of betrayal of the public trusts," Currie said. Republican leader Cross lashed out at the governor for making Illinois the "laughingstock of the country and, in fact, the world." Cross told colleagues, "You ought to be angry. You ought to be disgusted. You ought to be mad as hell because this is our state."[53]

The House voted 114 in favor of impeachment. One lawmaker voted against impeachment and one voted present. Both were leaving the House. The House needed to vote again on impeachment when lawmakers were sworn in a week later for a new legislative term. In the second round, the sole House vote against Blagojevich's impeachment came from his newly elected sister-in-law, Representative Deb Mell, the daughter of the Thirty-Third Ward boss. Impeachment passed the second time 117–1.[54]

The drama built up in the next few days as Illinois Senate President John Cullerton started the trial with Illinois Supreme Court Chief Justice Thomas Fitzgerald presiding. "This is a solemn and serious business we're about to engage in," Fitzgerald said.[55] But Blagojevich chose anything but a solemn and serious approach. Rather than defend himself in Springfield, he swept into New York for a national TV public relations tour. He said the outcome of the impeachment trial was a "fait accompli" and a "witch hunt." Madigan's legal team meticulously rolled out the prosecution. David Ellis, the speaker's chief counsel, who later would become an appellate court justice, took the role of lead prosecutor. Taking up two other positions were Heather Wier Vaught, an attorney for the speaker who one day would become Madigan's chief counsel and later a private lawyer and lobbyist, and Michael Kasper, a former chief counsel for the speaker who became the Democratic Party's lawyer and a major lobbyist.

The power trio walked senators through the case, using big white posters on easels in front of the full Senate to highlight Blagojevich's most incriminating statements—with "expletive" subbed in for the f-bombs. FBI agent Daniel Cain read a lengthy affidavit detailing the federal case. They played the four covert recordings about an attempted shakedown of a horse-track owner for campaign cash in exchange for signing legislation with Blagojevich's voice coming from loudspeakers and echoing eerily off the walls of the Senate chambers. "We will ask you to convict Governor Blagojevich because of his own words, not those of anybody else," Ellis told senators.[56] Interviewed on national television by Larry King and Barbara Walters, among others, Blagojevich begged for mercy, complained about unfair treatment, and hoped to get a sympathetic audience. Egged on by Joy Behar of *The View*, Blagojevich refused to do a Nixon impersonation. "Just say, 'I am not a crook,'" Behar said. "I'm not going to do that," Blagojevich replied, instead choosing another favorite Nixon phrase. "Let me make this 'perfectly clear.' I didn't do anything wrong."[57]

By week's end, however, Blagojevich reversed his PR strategy. He decided to show up at his impeachment trial after all. He would swoop in to the Capitol for an eleventh-hour appearance, where he would give his own closing argument without taking questions. He also would not take an oath to tell the truth. As he walked up to the well in front of the Senate president's podium, Blagojevich gave a quick glance at the press box, a crew of veteran scribes he tried to avoid so much in visits to Springfield that he would slip out side doors and run through basement hallways in order to dodge questions. He then turned forward to address senators.

Barely looking at notes, Blagojevich demonstrated the flair that made him a natural campaigner. "There was never a conversation where I intended to break any law," Blagojevich told his audience. He sought to knock holes in the criminal complaint, but then he tried to explain away conversations about getting a campaign contribution before signing legislation helpful to horse-track owners:

> I don't have to tell you what they say. You guys are in politics. You know what we have to do to go out and run—run elections. There was no criminal activity on those four tapes. You can express things in a free country. But those four tapes speak for themselves. Take those four tapes as they are, and you will, I believe, in fairness, recognize and acknowledge those are conversations relating to the things all of us in politics do in order to run campaigns and try to win elections.[58]

Clearly angered and insulted, the senators rejected the implication that everybody played the game the Blago way.

In forty-seven minutes, Blagojevich ticked off how he sought to provide health care to low-income parents, how he tried to arrange flu vaccines to save lives. He described how he sought to test the FDA by getting drugs from Canada at the suggestion of then U.S. Representative Rahm Emanuel and got advice from Republican U.S. Senator John McCain of

Arizona and Democratic U.S. Senator Edward Kennedy of Massachusetts. "If you're going to throw me out for something like this, then how can those guys stay in the office that they have?" Blagojevich asked defiantly.[59]

Seeking to undercut the inspector general's (IG's) report on hiring irregularities that the *Tribune* first exposed, Blagojevich said he wasn't personally involved in the improprieties. "This report from the inspector general alleges that some people, perhaps, may have—it's an allegation, nothing proven, nothing shown yet to be true, but an allegation that some people that worked for me violated some of the hiring rules. In that very report by the inspector general, there's never an allegation that I ever knew anything about it."[60]

Blagojevich implored senators to imagine how they'd feel if their presumption of innocence were "completely wiped out because of sensationalization of the media and other things." How, he questioned, could he be tossed when he couldn't bring witnesses or play all of the recordings the feds had accumulated against him? "This is not Richard Nixon and Watergate trying to keep the tapes from being heard," Blagojevich said. "I want all the evidence heard, and I want it sooner rather than later so I can clear my name."[61]

The Illinois Constitution gives lawmakers the ability to impeach a governor for "cause" without a definition of what that is, reasoning that the lawmakers would be able to figure out when to vote for impeachment and removal. This was not a criminal court, where a person must be guilty beyond a reasonable doubt. Blagojevich told senators he "cannot possibly admit to something I didn't do." But he also said, "If I felt I had done something wrong, I would have resigned in December."

The Senate took that option away. House prosecutor David Ellis, Madigan's top lawyer, methodically destroyed Blagojevich's arguments and excuses. He explained how Blagojevich would say one thing when the TV cameras were on him and another when the feds recorded him secretly. "Being governor is not a right," Ellis said. "It is a privilege, and he has forfeited that privilege. He has abused the power of his office. He has traded it for personal gain time and time again." Coles County Republican Senator Dale Righter sarcastically dismissed Blagojevich's "spellbinding performance." Righter maintained that the governor's arguments for acquittal belied a "devious, cynical, crass and corrupt politician." Democratic Senator James Meeks, a preacher of a major South Side Chicago church, had relied on Blagojevich's promises to improve funding for poor schools only to see the governor's words crumble. But Meeks looked to Blagojevich's own infamous words when he announced his vote to oust Blagojevich. "We have this thing called impeachment, and it's 'bleeping golden,' and we've used it the right way," Meeks said.[62]

Blagojevich didn't stick around to listen to the debate. He swiftly left the Senate chamber in order to catch the state plane back to Chicago before senators tossed him from office. He made it home, where he was met on his front lawn with a crush of reporters, TV cameras, and even sympathetic well-wishers. About two hundred miles away in Springfield, Lieutenant Governor Pat Quinn, the maverick who had made waves three decades before by championing the House cutback amendment, took the oath of office for governor. He would be sworn in, in the chambers of the Madigan-controlled House and at the speaker's podium. Administering the oath was Supreme Court Justice Anne Burke, the spouse of Fourteenth Ward Alderman Edward Burke. Quinn offered calming and encouraging words to a state caught up in the Blagojevich nightmare, saying, "The ordeal is over."

Not quite. Blagojevich kept denying he did anything wrong as he awaited his criminal trial, and he kept attacking the speaker. "He's more Machiavellian than Machiavelli," Blagojevich told James Ylisela Jr. for *Chicago* magazine. "When Machiavelli wrote *The Prince*, he had Mike Madigan in mind."[63] Ultimately, Blagojevich went on to win another term— this time to be served in federal prison in Colorado for fourteen years. In 2015 the Seventh U.S. Circuit Court of Appeals, for technical reasons, tossed five counts tied to the governor's attempt to trade his Senate appointment powers for a job for himself. But the court salvaged one of the most sensational allegations: that Blagojevich schemed to nominate then U.S. Representative Jesse Jackson Jr. to the Senate seat in exchange for $1.5 million in campaign contributions. They also upheld convictions for the attempts to shake down the horse-track owner and the CEO of a children's hospital for campaign cash. Justices called the overall evidence against Blagojevich "overwhelming" and sent the case back to U.S. District Judge James Zagel,[64] who held a second sentencing hearing on August 9, 2016. Attorney Leonard Goodman sought to play down the Jackson matter by arguing that the ex-governor "had almost certainly no intention of appointing him to the Senate seat." He contended Blagojevich wanted to raise campaign funds to "strengthen himself to defeat the opposition, mainly coming from Mike Madigan, to pass his priorities, which was a capital bill, a public works bill which he believed would benefit the people of Illinois."[65]

One key problem during Blagojevich's tenure as governor, though, was that Madigan stood with many lawmakers from both parties who didn't trust the governor to oversee a multibillion-dollar construction package. In contrast, new Governor Pat Quinn and the four legislative leaders put together the first major capital program in a decade within months of Blagojevich's ouster. When Blagojevich addressed his resentencing pitch to Zagel via video conference, he turned at one point to Abraham Lincoln. He said he taught fellow inmates to draw motivation from how Lincoln overcame personal struggles, including the death of a son in the White House, and the hardships of the Civil War. "There's nothing like Abraham Lincoln, who persevered through such difficulties, perhaps this—perhaps this could help you get through some of the difficulties that you have," Blagojevich recounted. Zagel was unmoved. He gave the imprisoned ex-governor the same fourteen-year term.[66] Once the U.S. Supreme Court justices turned their thumbs down on a subsequent Blagojevich appeal in 2018, he and his wife, Patricia, double-teamed President Donald Trump and doubled down on clemency.

Way before he became president, Trump donated five thousand dollars to Blagojevich in his 2002 campaign for governor and tossed him a few thousand more after he was elected, records showed. Blagojevich met Trump at a 2002 fund-raiser for the governor candidate at Yankee Stadium, and Blagojevich would appear as a contestant on *The Celebrity Apprentice* series after his impeachment. The future president would send the ex-governor on his way with the show's catchphrase: "You're fired." Years later, with Trump the last hope for an early release of her husband, Patti Blagojevich showed the president the real art of making a deal. She took to the airwaves, stroking Trump's ego and pushing his Twitter-exhausted buttons with pleas on Fox News, the network then holding the president's most-favored-station status. She spoke of how "kind" Trump had been to the Blagojevich family during the taping of his reality show, and she argued that the Deep State that took down her husband was now trying to take down Trump with the Russian election interference investigation. With Trump himself deeply suspicious of the U.S. Justice Department, the president began to hear a story that fit within his own worldview.[67]

Off and on, Trump had dangled the idea of cutting Rod Blagojevich free since early in his presidency. But even by May 2018 the president didn't show a strong grasp of the case, making statements that Blago-jevich received an eighteen-year sentence rather than fourteen. Robert Grant, the ex-boss of the FBI's Chicago office during Blagojevich's arrest, said it was clear that Trump "has never seen the evidence."[68] Trump said Blagojevich got unfair treatment from "the same gang, the Comey gang and all these sleazebags that did it."[69] No matter that former FBI Director James Comey, who was ousted by President Trump in May 2017, had been in private practice from 2005 to 2013—most of the time that Blagojevich was under scrutiny.[70]

Blagojevich wrote an essay for the *Wall Street Journal,* saying that he was only doing what other politicians do and that the feds made up crimes against him because they couldn't prove anything illegal. "Politically mo-tivated prosecutors can now interfere with and undo free and fair elec-tions," Blagojevich wrote in a piece titled "I'm in Prison for Practicing Politics."[71] Watching Patti Blagojevich on television, Trump took note of her own arguments. "She's one hell of a woman," Trump said.[72]

In February 2020, after several hints, Trump commuted Blagojevich's sentence to the roughly eight years he had served rather than pardon him of the crimes, saying the fourteen-year term was a "tremendously, power-ful, ridiculous sentence in my opinion." When he returned to his home in Chicago, the former Democratic governor thanked the Republican president. They'd made history. An impeached president gave clemency to an impeached governor. Blagojevich declared himself a "freed political prisoner" and called himself a "Trumpocrat."[73] Madigan still remained speaker.

5

PARTISAN MATH

"People in this chamber did not do what
was easy today, but we did what was right
for the future of our state."
—Speaker Michael Madigan, July 6, 2017

Nearly two decades had gone by since Speaker Madigan had unleashed
Operation Cobra in 1989. But with the Great Recession of the late 2000s
and rising pension costs contributing to the state's already rocky finances,
the pressure for a new income tax hike began to build. Once again it
would be up to Madigan to supply the muscle, but it would also be largely
up to him to decide when the time would be right. Democratic Governor
Pat Quinn had taken over for ousted predecessor Rod Blagojevich in
January 2009. After six years of Blagojevich refusing to raise the income
tax while wanting to spend more, Quinn learned that the potential state
budget deficit had hit $9 billion—nearly twice the size that Democrats
thought it was. Democratic Comptroller Dan Hynes blamed Governors
George Ryan, a Republican, and Rod Blagojevich, a Democrat, for failing
to prepare the state for a national recession. Nobody likes to pay more
taxes, but there was a built-in excuse to cite the two consecutive corrupt
administrations as the reason tax hikes were needed. Quinn called the
deficit a "giant hole to fill."[1]

As Quinn prepped for his first budget address, in March 2009, the *Tribune*
broke a story reporting that he was looking at a 50 percent increase in the
Illinois income tax. A giant headline topped page 1: "Big State Income Tax
Hike?" The story explained that Quinn's plans would move the personal

income tax rate to 4.5 percent from the 3 percent tax, where it had remained almost since the moment Madigan yelled "Banzaiiiii!" to Governor James Thompson in 1989. Quinn also wanted to boost the exemption for low-income folks, an attempt to cushion the blow for the poor.[2]

With airtight sources behind our reporting—and despite a top Quinn aide shouting into the phone that the administration wanted to wait a while longer to tell the public about the tax hike plans—we had our story nailed down and pushed ahead. Ashley Rueff, an intern in the *Tribune* statehouse bureau, added a few paragraphs about the prospects of a gas tax hike, and we hit the send button. As the story was being edited in Chicago, she stood two hundred miles away in the *Tribune* statehouse bureau, where we had written and filed the story, and marveled that only a handful of people in Illinois knew what we would soon tell everyone. Veteran reporters can get used to the buzz of popping stories onto the front page, even big scoops like the tax hike proposal. But Rueff's genuine enthusiasm about breaking a big story reinforced the idea that journalists are the eyes and ears for the public at large.

When the story rolled off the presses the next morning, the chase was on. A pack of reporters descended on Quinn in Chicago, but the governor would acknowledge only that he planned to seek a tax increase. He did not give specifics, preferring to emphasize potential breaks for the poor. "This is a once-in-a-lifetime chance for the people of Illinois, the hardworking taxpayers of Illinois, to get tax reform that produces tax relief for millions and millions of people," Quinn said. It was a political gamble for Quinn to take a tax-increase stance only weeks into office. He counted on voters giving him credit for being up front with them, but blowback was swift. Republicans denounced Quinn's proposal. House Republican leader Tom Cross declared Quinn's plan "pretty much of a long shot."[3]

Five days after the *Tribune* story broke his game plan, Quinn made it official. He proposed increasing personal and corporate income tax rates by 50 percent and tripling the personal exemption for lower-wage-earning residents to six thousand dollars. Senate President John Cullerton said "it's very likely" a tax increase would emerge but noted that the size and shape of the taxes and exemptions were "all negotiable." Both Cullerton and Madigan said they needed to see budget cutting and reforms in a government that had been tainted by the back-to-back Ryan and Blagojevich scandals. But Senate Minority Leader Christine Radogno, R-Lemont, labeled the Quinn tax-hike proposal "premature and irresponsible." With Democrats holding majorities in both houses and the governorship, Rado-gno said supporters of Quinn's tax hike should at least consider making it temporary. With Ryan in prison and Blagojevich charged with corruption, Quinn told lawmakers during his budget address that he wanted to talk to voters "honestly and directly." But passing the tax hike with the votes of nervous lawmakers would not be a slam dunk, particularly with different ideas coming from the House and Senate.[4]

One major alternative that emerged that spring might have been one of the better plans to put the state on sounder fiscal footing without relying on cuts alone. Cullerton shepherded through his chamber a 67 percent increase in the personal income tax rate and a broader sales tax covering more services. The Senate president's move asserted his independence from Madigan, drawing appreciation from a Senate majority that too often felt the speaker ignored senators' wishes. "I think it's time we step up," Cullerton said. But Madigan's House Democrats said they didn't have the votes for the Cullerton plan, and the House overwhelmingly rejected a two-year version of Quinn's 50 percent increase. When his first spring session as governor ended, Quinn's call for higher taxes had failed.[5]

As the calendar turned to 2010, the biggest political question was obvious: Would this be the year the income tax would go up? First, Quinn had to hold on to his job. In the 2010 Democratic primary, Quinn narrowly beat Dan Hynes, the state's comptroller, who challenged the governor. Despite steadfastly pressing for an income tax increase in the general election, Quinn then beat Republican Bill Brady of Bloomington. Quinn had lowered the size of the income tax he wanted, calling for a 33 percent tax increase in his March 2010 budget address. The increase he proposed would bump up the personal income tax rate from 3 percent to 4 percent. But Madigan didn't give the plan much hope. "The people of America don't want tax increases. . . . They're hurting," the speaker said on the public television show *Illinois Lawmakers*.[6] Madigan had another reason to be cautious: He needed Quinn to win. He needed a Democrat sitting in the governor's chair to sign a legislative redistricting proposal that Madigan and Cullerton would draw to their liking. A preelection tax hike could jeopardize the Quinn candidacy—and Madigan's all-important need for a Democratic map to maintain his power.

When Quinn won in November 2010 and Democrats won solid majorities in both chambers, Madigan and Cullerton quietly began working with the governor on how to construct a postelection income tax hike. They waited as long as they could to spring it—until January 2011, just before the governor and lawmakers would be sworn in to a new term. That meant lame-duck lawmakers, members of the General Assembly defeated in the election or deciding to leave on their own, could put their votes up for grabs without worrying about a voter backlash. Waiting until the beginning of the year meant the two houses needed only simple majority votes rather than a three-fifths supermajority vote to pass an income tax that would take effect immediately.

Madigan, Cullerton, and Quinn looked at raising the income tax even higher than the governor had publicly embraced. One idea would raise the personal income tax from 3 percent to 5 percent, possibly for three to five years, and possibly even higher to help borrow money to pay down bills. Madigan took the rare step of walking desk to desk in the upper chamber as he and Cullerton fanned out to gauge support among Senate Democrats. "This is Madigan's . . . way of telling you that, 'Something has to be done, and I'm going to be the one to do it,'" said Senator Lou Viverito, a longtime Madigan ally from southwest suburban Burbank. Madigan blamed Republicans for refusing to help pay down the growing multibillion-dollar deficit and mountain of backlogged bills. "They are continuing on a campaign plan, which means they are not participating in governmental decisions," Madigan said.[7]

The trio of top Democrats considered a 75 percent increase in the income tax rate, a proposal that would have pushed the 3 percent rate to 5.25 percent for four years and then fall to 3.75 percent. Republican Brady pointed out that all of the Democratic ideas would break Quinn's campaign promise to veto any tax hike higher than his proposed 33 percent increase. But as key House lawmakers questioned whether they had the votes to pass a major increase, Democratic Representative Joe Lyons of Chicago still had faith in the speaker: "Never doubt what Madigan can do when he puts his mind to it. When we mere mortals don't think it can get done, he gets it done."[8]

Madigan, Cullerton, and Quinn did get it done, but they scaled back the income tax proposal from a 75 percent rate hike to 67 percent. The Illinois Constitution calls for the term of a governor to begin on a different day than that of the General Assembly. That meant Quinn was giving his inauguration speech at Springfield's convention center a few blocks from the Capitol while Madigan and Cullerton worked on the final details of the tax proposal at the statehouse. Quinn said he was negotiating on the tax legislation the same day he was dealing with the pomp and circumstance of the swearing-in ceremonies. "And then the next day was a Tuesday," Quinn said, recalling the high-wire negotiations years later. "That was all day. . . . Many of the members, definitely Democrats, were very wary and skeptical. By that time, Illinois had huge amounts of money of unpaid bills. It had to be done in order to straighten out financing." Quinn could not convince Madigan and Cullerton to go for a permanent income tax hike and settled for the temporary approach. "That was all we could get," Quinn said.[9] In the middle of crafting the tax legislation, Madigan called the moment "do or die."[10]

On the last full day of the General Assembly's outgoing term, Madigan took his place at the speaker's podium and turned to House Majority Leader Barbara Currie, a legendary debater from Chicago, who presented the tax increase legislation. "Illinois is in a crisis, absolute financial crisis, and there is no way we can dig ourselves out of the crisis without increased revenues," Currie said.[11] The Madigan-led Democrats then pushed the 67 percent rate increase through the House on a razor-thin 60–57 roll call—without any Republican votes. "They're on the sidelines," Madigan said of Republicans. "They don't want to get on the field of play."[12]

Gathering sixty House votes required creativity, but Madigan was up to the task. Twelve lame-duck House Democrats voted for the 67 percent increase in the income tax rate. Having lost their elections or opting not to run in 2010, their terms would soon be over. They voted for the tax increase without having to worry about facing a public backlash at the ballot box.[13] The impact of the carefully constructed Democratic roll call was lost on no one. A sarcastic downstate, antitax Republican Representative David Reis of Willow Hill told colleagues, "Well, happy new year from the lame duck General Assembly."[14]

The Senate Democrats eventually voted for passage after a long night—again without any Republican help. The final votes came together in the Senate when African American lawmakers huddled in the governor's office and extracted a promise from Quinn that they could get more money for public education out of the deal. Quinn quickly signed the bill, and the personal tax rate rose to 5 percent from 3 percent for four years and was scheduled to drop to 3.75 percent in 2015.[15] Though Quinn denied horse-trading jobs for votes on the tax hike, at least four lame-duck lawmakers who voted for the tax hike ended up with jobs in his administration. Each one drew criticism for their votes, because the jobs they landed looked like more than a coincidence. The *Tribune* editorial board came up with its own name for these cozy Quinn appointments: "Quinncidences."[16]

During the four years of higher tax revenues, the state coffers would benefit. But Madigan, Cullerton, and Quinn would be razzed repeatedly for raising taxes with all Democratic votes. Though Madigan was among lawmakers insisting upon making the tax increase temporary, the move put pressure on Springfield politicians to explain what would happen when the tax fell off.[17] Doubts grew about the wisdom of the decision to let the income tax go down after four years. Yet all but one Democratic legislator who sought reelection after voting for the increase won another term, and that was in a primary that was all about West Side politics rather than a tax vote. In comparison, six Republicans who voted against the increase lost races—two in the primary and four in the general election.[18]

Flash forward to 2014, and Quinn had a critical decision as he ran for reelection: Would he seek to make the temporary tax hike permanent when it was due to decrease in January 2015? He knew the political risks, but the state's finances were still in bad shape. On the eve of Quinn's tightly guarded budget speech, the *Tribune* once again nailed down his plans and put them on the front page before he could unveil them himself. Quinn had made his decision: He would propose making the four-year tax hike permanent. Hoping to ease the pain, Quinn sought property tax relief in the form of a five-hundred-dollar annual refund. Working the phones and capitol corridors late into the night, my *Tribune* reporting partner Monique Garcia and I secured confirmation from sources before his budget speech and slammed together a story that garnered a top corner of the front page and a spot for the full story inside.[19] After Quinn's speech, Madigan told public television that the governor had "laid the cards on the table." But Madigan also outlined his election-year conditions: "If we wish to continue to provide the level of services which we've become accustomed to for education and other purposes, then the income tax increase should be extended. My demand as part of this program is relief for homeowners on their real estate taxes."[20]

Despite his own supportive remarks, Madigan could not—or would not—use his considerable persuasive skills to round up the House Democratic votes necessary to pass Quinn's tax plan in a volatile election year. The most critical moment for Quinn's income tax pitch came on May 19 in a closed-door House Democratic caucus. He pleaded his case for a permanent tax increase for more than two hours, but he could not squeeze sixty votes from Madigan's seventy-one troops. "We are significantly away from 60 today," Madigan said after the caucus ended. "It's going to take a great deal of persuasion."[21]

Standing outside of the room where he had just faced a battery of questions from lawmakers, Quinn flatly denied that his mission to pass the signature piece of his budget plan was over. But it was. For all practical purposes, his campaign was over too. The Democratic-controlled House and Senate passed a budget that funded programs at levels Quinn proposed to go along with the higher tax rates he wanted but used short-term gimmicks rather than providing any extra, sustainable dollars to cover costs.[22] Only later did Quinn find out that Madigan's ground troops in some close suburban House races had asked voters to sign petitions opposing Quinn's tax increase. Out of office years later, Quinn made clear the political maneuver to help Democrats in tough races maintain Madigan's House majority still stung the ex-governor. Quinn said in a 2021 interview that he found the House Democratic politics "pretty hard to put up with. It was pretty clear that they were more interested in retaining the majority than reelecting the governor. But you could do both."[23]

Quinn would lose the November 2014 general election to Republican tax-hike foe Bruce Rauner. Had Democrats used the postelection lame-duck session to pass a tax increase, as they did four years earlier, they undoubtedly could have avoided many painful social service cuts over the next few years. But Democrats provided no help for the incoming Rauner. They would let him figure out how to solve the budget mess—a form of payback for a Republican candidate who said the state could afford to let the temporary income tax hike expire. In his campaign, Rauner had said he wanted to push the income tax rate back down to 3 percent over his four years in office. But Rauner also opened the door to the "possibility" of increasing the rate above 3.75 percent if it were part of a tax code overhaul.[24]

Madigan kept his options open, but he stood to gain politically if he could pressure Rauner into breaking his antitax stance—as Republican President George H. W. Bush did following his words "Read my lips. No new taxes." The makings of future historic fights between Madigan and Rauner were planted, but the next four years turned ugly.

Nobody was prepared for the war that Madigan and Rauner would wage. Rauner's ideological fight counted on being able to pressure the speaker into submission. The speaker fought and pushed around other governors. But Rauner clearly was different. He had outspent Quinn two to one in a $100 million race for governor, including nearly $28 million from Rauner's own funds. With no love lost for unions, Rauner disparaged the American Federation of State, County, and Municipal Employees—now known as AFSCME, the state's largest public employee union—as "Afscammy." He'd made big money as a hard-nosed businessman, one who stood up to adversaries and beat them down. In his campaign, Rauner showed no sign that he lacked self-confidence: "I've been a success at everything I've done."[25]

Rauner foreshadowed his Capitol playbook on the weekend before the election. From the site of the high-minded 1858 Lincoln-Douglas debate at Quincy, Rauner sought to exploit Illinois' regional rivalries. He condemned the Chicago Democrats running the state, much to the delight of the sign-waving crowd. He told of plans to "shake things up" in Springfield. "We can't deal with these tax hikes," Rauner said. "We need value for our taxes. We need the best schools in America. . . . We're going to rip up that patronage-corruption-cronyism system in Springfield, and we're going to get the government right, to run right for your benefit."[26] When the Rauner campaign hit Springfield two days later, he stood on a platform with the shiny silver Capitol dome as his backdrop and former GOP Governor Jim Edgar at his side. Rauner lumped together Madigan, Cullerton, Quinn, and Blagojevich, saying their combined "one hundred years of failure is more than enough."[27] Rauner won the election the next day. Many Illinois voters felt that after six years of Blagojevich and six years of Quinn, it was time to try something else.

A few weeks before he was sworn in, Rauner struck a statesmanlike tone when he stopped by the Capitol. Illinois, he said, was in dire financial straits. His words echoed past governors who acted surprised upon discovering that the state finances were worse than they had imagined when they were campaigning. Democrats and Republicans were both to blame, Rauner said, and bipartisan fixes were needed. As lawmakers soon would discover, Rauner's view of bipartisanship was a lot different from that of Madigan. The incoming governor's financial ideas were different too. In Quinn's exit interview with the *Tribune*, the outgoing governor was still smoldering from Rauner's vow that the state's yawning budget gap could be fixed without the higher tax rates Quinn supported. "It's all about arithmetic—as folks will find out in the coming year," Quinn said.[28]

About two weeks into his term, Rauner pulled his beloved old beater van up to the Executive Mansion, strode onto the driveway with two family dogs, and talked once more about big plans, again in vague terms: "We are going to overhaul our entire tax code so we can have the growth to make sure we have the revenues to fund everything that we need to fund and that the government is properly financed." Skeptical, public radio reporter Amanda Vinicky pressed Rauner on whether he planned to make the changes in the upcoming year or over the long haul, noting that the state's constitution puts some restraints on what can be done with the tax code. "Our reforms will be both short term as well as long term," Rauner replied. "We're going to focus on both. The critical thing of concern to me is too often politicians really focus on the short term and the next election, and that means they patch things together, Band-Aids and chewing gum, to get through a particular budget year," a move that means "they kick the can down the road" rather than make wise structural budget reforms.[29]

Madigan brought his own ideas from decades of experience, and soon he and Rauner would clash in a monumental power struggle. Though they worked to close a funding gap in the budget he inherited, Rauner ultimately wanted a platter of antilabor changes that Democrats—and some Republicans—would never accept. Rauner called it a "Turnaround Agenda," dozens of items highlighted by plans to rein in workers' compensation costs, push for government contracts that didn't require union labor, put limits on civil damage awards, and make changes to public employee pension costs. Madigan later recounted how Rauner threatened to unleash a campaign-style assault aimed at tearing down the speaker if he didn't go along, a vow Madigan said played out as Rauner fired off tens of millions of dollars in attack ads.[30]

Neither Madigan nor Rauner liked to capitulate. "The governor has said that he feels that he can eliminate the deficits just by cutting state services. I disagree," Madigan said. "I think that the elimination of the deficits will require a blend. Service cuts, plus new revenue."[31]

Their standoff reached unprecedented levels of enmity. For slightly more than two years the state went without a budget—a freakish rarity among states. Rauner persisted on seeking the antiunion changes before discussing how to raise revenue. Madigan maintained that Rauner's ideological changes should not be linked to the budget. Legislators from both parties watched the social services safety net tear apart; state universities suffer from cuts; road projects put on hold; and doctors, pharmacists, and dentists who served the poor wait months to be paid. At an appearance at Southern Illinois University's Carbondale campus, former Governor Edgar acknowledged that Madigan could be "extremely difficult to negotiate with" but would not put the majority of the blame on the speaker for the standoff. "He is not the problem," Edgar said. "He might be a little bit of the problem, but he is not the big problem."[32]

As the state began its third fiscal year without a budget on July 1, 2017, Madigan waited no longer. School payments were in jeopardy. The bill backlog had risen to $15 billion—almost half the size of an annual operating budget. The speaker himself wrote a letter asking Wall Street bond houses to hold off on giving Illinois an ignominious junk-bond designation—a rock-bottom ranking that no state wants. The lower the ranking, the more it costs for a state to borrow money—millions of dollars for higher interest rates rather than spending that money on state programs.[33]

What Madigan pulled off in the next few weeks turned out to be as much of a show of political strength and strategy as the secretive Operation Cobra nearly three decades before. However, unlike Governor James Thompson, who had been blindsided by a lightning-quick passage of Madigan's income tax increase plan, Rauner could see what was coming and couldn't do anything about it. Madigan pulled together a bipartisan coalition to put up a supermajority vote to pass a major tax increase once again. With the state's finances reeling and small businesses going unpaid, fifteen Republicans defied Rauner and voted for the tax increase. Representative David Harris, a longtime suburban Republican from Arlington Heights, supported the tax increase and called on Rauner to have the courage to sign the bill, pleading, "Bring this madness to an end."[34] The Senate quickly went along, but Rauner vetoed the bill. In a dramatic display of defiance, the Senate and the House then overrode the governor, making the tax hike permanent. It raised the individual income tax rate from 3.75 percent, where it had been since Quinn left, to 4.95 percent. The corporate rate rose from 5.25 percent to 7 percent. All told, the increase was projected to generate roughly $5 billion a year. Rauner's response: "Today was another step in Illinois' never-ending tragic trail of tax hikes."[35]

Addressing the House, Madigan praised lawmakers on both sides of the political divide: "Republicans and Democrats stood together to enact a bipartisan balanced budget and end a destructive 736-day impasse." Taking a shot at Rauner without using his name, Madigan said the budget put the best interests of the state first and showed what can be accomplished when people work cooperatively and negotiate in good faith. "People in this chamber did not do what was easy today, but we did what was right for the future of our state," Madigan said, adding that he hoped to "continue to work to heal the wounds of the last three years. . . . Thank you to all of you for persevering through this unbelievable struggle."[36]

6

THE ART OF PERSUASION

"Pope Francis has spoken, and he has
articulated the basics of my thinking on
this issue."
—Speaker Michael Madigan,
    November 5, 2013

Every decision made in the General Assembly revolves around right and
wrong—what's right for the politics, what's right for the politicians, what's
right for the citizens. Will it hurt a lawmaker's chances for reelection? Will
it help? These are simple equations, but they get complicated fast. Over
the years, the lines move, society evolves, lawmakers change attitudes.
Constituents speak up. Special interests weigh in. And Speaker Madigan
would put his thumb on the scale.

Few issues showcased such an evolution more than gay marriage. This
was an issue that divided Illinois Democrats when they were on a bigger
stage in 1996, the year Chicago hosted the Democratic National Convention. Chicago's Seventh Ward Alderman William Beavers, a former cop
who later went to prison, told me on the floor of the United Center that
God made marriage for "Adam and Eve, not Adam and Steve," a point
he had also made on the Chicago City Council floor eight years before.[1]

For decades, state lawmakers got little traction with gay rights. Then the
state moved to approve legislation that banned discrimination against sexual orientation in housing and employment, allowed civil unions among
people of the same sex, and approved gay marriage. An antidiscrimination
bill was introduced in 1974 but didn't become law until 2005. It took six

more years for civil unions to be approved, but lawmakers moved swiftly to approve gay marriage.[2] That last step took place in 2013, making Illinois the sixteenth state in the nation to legalize marriage between two people of the same gender. The development partially opened a window into the way Madigan worked when he needed to help a lawmaker with an important constituency to seal the deal.

The Illinois Senate, a much more liberal body under the lopsided Democratic majority of Senate President John Cullerton, passed gay marriage legislation with four votes to spare following a passionate debate on Valentine's Day 2013. But the bill stalled three months later in the House, where sponsoring Representative Greg Harris, D-Chicago, would not force a roll call when he thought he was short of the sixty votes needed to pass. Harris, who is openly gay, received brutal criticism and heckling from the House gallery when he made the decision to hold off on voting on the last day of the spring session. But when he returned in the fall for the veto session, Harris gathered in his cramped office with several advocates, lobbyists, and lawmakers. They debated whether they should risk taking a vote in the full House when they estimated they had locked in only fifty-eight or fifty-nine votes. That would be one or two votes short—unless unknown supporters would get caught up in the moment and vote for the bill.[3]

After an hour-and-a-half discussion of the risks of failing versus the chances of winning, Harris decided to go for it. He made his case on the House floor and heard out the opponents. But just before Harris closed, Madigan weighed in. Walking through his reasoning, the speaker gave political cover to Catholics wrestling with their faith. He cited the words of Pope Francis of the Roman Catholic Church that gave gay marriage advocates a boost when he spoke out only months before: "If someone is gay and he searches for the Lord and he has good will, who am I to judge?"[4] Madigan then told his colleagues:

Vatican experts were quick to point out that Pope Francis was not suggesting that the priest or anyone else should act on their homosexual tendencies. But Pope Francis has spoken and he has articulated the basics of my thinking on this issue. The history of civilization is a history of people finding each other. Two people find each other. They get to know each other. They come to a judgment that they love each other, they want to be with each other, that each will help the other move through life and then, hopefully, each will help the other in the raising of children. That's the simple history of civilization and people have found each other over all of these centuries; people that are straight and people that are gay. Those that are gay, living in these relationships, under the law are illegal. And so that brings me to my personal thought for those that just happen to be gay living in a very harmonious, productive relationship, but illegal; who am I to judge that they should be illegal? Who is the government to judge that they should be illegal? And for me, that's the reason to support this Bill.[5]

The legislation passed with sixty-one votes, more than proponents thought they had going onto the floor. At a capitol press conference, the speaker said he helped persuade "over five" lawmakers to vote yes but not more than ten. He didn't name them. He didn't say how he had convinced them. He's not precise when he doesn't want to be, of course—again part of the Madigan Mystique.

Governor Pat Quinn signed the measure a few weeks later to great fanfare in a ceremony in Chicago.[6] On the same day, the head of the Springfield Diocese offered prayers of exorcism, saying that politicians are "morally complicit" in assisting the sins of same-sex couples. "Be gone, Satan, father of lies, enemy of human salvation. Give way to Christ," Bishop Thomas Paprocki said in Latin to a large crowd at the cavernous Cathedral of the Immaculate Conception, just a short walk from the state Capitol. "I exorcise you, every unclean spirit, every power of darkness, every incursion of the infernal enemy, every diabolical legion, cohort and faction, in the name and power of our Lord Jesus Christ."[7]

In the pantheon of exorcisms, this was a minor one, something akin to renouncements of the devil during baptisms and confirmations, Paprocki said. He warned that "legal redefinition of marriage is contrary to God's plan," in which marriage should be only between a man and a woman. Yet Paprocki also contended that "politicians responsible for enacting civil same-sex marriage legislation are morally complicit as co-operators in facilitating this grave sin." Paprocki said he hoped the gay marriage law would be repealed.[8]

Less than two years later, the U.S. Supreme Court ruled by a 5–4 vote that the U.S. Constitution guarantees a right to same-sex marriage. "No longer may this liberty be denied," Justice Anthony M. Kennedy wrote. "No union is more profound than marriage, for it embodies the highest ideals of love, fidelity, devotion, sacrifice and family." Marriage is a "keystone of our social order," Kennedy added, noting that the plaintiffs sought "equal dignity in the eyes of the law."[9] Celebrants at Chicago's gay pride parade carried large posters of the five justices who supported the opinion. Governor Quinn drew wild cheers as he walked the parade route.

The times that Madigan needed to help forge a compromise, as he did on gay marriage, are virtually uncountable, but more than a few are notable. He drew upon the lessons of Richard J. Daley, the powerhouse mentor. In his Springfield and Chicago offices, Madigan kept a mass card featuring a picture of the mayor and his wife, Eleanor "Sis" Daley, that was handed out following her death. "When I'm sitting there and trying to make a tough decision, I'll look over at him and just ask myself, 'What would he do?' It's very helpful," Madigan said.[10]

Madigan had bountiful opportunities to draw strength from that card in Springfield. One in particular was forced on the General Assembly in the always volatile debate over gun laws in Illinois. For half a century, it had been illegal in Illinois for a person to carry or possess a firearm in a vehicle or conceal one on their body except on the person's own land or place of business. The U.S. Seventh Circuit Court of Appeals changed all of that, ruling in December 2012 that the state ban on concealed weapons was unconstitutional.

The court voted 2–1 in support of a decision written by Judge Richard Posner, a Reagan appointee, to go against two downstate federal judges that had upheld the law. "We are disinclined to engage in another round of historical analysis to determine whether eighteenth-century America understood the Second Amendment to include a right to bear guns outside the home. The Supreme Court has decided that the amendment confers a right to bear arms for self-defense, which is as important outside the home as inside," Posner wrote, adding, "Illinois had to provide us with more than merely a rational basis for believing that its uniquely sweeping ban is justified by an increase in public safety. It has failed to meet this burden." He continued, saying, "A Chicagoan is a good deal more likely to be attacked on a sidewalk in a rough neighborhood than in his apartment on the 35th floor of the Park Tower." In his majority opinion, Posner acknowledged that a "gun is a potential danger to more people if carried in public than just kept in the home. But the other side of this coin is that knowing that many law-abiding citizens are walking the streets armed may make criminals timid."[11]

The dissent came from Judge Ann Williams, who called the state's decision to ban firearms in public constitutional. "Guns in public expose all nearby to risk, and the risk of accidental discharge or bad aim has lethal consequences," she wrote. "Allowing public carry of ready-to-use guns means that risk is borne by all in Illinois, including the vast majority of its citizens who choose not to have guns."[12]

The state's geographic split over the issue of guns—one of the most prominent political divides in Illinois—flared up immediately. Democratic Representative Eddie Acevedo, then a Chicago police officer, explained to me that parts of Chicago could become the "wild, wild West." He feared that "honest, law-abiding citizens are going to get themselves into predicaments where an individual has a weapon, and they unload on someone else they think may be armed, when in fact they may just be reaching into their pocket for a cellphone."[13] But Chicago's Twenty-First Ward Alderman Howard Brookins, who chaired the City Council's Black caucus, hailed the decision because some citizens wanted to carry guns for protection. And downstate Democratic Representative Brandon Phelps, who previously sought unsuccessfully to allow a concealed carry law with numerous restrictions, suggested that the antigun lawmakers should have taken what he'd offered.[14] The state's regional divide on gun issues in the General Assembly had long prevented either pro-gun or antigun lawmakers from tipping laws too far one way or the other. Neither extreme got its way. The court decision gave the pro-gun folks a major victory and forced the General Assembly to move into unfamiliar territory.[15]

That's where Madigan was needed. The divide meant the speaker played an outsized role. He spent months in Springfield testing which provisions the different factions in the Illinois House would support. He looked for consensus in multiple roll calls. Would lawmakers support carrying concealed guns on mass transit buses and trains? Put it up for a vote. What would the antigun lawmakers prefer to see in a bill? Put it up for a vote. What would the pro–gun rights folks prefer? Put their ideas up for a vote. But that's where Madigan's muscle began to show. By late May, Madigan was prepared to support a compromise arising from the House, where Phelps had worked with the speaker to bring sides together.

In remarks on the House floor, Madigan first sought to explain himself after racking up a decades-long, antigun track record. "I plan to support the Bill," he said, "and I think it's a legitimate question to ask, well, after all of these years fighting against Bills just like this, 'why have you changed your position?' It's very simple."[16] He explained that antigun lawmakers could round up only about half of the votes they needed to pass their preferred, stricter version of the new concealed carry legislation. But then he gave a rare taste of his behind-the-scene maneuvers. The bill supported by gun-rights lawmakers would have fared much better had he not intervened. That pro-gun bill, which needed seventy-one votes to pass with a supermajority for technical reasons, eventually fell short because Madigan successfully talked some lawmakers out of supporting the measure. When Madigan started, the bill had seventy-five supporters—enough to pass with votes to spare. But he whittled the number of supporters down to sixty-four—far too few to pass. "Those vote counts are very telling," Madigan said:

> They tell the reason why I stand before you today changing a position which I have advocated for well over 20 years. But that's what happens in a democracy where there's free and open debate and people are called upon to cast votes in Legislative Bodies because over time, the people that send them to these Legislative Bodies change their thinking. And in a democracy, it's not only okay to do that, it's expected that there would be changes in thinking by people and Legislators consistent with how the people of the country feel.[17]

The compromise bill that Madigan forged would have required a strict-est-in-the-nation sixteen hours of firearms training to get a permit to carry. It would have required law enforcement, doctors, mental health workers, nursing home professionals, and school employees to report people who pose a clear and present danger to themselves or others. It would have set up a board of professionals to screen license applicants, and it would have used some of the funds from a $150 fee to reduce backlogs at overworked crime labs.[18] The House approved that compromise with eighty-five votes, but it ran into immediate trouble with Senate President Cullerton, Mayor Rahm Emanuel, Governor Quinn, and Attorney General Lisa Madigan. Cullerton asserted that he "violently opposes" a provision that would override home-rule powers of Chicago and other bigger communities to have stricter gun laws. Quinn's strong opposition to the bill became evident fast: "We're going to fight it with every fiber of our being."[19]

Cullerton, Quinn, and Emanuel backed the Senate version. The National Rifle Association registered as "neutral" on the Madigan-backed bill but opposed the Senate legislation.[20] To come together, the disparate sides—Republicans, downstaters, city Democrats, antigun, and pro-gun—looked again to the speaker. Years later, Phelps, long a Second Amendment advocate and himself a hunter from Southern Illinois, recalled the intensity of Madigan's determination to find enough common ground in closed-door negotiations to get support from all sides. "Madigan was trying to keep everything together because he knew we had to get something done. That's why we got something done," Phelps said. He recalled that Madigan "very rarely, rarely talked in those meetings. He just took everything in like a sponge." Madigan brought a keen ability to weigh the multiple positions of various gun proponents and gun opponents, Phelps said. "He mastered that art of negotiations. The thing of it is, he did listen to everybody." But through it all, Phelps said, Madigan kept the negotiations on track: "He was driving. He was driving. He was the conductor of the train. There's no doubt about it."[21]

Once a deal was worked out, Senator Kwame Raoul, a Chicago Democrat who later would become attorney general, said one of the closed-door meetings netted a "tentative agreement." That included reining in the House provision for a statewide preemption of all local gun laws so that it would void only local laws involving concealed weapons, as we wrote at the time. They banned concealed carry in many places, such as buses and trains, casinos and government buildings.[22] "Look," Phelps recalled, "my pro-gun guys, they didn't get everything they wanted. The anti-gun groups, they didn't get everything they wanted. It was just one of those things that we had to get done. Because of his leadership, he kept everything together and made sure that we did get something done in a timely manner. We had a clock."[23]

In effect, Cullerton's Senate won out on a major point, keeping the provision that gave Chicago and other big cities leeway on stricter laws.[24] When the Senate voted the next day, on its May 31 deadline, Senator Bill Haine, a former Madison County state's attorney, gave accolades for the "timely and extremely perceptive intervention of the speaker of the House, Mr. Madigan. Without his calm and competent focus on these issues of different, competing views, we would clearly not be here today."[25]

Haine recalled during a 2021 interview that the summit in Madigan's office illustrated the speaker's overall negotiating skills. Madigan didn't have to pound his fists or tell the players on both sides of the concealed carry issue that it was his way or nothing. "He went back and forth. He listened to everybody. He wasn't overbearing," Haine said. "He was conciliatory. He was very accommodating." In a conference room loaded with Republicans and Democrats from the House and Senate as well as pro-gun and antigun lobbyists, Haine said the speaker made it clear that a bill would come together for a vote. "He did his homework, and he was willing to give for what he wanted," Haine said. According to Haine, the speaker wanted to make sure people had training in how to handle firearms and background checks. Madigan also wanted to make sure the guns would be concealed rather than out in the open, Haine recalled.[26]

Both chambers finally voted with three-fifths supermajority roll calls that could defeat Quinn if he decided to veto the bill or put in changes with his amendatory powers to make it tougher. Given the balancing act he had just performed between pro-gun and antigun interests, the speaker warned, "At the end of the day, if the governor were to veto or to offer an amendatory veto, he'll be overridden."[27]

Never too shy to tilt at windmills, no matter how firmly they were planted in the ground, Quinn did not take the speaker's advice. He might have been wary. A complicating factor was the lingering question of whether the speaker's daughter, the attorney general, would decide to run against Quinn as he sought reelection in 2014. The speaker suggested that Quinn would rewrite the concealed weapons bill "to advance his campaign for re-election."[28]

But Quinn didn't play around the edges of the bill. He wrote in what he called wholesale "common sense" changes, saying the legislature's bill would allow people to carry as many guns as they wanted in too many places. "I think this is an example of a situation in Illinois where the legislature passed a bill in a hurried way at the inspiration of the National Rifle Association, contrary to the safety of the people of Illinois," Quinn said. The governor appeared in full campaign mode when he announced his changes, surrounding himself with family members of gun victims and antigun advocates. But he met resistance. One other candidate ramping up for a 2014 challenge to the governor was Bill Daley, another son of Richard J. Daley and a former chief of staff to President Barack Obama. Daley dismissed Quinn's attempt to change the carefully constructed plan as a "stunt."[29]

In reality, Quinn's ideas were not all wildly radical. He wanted to limit a person to carrying one concealed weapon at a time. He wanted to make sure the guns could hold a maximum of only ten rounds. He wanted a ban on guns at all places that serve alcoholic beverages, not just places where that makes up a majority of sales. Taken alone, those ideas and others could be considered reasonable in many quarters. But the geographic breakdown, where downstate hunters and suburban Republicans took pro-gun stances and Chicago lawmakers lined up for tougher gun laws, required Madigan to strike a balance. Both chambers quickly overrode Quinn's veto changes on overwhelming votes.[30]

Of course, coalition building, rather than conflict, is one of Madigan's preferred methods of garnering support for legislation, another tip of the cap to his mentor. "Mayor Daley's greatest strength was his ability to work with people and to satisfy as many elements of his coalition as he possibly could," Madigan said as he first became speaker. "You hear independents talk in terms of building coalitions. Well, Daley was a coalition builder."[31]

In public, Madigan has long rejected the idea that he bludgeons his lawmakers into submission when he needs them to vote one way or the other, a reputation that preceded him into the speakership in 1983. He blamed his Republican predecessor as House speaker for suggesting his arm-twisting got out of hand. "I don't hit people over the head," Madigan told the Associated Press, saying, "That's a label George Ryan put on me many years ago."[32]

Insisting his art of persuasion is above reproach, Madigan has welcomed his critics to come and watch how bills come together. "For those people who think that there's too much arm-twisting in the legislature by the leaders, those people ought to come to Springfield, they ought to come to the Capitol building, they ought to spend some time at the Capitol building, interact with members of the legislature," he said in an interview at Southern Illinois University.

> Observe how business is done in the legislature. And most of them, the strong majority of them, would come to the view, "Well, if there is arm-twisting, it's not undue. It's just persuasion, it's conversation. . . ." Spend time with the Democratic members of the House, people that I interact with day in and day out, and they will be told Speaker Madigan does not threaten people. He does not intimidate people. He will come out on the floor. He will go into a Democratic caucus. He will attempt to articulate a Democratic position on certain issues. But there's never threats, there's never intimidation, just doesn't happen.[33]

There are lawmakers who dispute Madigan's assessment, of course. But Madigan provided a contrast to his style and that of Republican George Ryan during a forum at Elmhurst College, noting a time when Madigan and the three other legislative leaders huddled in summit while Ryan was governor: "One of Governor Ryan's favorite approaches and favorite statements would be to convene the leaders. He and I would be in the room with the other leaders, and George would just say, 'Well, look, we've got problem A. What do we have to do to solve this problem?' He'd say, 'Mike what do we have to do? Lee, what do we have to do?' . . . And George would just pursue, persist, you know: 'I want an answer.'"[34]

When Ryan wanted a new construction program, Madigan recalled, the governor gathered the legislative leaders into a room and started to outline a variety of fee and tax increases. "I think he started with me, and I told him, I said, 'I'm for it. I think you ought to make it bigger.'" As Ryan went around the room, he came to Philip, who fell back into what Madigan called a "favorite method" of legislative leaders when they don't want to say no and reject a governor's request outright. "So they blame their caucus members," Madigan said. Noting that Philip would refer to his Senate Republicans as "gorillas," the speaker recalled. "He would say, 'My gorillas don't like that.' And so there's this pause, and Ryan just looked at him, and he said, 'You said that to me after everything I've done for you?' And then [Ryan] took [Philip] out of the room. Took him into a separate room, closed the door."[35]

"There was a lot of screaming and shouting," Madigan said. "And they both came back and sat down, and George just looked at Pate, and Pate said, 'Well, governor, there will be enough votes to pass your bill.' That was George's method. Very effective."[36]

Nearly two decades removed from when he served as governor, Ryan recalled in a fall 2021 interview for a Better Government Association podcast that he worked with Madigan and accomplished "some good things done for the state of Illinois." Despite their clashes over the years, particularly over politics, Ryan told BGA interviewer Justin Kaufmann that he "never had a bad experience with Mike Madigan."

> And every time I worked with him, he knew what he was talking about, knew what he wanted. And he was not difficult to work with. If he told you he was going to do something, he did it. You know, we didn't always agree on things. But the major things we did, you know, things that the city of Chicago needed, why, they'd come to me. And, of course, I'd have to appease a lot of the Downstate guys. But we always managed to get things worked out for the benefit of the state.[37]

Lee Daniels, who sat across the table from Madigan in negotiations longer than any other House Republican, acknowledged in an oral history interview that his relationship with Madigan was "strained at times," but Daniels said he always liked and respected Madigan. "There were times that we would have shot each other, if we'd had guns, because we were fierce competitors," Daniels said. "In a sense, we were fighting for our individual and collective beliefs, and we were representing, not only our own beliefs, but our caucuses' beliefs and our party's beliefs." Daniels, whose Republicans gained the majority in the 1994 election that drove Madigan from the speakership for two years, said Madigan "never made the same mistake twice. He learns from his experience. He's very disciplined, very focused, very knowledgeable on the retention of power, and that's one of his strongest points." Daniels said both could count votes and deliver them when they struck a deal. But just as Daniels calls Madigan the "best power player in the game of politics," he also said, "One of the criticisms that is leveled against Mike is that he doesn't utilize this to help solve the [state's] problems in a responsible and efficient manner."[38]

Quinn questions whether Madigan negotiates only when he wants—and if it's in his best interest politically. To this day, Quinn blames Madigan for delaying an increase in the state's minimum wage. After he lost the race for governor in 2014, Quinn wanted Madigan's lame-duck House to take up legislation that would raise the minimum wage—an issue the governor had campaigned on and one that had received overwhelming support in an advisory referendum. The referendum asked if the minimum wage should rise from $8.25 to $10. Cullerton's Senate passed legislation to raise the wage, but a Madigan spokesman said there was not enough support to pass it in the House.[39] Business groups called the minimum wage hikes a "job killer." No progress was made under Republican Governor Bruce Rauner. Eventually, though, Madigan and Cullerton sent Governor J. B. Pritzker a bill that phased in a minimum wage hike from $8.25 to $15 by 2025, and he signed it. Still, the minimum wage didn't hit $10 until July 1, 2020—a delay that, according to Quinn, was five years too long.[40] "That's one of my biggest disappointments," he said.[41]

Madigan long demonstrated that his longevity gave him an extra edge, particularly when negotiating with Rauner, a governor who the speaker believed was too extreme for Illinois. Rauner's Turnaround Agenda, for one, would have hurt too many regular citizens because of changes he wanted in workers compensation, collective bargaining, and the prevailing wage, Madigan said. "I don't think America likes extremism," Madigan said in a 2016 interview with radio reporters Amanda Vinicky of WUIS-FM 91.9 and Craig Dellimore of WBBM-AM 780. "I think America wants a full, healthy debate and then they want people to come together and settle somewhere in the middle."[42]

Pressed on whether Rauner was trying to exploit differences between Madigan and longtime associate and Senate President John Cullerton, Madigan harkened back to his Irish roots: "What the governor should understand is that's an old divide-and-conquer theory which was practiced by the British against the Irish. And he's working with two Irishmen, Madigan and Cullerton, who are very aware of the British history of divide and conquer, and we're not going to permit that to happen."[43]

Until Rauner, Madigan said, the Democrats in the legislature found ways to work together with Republican governors, such as Jim Thompson for fourteen years, Jim Edgar for eight years, and George Ryan for four years. "So the record of those three prior Republican governors is a record of cooperation," Madigan said, "recognizing that there are competing interests in the state, but there can be shared agreement on the solution to problems."[44]

Looking back, Edgar acknowledged that he had worked with Madigan during the first half of his speakership and that "he became much more this mythical power person" in the last half of his time as speaker, when it "may have been a little harder to compromise." Edgar conceded he could get frustrated waiting for Madigan to make his move, because many unrelated issues could be coming to a head. "As far as getting the votes, I think he always thought there were trade-offs," Edgar said. "He wanted as many things on the table that you could do trades with. If there was just one thing, you're limited to how much you can trade. Also, at times he was just trying to assess what could he get and what couldn't he get and what did he have to do to bring his members along."

With Madigan, Edgar felt confident that a deal cut was a done deal. "The thing great about Madigan, if you had a deal with Madigan, that meant he brought the votes from his side," Edgar said. "Though it was pure torture sometimes trying to get it done, you could finally get to the point where you had something worked out."[45]

On one of the most historic bills of his governorship, Quinn recalled that Madigan was particularly coy when asked in a private meeting about legislation to ban the death penalty. The bill was pending in the House during a lame-duck session following the 2010 election. Governor Ryan had placed a moratorium on executions in Illinois in 2000 because 13 condemned inmates had been cleared since Illinois had reinstated the death penalty in 1977. A dozen people had been executed in that same period.[46] Two days before the end of his term in January 2003, Ryan cleared Death Row and commuted the sentences of more than 160 inmates to life in prison. Momentum had been building for a ban on the death penalty, though neither the House nor the Senate had passed the legislation. Quinn and Madigan were alone in the governor's office addressing other issues when the governor asked how the speaker planned to handle the death penalty bill. "There was a very long pause," Quinn recalled in a 2021 interview. "Complete silence." In the back of his mind, Quinn knew the speaker's friends and colleagues sometimes referred to Madigan as "the Sphinx from Pulaski Road," a nod to his silence and his ward headquarters at Sixty-Fifth and Pulaski. "I was quiet," Quinn said. "I wanted the sphinx to speak. So after a long delay, Madigan goes . . . 'What do you think I should do?' Not exactly an answer. But I was ready. I said, 'Well, I think you should have them vote their consciences.' And that's all I said. But I figured by saying that, he would call the bill. . . . I didn't say anything about what I would do with the bill—but I think his surmise, which was correct, was that if it did pass the House, that I would sign it."[47]

The bill passed both chambers following robust debate. After weeks of meeting with opponents and supporters of the ban, Quinn signed the legislation. "I gotta give him credit," Quinn said. "He called the bill."[48]

7

PENSION FAILURE

"I think there will be at least four
members of the Illinois Supreme Court
that will approve the bill."
—Speaker Michael Madigan, May 1, 2013

The time to repair the state's broken public employee pension system
had already come and gone by 2013, but that was the last year a serious
attempt was made to fix it. Governor Pat Quinn had declared more than a
year before that he was "put on earth" to solve the pension mess, a destiny
that the Democratic chief executive saw for himself.[1] He would go so far as
to suspend lawmakers' paychecks in hopes of forcing them to act, a move
popular with the public but one that peeved Speaker Madigan, who went
to court with Senate President John Cullerton to block the governor's
populist move. Yet the massive hole the state had dug for itself kept getting
deeper. The pension debt—what the state owed, mostly because governors and lawmakers for close to a century had failed to set aside enough
money each year to pay for the future pension benefits workers earned
that year—crept closer and closer to the $100 billion mark. Sweetheart
pension deals, early retirement packages, and lackluster investments also
played roles over the years for the five retirement systems—judges, lawmakers, university employees, rank-and-file state workers, and teachers
outside the city of Chicago. But the failure of too many governors and
lawmakers to take the pension problem seriously gave Illinois the title of
the worst-funded state pension system in America.

The mathematics boggled the minds of many lawmakers: How many more billions of dollars must be pumped into the pension system each year to pay for the sins of shorting the retirement funds for so long? The Teachers Retirement System of the State of Illinois, for example, had to sell assets for several years to make the required annual payments to retirees.[2] The cost of playing catch-up on pension payments eventually meant the state was holding back money for schools, social services, and health care in order to fill the shortfalls in the retirement systems. Illinoisans kept wanting more services than they were willing to pay for, and politicians accommodated them by shorting pension systems. Short-term thinking, so often the bane of politics, meant lawmakers could use money to fund popular programs today that would make voters happy the next time they cast their ballots rather than making long-term investments in pensions. Math wizards wrangled with the astronomical costs for the years of neglect, but Speaker Madigan had a much simpler equation on his mind.

The Illinois Supreme Court had seven justices: four Democrats and three Republicans. The biggest hurdle in finding a quick fix to the state's pension woes was the Illinois Constitution, which effectively banned reductions in public employee pension benefits once they were put in place. The constitution said state and local public workers' pension systems "shall be an enforceable contractual relationship, the benefits of which shall not be diminished or impaired."[3] In short, once a person is given a pension benefit, it can't be taken away. Madigan believed he saw a path that could meet the constitutional test. His ideas included scaling back 3 percent annual cost-of-living increases, requiring workers to chip in more from their paychecks, and raising the retirement age for public workers. Before he finished, he would justify the major changes in a preamble to the legislation stating that far-reaching reforms are "necessary to address the fiscal crisis without incurring further severe and irreparable harm to the public welfare."[4] All he had to do was convince four of the seven justices to go along. And he sounded confident.

Speaking to reporters, Madigan made a rare prediction. In a large, ornate Capitol hearing room, he had just advanced his pension proposal through a committee on a 9–1 vote on May 1, 2013. "I think there will be at least four members of the Illinois Supreme Court that will approve the bill," Madigan said.[5]

Given that four elected Democrats represented a majority of the Supreme Court and that Madigan chaired the Democratic Party, the calculation looked like a pretty easy formula: write the legislation, scale back the benefits, cut the costs, explain the state's disastrous financial woes, and let the Democratic majority on the court uphold the plan as constitutional. He might have thought four of seven justices of any political stripe would come around. And he might have thought he could get a Republican justice to buy in if one of the Democrats strayed. But it was lost on no one that the prediction came from the man who had helped the Democrats hold the majority on the high court. Only one day after his prediction, Madigan put the bill up for a vote in the full House, where it passed 62–51, with two votes to spare. "I'm committed to the bill. I'm committed to solving this issue," Madigan said. "I've spoken to this publicly, that the state's fiscal problems are so bad that they require radical surgery, and this is the first step. We've taken the first step in the House. My expectation is the Senate will approve this bill."[6]

So much for great expectations. The Senate did not go along. Perhaps no other moment defined the differences between the two veteran politicians, Madigan and Cullerton, as well as the pension conundrum. More than virtually any other topic, their approaches to resolving the issue opened windows into what the two longtime friends were thinking. The Senate president searched for ways to outwit the system, looking for the magical phrasing and formula that would fit within the narrow confines of a tightly drawn constitutional standard. And he also sounded confident that he'd figured it out.

For Madigan, though, it was more a matter of clout. By projecting the support on the high court, he showed that winning votes was what mattered most. In the House the question is how to get sixty votes to pass a bill; in the Supreme Court it's how to get four to uphold a law. The wording, arguments, and other niceties in the legislation would give justices enough to hang their robes on when writing their decision, but his prediction suggested that he believed that a court led by a 4–3 Democratic majority would side with the Illinois Democratic Party chair. The speaker's words—always dissected to the nth degree by the Capitol crowd—rocketed around the rotunda. Some lobbyists weighed each of Madigan's syllables against their law degrees and pondered whether the speaker's bill could clear the constitutional hurdles. But his fan club of lawmakers, lobbyists, and staffers reveled at the boldness of the prediction.

Even if the speaker had private doubts about his plan—as some observers suspected—Madigan's effort would quiet the loud and constant calls for action from Quinn, business groups, editorial writers, and innumerable critics begrudging public workers' pensions. Despite the closeness of the two legislative leaders, Cullerton long had doubts that Madigan's plan would be upheld as constitutional. Cullerton had argued that he had a "constitutionally sound" pension proposal, one that he negotiated with a coalition of unions. Yes, Madigan's plan would save $150 billion or more. And Cullerton's proposal theoretically would save about a third as much as the speaker's bill, but any plan, first and foremost, needed to pass constitutional muster. "We must calculate the risk associated with passing a plan that could save zero if the court throws it out," Cullerton said. "We need to remember that the unilateral approach is a gamble. Betting against the Constitution is risky."[7]

Cullerton's proposal incorporated his belief that public employees must be offered a choice when it came to changing benefits, an exchange necessary to meet legal and contractual considerations baked into the state's constitution. He offered various options, basically looking to give employees and retirees a chance to choose between scaling back their generous 3 percent compounded, automatic annual cost-of-living increases and keeping state-subsidized health care in retirement. Among the unions in agreement with Cullerton were the American Federation of State, County, and Municipal Employees; the Service Employees International Union; the Illinois Federation of Teachers; and the Illinois Education Association. Michael Carrigan, the president of the Illinois AFL-CIO, spoke for the unions, declaring, "This agreement is our coalition's bottom line." In contrast, Carrigan said, the Madigan plan "threatens to rob the retirement savings of teachers, police officers and others in public service by 20–40 percent. His proposal is not only drastically unfair, but it is blatantly unconstitutional, rendering any advertised savings fictional."[8]

Many observers thought the Cullerton plan also had flaws. For one, it "conveniently overlooked the constitutional language that says membership in, i.e., a person's relationship with, a pension system is a contractual relationship whose benefits cannot be diminished or impaired," said Charles N. Wheeler III, the retired statehouse reporter and journalism professor who specialized in state finances. Cullerton's plan required an employee to choose between two options—either of which would diminish benefits—which the state constitution prohibits, Wheeler noted.[9] One remedy might have been to give workers a third option—choose to keep all of the benefits—which likely would have resulted in little or no fewer savings, Wheeler said. While union leadership could agree with a public employer, such as the state, to cut retirement benefits, an individual worker would not be obligated to accept the cuts, Wheeler said. It's a roadblock that Chicago Mayor Rahm Emanuel ran into when the Illinois Supreme Court in 2016 tossed a benefit-cutting deal he made with some of the city employee unions—only to have individual workers challenge the reductions.[10] Despite such reservations, Cullerton kept pressing. He quickly won the backing of the Senate, but Madigan held fast. He said the Senate should pass his plan and predicted it would, saying, "I have faith." In a statement, Cullerton again warned the Madigan plan's "ambitious savings projections should always be balanced against the prospect of netting zero with an unfavorable court decision."[11]

But now the Cullerton plan was in the House, and the Madigan plan was in the Senate. Like many of her colleagues, Senator Heather Steans, a Democrat from Chicago's North Side, worried the costs of failing to reach a pension deal would squeeze tight budgets for schools, health care, and social services. "It's really dark to even think about it," she said.[12]

In the end, Madigan did not call Cullerton's plan for a vote in the House. But he did get a vote on his plan in Cullerton's Senate. The upper chamber, however, didn't follow Madigan's wishes. Senators soundly rejected the speaker's proposal—with forty-two opposed and only sixteen in favor. The spring session closed without a pension deal, with Madigan's wrap-up statement contending for the understatement of the year. "Obviously," Madigan said, "this is a session where we have not enjoyed a great deal of success."[13]

Breaking the logjam took time. At Quinn's suggestion, the House and the Senate put together a conference committee designed to iron out the differences between the chambers. Rank-and-file stalwarts who had spent countless hours working on a pension fix took part, including Senator Kwame Raoul, D-Chicago; Representative Elaine Nekritz, D-Northbrook; Representative Darlene Senger, R-Naperville; Representative Jil Tracy, R-Quincy; and Senator Daniel Biss, the Evanston Democrat who worked in the House on the issue before joining the upper chamber.[14] In the summer of 2012, then Representative Biss, who had both a bachelor's in math from Harvard and a doctorate in math from the Massachusetts Institute of Technology, famously let out his frustration on the House floor when nothing got done in a special session that Quinn called to address pensions. "Guess what? We all look like idiots," Biss declared.[15] After months of wrangling, the new 2013 conference committee could get close to an agreement, but the legislative leaders would have to bring it over the goal line. Madigan played shuttle diplomacy, incorporating Senate Democratic desires to tweak proposed changes in cost-of-living adjustments to protect those with smaller pensions and Republican wishes to achieve substantial savings. They all came together in early December 2013 with a proposal looking more like Madigan's unilateral approach to benefit cuts than Cullerton's contractual consideration model. Madigan said the bill he'd passed earlier was the high bar in savings, with an estimated $163 billion, while Cullerton's would have tallied $58 billion. Madigan said the new bill emerging in December would still save $160 billion.[16]

The historic overhaul received robust debate, with the speaker saying the pensions are "just too rich" for the state to afford. "Something's got to be done," Madigan said. "We can't go on dedicating so much of our resources to this one sector, pensions." The legislation made it through the House 62–53, with one lawmaker voting present. The Senate passed the bill 30–24, with three casting present votes. One opponent, Senator Linda Holmes, criticized the speaker's "too rich" description and slammed prior state officials for failing to keep the pensions in better shape. "What we are doing is quite simply wrong," Holmes, an Aurora Democrat, told Senate colleagues. "This is actually no different than a thief coming into your house at night and stealing your valuables. The difference is this isn't a thief coming in the night. This is your elected representatives coming to you, looking you straight in the eye and saying, 'I'm going to take away your future.' That is more than a promise broken. That is reprehensible."[17] After the bill's passage, Madigan stood by his position: "The bill would not have passed without me. I was convinced that standing fast for substantial savings, clear intent and an end to unaffordable annual raises would result in a sound plan that will meet all constitutional challenges."[18]

Though Cullerton worried aloud that the legislation would violate the constitution's ban on diminishing or impairing pension benefits, he voted for the measure in hopes of settling the question. "I think the bill has serious constitutional problems," Cullerton said. "I've made that clear from the start, but now it's in front of the court, and they can decide."[19]

Quinn signed the legislation two days later, spurring an onslaught of union and retiree lawsuits challenging the law. The validity of the pension law's changes came into doubt when the Supreme Court ruled on July 3, 2014, that subsidized health-care premiums for retired state workers were guaranteed under the pension protection clause.[20] The court voted 6–1, with the only dissenter being Justice Anne Burke. Less than a year later, a Sangamon County judge made Cullerton's warnings about the pension law look prescient. Judge John Belz tossed out the law. "The state of Illinois made a constitutionally protected promise to its employees concerning their pension benefits," Belz wrote in November 2014. "Under established and uncontroverted Illinois law, the state of Illinois cannot break this promise." In response, the Madigan team still maintained the Illinois Supreme Court eventually would uphold the law. But Cullerton said Belz's ruling "confirms that, while the need for reform is urgent, the rule of law is absolute." In arguing to uphold the pension reform statute, Attorney General Lisa Madigan's office called the law constitutional because the state has the ability to change the pensions under extraordinary conditions, such as the huge pension debt and economic woes.[21] But the Supreme Court disagreed.

Despite the speaker's prediction, the high court's justices unanimously ruled the law was unconstitutional, voting 7–0 on May 8, 2015—a year and a half after the law passed. "Our economy is and has always been subject to fluctuations, sometimes very extreme fluctuations," Republican Justice Lloyd Karmeier wrote on behalf of all seven justices. "The law was clear that the promised benefits would therefore have to be paid and that the responsibility for providing the state's share of the necessary funding fell squarely on the legislature's shoulders. . . . The General Assembly may find itself in crisis, but it is a crisis which other public pension systems managed to avoid and . . . it is a crisis for which the General Assembly itself is largely responsible," Karmeier wrote. "It is our obligation, however, just as it is theirs, to ensure that the law is followed. That is true at all times. It is especially important in times of crisis when, as this case demonstrates, even clear principles and long-standing precedent are threatened. Crisis is not an excuse to abandon the rule of law. It is a summons to defend it," he said.[22]

Karmeier explained that there were other ways to address the pension system's fiscal problems besides taking money away from retirees. He noted, for example, that lawmakers could have adopted a new schedule for paying down, or amortizing, the unfunded liabilities. But he also noted that the General Assembly refused to extend a temporary income tax that expired right before Republican Bruce Rauner became governor, a decision costing the state roughly $4 billion a year. Sure, Rauner ran against extending the temporary income tax hike, and Madigan would have done him a big fiscal favor if the speaker had renewed the tax for the incoming GOP governor taking office in January 2015—something the speaker didn't rush to do. But it was largely a choice. Rounding up votes from nervous lawmakers is always a chore, but the Democrats had passed a temporary income tax hike four years earlier in a lame-duck session. "The General Assembly could also have sought additional tax revenue," Karmeier wrote. "While it did pass a temporary income tax increase, it allowed the increased rate to lapse to a lower rate even as the pension funding was being debated and litigated."[23]

In case there were any doubters, Karmeier went into a historical review of the state's woeful record of shorting the public pensions. The justice cited the arguments in the 1970 constitutional convention, whose members included a twenty-eight-year-old Michael Madigan, who voted for the pension protection language.[24] In his decision, Karmeier essentially rejected the General Assembly argument that it could exercise, as he described it, a "'reserved sovereign power,' i.e, its 'police power'" to override the constitution. In other words, the state could just blame the state's financial mess on the Great Recession, the growing pension costs, the state's poor economy, and a deterioration of its once-mighty AAA credit rating that now hovered around junk status and cost the state more and more dollars when it borrowed money. But that's a tough call. "Indeed," Karmeier wrote, "accepting the State's position that reducing retirement benefits is justified by economic circumstances would require that we allow the legislature to do the very thing the pension protection clause was designed to prevent it from doing."[25]

The reluctance of lawmakers to tackle the pension woes didn't just begin overnight. An incisive analysis for Chicago-Kent College of Law by Eric Madiar, who performed deep legal and historical research on pensions while serving as Cullerton's chief legal counsel, pointed out that the problems with underfunding pensions dated to at least the early 1900s.[26] Madiar cited a 1917 report commissioned by the General Assembly that described the state and municipal pension systems as "one of insolvency" and "moving toward crisis." From 1947 through 1969, a General Assembly pension laws commission sent "dire warnings of the pension systems' impending insolvency, the growth of unfunded pension liabilities, and the significant burden these liabilities posed for 'present and future generations of taxpayers.'"[27]

The warnings never really stopped. In 1970 the five state pension systems had unfunded liabilities of $1.46 billion—a figure Madiar compared to the $97.4 billion in the fiscal year ending June 30, 2013.[28] In the 1970s and 1980s, Madiar wrote, a state pension commission recommended making contributions that covered the current costs of benefits accrued by employees each year, meaning the normal cost, as well as the cost associated with the interest due on unfunded liabilities.[29] But in a plan criticized for ignoring the rising overall costs and potentially leading to insolvency, the state started making pension payments based on the amount of money it spent on paying out retirees' benefits for each budget year. That meant state officials made their employer contributions to the pension systems "equal to 100% of what the systems were expected to 'pay-out' in benefits each year."[30] By 1979 Republican Governor James R. Thompson's third year in office, his administration received an outside consultant's report warning that pension problems had "reached crisis proportions" because funding the benefit payouts had "increased dramatically."[31] The state risked putting its AAA bond rating in jeopardy.

Leading up to his third term, Thompson was juggling the state's finances as the economy teetered toward recession. In March 1981 he announced that the state would move from the "100% payout" policy to one that covered only 60 percent of the costs of benefits to be paid in one year.[32] In covering budget negotiations over the years, reporters had observed that Thompson and the four legislative leaders would go to the pension funds when they needed money to shore up a budget. "Indeed," Madiar noted, "between fiscal years 1982 and 1995, pegging the state pension contributions to at or below 60 percent of payout became the state's de facto funding policy."[33]

The moves under Thompson didn't all happen in a vacuum. By 1982 Thompson was fighting a recession, struggling with the state's finances, and battling former Democratic U.S. Senator Adlai Stevenson III, Madigan's candidate for governor. Thompson squeaked out a win with 5,074 votes. But Democrats throughout the state drove voters to the polls in races at all levels—even to the point that they gave a scare to U.S. House Minority Leader Bob Michel, R-Peoria, who barely won reelection in what was seen nationally as a "referendum on Reaganomics." In the tumultuous political two years before the election, Thompson signed pension legislation making "investment returns the largest funding source for the pension systems" and permitting the retirement systems to "invest in mortgage-backed securities," changes that added the volatility of the markets into the pension mix.[34]

By 1985 a Thompson task force searching for new strategies noted that Standard and Poor's had cut the state's rating to AA+ from the healthier AAA standard because the state was refusing to put enough money into pensions.[35] His 1983 temporary eighteen-month income tax hike, one for which Madigan's Democrats put up forty votes, was expiring. The credit ratings slide had begun. The Illinois Economic and Fiscal Commission said the 60 percent "payout policy" each year would eventually cause the state to start siphoning money from schools, human services, and other operations. The commission recommended paying normal annual pension costs and put in money to pay down the unfunded pension costs caused by years of shorting the retirement system.[36]

In 1989 the General Assembly approved a proposal that had the goals of better funding but not the hammer to force the necessary payments. Democratic state Senator Dawn Clark Netsch of Chicago, who advocated the plan, said later that it had failed because Governors Thompson and Edgar and the legislature never put in enough money. Thompson also signed costly union-backed legislation that allowed retirees and their survivors to collect 3 percent compounded increases every year, pushing the five systems' unfunded liabilities deeper into the red as the politicians declined to provide full funding.[37] Madiar noted that from fiscal years 1990 to 1995 more than $1.4 billion that the pensions needed was "used on other state budget priorities." The impact of underfunding was becoming clearer. The pension systems saw their unfunded costs grow from $8.2 billion in 1989 to $17 billion in 1994.[38]

The pension problem became more volatile as a political issue when Governor Edgar geared up for his 1994 reelection campaign. Netsch, the Democratic challenger, who by then had risen to state comptroller, long had made pension funding one of her major concerns. Edgar called for his own pension funding plan, but Netsch wanted more money pumped into the retirement systems than Edgar. She said her proposal, over the long term, would save $38 billion more than the Edgar plan. Netsch contended that Edgar's plan would "saddle our children" with debt.[39]

Edgar eventually negotiated with House Democrats and Senate Republicans, the majority parties from the two chambers, to come up with a plan that he called "fiscally realistic." It contained what in hindsight has been called the "Edgar ramp," which called for starting low and pushing payments progressively higher for about fifteen years. Payments were supposed

to level off for the final thirty-five years of a fifty-year plan to take funding to 90 percent by 2045.[40] The idea was buoyed at the time by healthy
annual state revenue increases—sometimes by double-digit percentages.
The notion that state general funds would see year-over-year decreases was
unheard of. Yet since fiscal year 2000, Illinois has seen four instances in
which general funds receipts went down year to year, the most recent being the fiscal year that ended June 30, 2020, according to the legislature's
Commission on Government Forecasting and Accountability.[41]

One more pertinent note: Unlike the 1989 Netsch-backed law, which
was largely ignored, the Edgar plan made the ramp's annual contributions
a continuing appropriation. What that means is that, even if governors
and lawmakers choose not to fund pensions in a given year, comptrollers
still must shift the required amounts to retirement systems automatically.
The pension systems were more than 50 percent funded when Edgar
took action. The debt? Only $18.7 billion. "We had a time bomb in our
retirement system that was going to go off sometime in the first part of
the 21st Century," Edgar said. "This legislation defuses that time bomb."[42]

A quarter century later, plenty of folks would beg to differ. The pension
plan that passed with bipartisan cheers gets more than its share of jeers
because that long ramp allowed the debt to grow bigger than it would
have if more money had been put in sooner. "I still think it was a good
proposal," Edgar recalled in a 2021 interview. "We put it in the statute
that you've got to pay money into the pension fund. It never had been
required before." He said he believed inflation and proper preparation
by officials would have allowed for the state to handle bigger payments.
But the pension problem got worse with more than a little help of state
officials who followed Edgar into office and a volatile stock market. As
Governor George Ryan headed out the door, he worked on rolling out
an early retirement program. In theory the program would save the state
money by allowing about seven thousand workers to retire early following
the post-9/11 and dot-com bubble recessions. That would conveniently
take care of many of the employees hired at the beginning of the quarter-
century reign of Republican administrations starting with Thompson.

In practice, though, the early retirement program was made so sweet
that 11,372 state workers took the deal, costing the pension systems hundreds of millions of dollars more than anticipated.[43] The final calculations
were not made before lawmakers voted on the plan. "I don't think there
were very many lawmakers who knew that the package was sweetened so
much after the actuarial projections were completed," said former Senator

Jeff Schoenberg, an Evanston Democrat, when the deal was cut by Ryan and legislative leaders. "Virtually nobody anticipated the profound effect the proposal would have."[44]

Following Ryan's departure, Democratic Governor Rod Blagojevich, with Madigan's willingness to help the rookie chief executive, took out a $10 billion pension bond to infuse money into the retirement funds in 2003, but the loan was not as effective as it could have been, because he only used about $7.3 billion to buttress the pension funds and used most of the rest to plug holes in his budget, pay investment fees, and cover other costs. In the two budget years running up to Blagojevich's 2006 reelection bid, the governor also cut a deal with the cochairs of his campaign, Madigan and then Senate President Emil Jones, a fellow Chicago Democrat. They would slash contributions by about $2.3 billion over the two years to free up money to cover other government programs. It gave the illusion that the annual state budgets were in better shape than they really were and hurt the pension funding even more.

The long-term costs of shorting those funds added to the debt. But Madigan's House Majority Leader, Barbara Currie, D-Chicago, defended the efforts. She said lawmakers weigh the competing demands on a state budget, and the unfunded pension liability "may not be the most immediate problem."[45]

Though the courts shot down the big pension deal of 2013, Madigan and Cullerton did combine with Quinn to make a sizable dent in the state's future pension costs. In late March 2010, before unions could gear up to stop the package, Madigan and Cullerton sent Quinn legislation that set up a much cheaper pension plan with lower benefits for new state employees. Republicans happily embraced it, and Quinn signed it. Just boosting the retirement age for future employees from sixty-two to sixty-seven was estimated at the time to save $40 billion over several decades.[46] The state gets a little more savings each year because benefits are lower down the line. Overall, early estimates showed that state contributions would go down by more than $70 billion and that the total pension liabilities would be sliced nearly in half—by $256 billion down the road.[47] As a result, the Madigan-Cullerton-Quinn combo did get to say they did something major even though they blew their chance on the big one.

By 2020 the failure of the Madigan-orchestrated 2013 pension fix was adding up fast, according to the legislature's Commission on Government Forecasting and Accountability. From a $97.5 billion gap in fiscal year 2013, "based upon the market value of assets, the combined unfunded liabilities of the State systems totaled $144.4 billion on June 30, 2020," the commission noted. "The aggregate unfunded liability has been growing significantly over the past 15 years. One of the main drivers continues to be actuarially insufficient State contributions determined by the current pension funding policy . . . . [I]f all other actuarial assumptions are met, unfunded liabilities will still increase due to the State contributing an amount that is not sufficient to stop the growth in the unfunded liability." Other factors that could hurt the pension funds included poor performances by investments and poor actuarial calculations, the report noted. On June 30, 2020, the market value of pension assets showed the retirement systems were funded at only 39 percent.[48]

Why does all of this matter? In the big picture of state finances, deferring payments is costly in the long term, and making up for short-changing the pensions draws dollars that could have been used on other programs. The short-changing freed up money to spend on immediate needs. But it's like making interest payments on a home mortgage. The overall amount of money one spends depends on how fast the principal is paid down.

Are there ways out of this mess? In addition to giving new employees smaller benefits, there have been other changes enacted to cut long-term costs. For example, a buyout option offered workers retiring or quitting state government a one-time opportunity to take a lump sum in lieu of a future pension. That has saved $786 million, the commission said.

One potential approach to attacking the pension problem would be to reamortize the pension debt, as Justice Karmeier noted in writing his high court decision. It's kind of like refinancing a home with a long-term fixed mortgage—as opposed to an adjustable-rate deal with a balloon payment later. The Chicago-based Center for Tax and Budget Accountability's Ralph Martire long promoted putting in place a new repayment plan, saying the Edgar law "had nothing to do with actuarial science."[49]

Beyond the math, the state's five pension systems provide retirees with their rocking-chair income, help pay the bills for their nursing home costs, and give them a better chance to enjoy retirement from a state job. Is the system fair? The rules are bent to help the politicians, who get the most lucrative deals, and their friends. Anomalies between annual increases for older workers and new retirees with fatter salaries raise questions of fairness. A striking example comes from a 2013 story looking at the oldest retired educators in Illinois.

Consider Daisy Rittgers. She rode a horse named Prince to a one-room wooden schoolhouse where she taught in Shelby County during the Great Depression. She spent more than four decades teaching and retired in 1972 with an annual pension of $6,327. Forty-one years later, she was 105 years old and collecting only $20,796 a year. In comparison, retired New Trier Township High School District 203 superintendent Henry Bangser, then age 63, received $277,617 a year from the Teachers Retirement System, the fund for public school teachers outside of Chicago. Granted, superintendents are usually paid more than teachers, and suburban school folks generally make more than their rural and downstate counterparts. But their comparison demonstrated that there are no one-size-fits-all solutions when lawmakers come to the bargaining table. Bangser's pension broke down to $23,134 a month—more than what Rittgers received in one year. The annual 3 percent automatic increase boosted Bangser's pension by $673 a month. That monthly boost for Bangser also was more than the $605 total increase Rittgers saw for the entire year. Rittgers had the good fortune of living a long life, but her tiny pension on a much smaller salary left her way behind despite the 3 percent compounded interest.[50] Outlined in the *Tribune*, her story resonated.

Along the way, of course, there are always golden parachutes that anger the public. Two teachers union lobbyists, for instance, managed to jump through a brief window in a bill that allowed them to count their time in the Illinois Federation of Teachers toward a taxpayer-supported teacher pension. They each spent one day as a substitute teacher in a Springfield school to get into the pension plan. When lawmakers sought to scale back the lucrative deal, one lobbyist took it all the way to the Illinois Supreme Court—and won the right to let him include the union time he had racked up before the law took effect. It fell under the iron-clad constitutional rule that once a benefit is given it cannot be taken away.[51]

At almost every turn, there are lawmakers leaping through loopholes placed intentionally into the pension statutes to benefit them. A number of older lawmakers were grandfathered into a provision in the General Assembly pension plan that allowed them to peg their legislative pensions to their highest public salary—meaning much-higher-paid government jobs than what they received as lawmakers. That has meant big boosts for former legislators, such as Richard M. Daley, who rose to mayor of Chicago and used his more than $200,000 city salary to raise his General Assembly pension.[52] When Madigan retired from the General Assembly, he started collecting his pension check in March 2021 at an annual pension rate of

$85,117. But thanks to a provision slipped into the law during his long tenure, Madigan stood to gain from 3 percent cost-of-living increases for each year beyond twenty in the General Assembly. The sweet formula meant that Madigan, with half a century in the legislature, was eligible to start collecting $148,955 a year on July 1, 2022. Given that his final salary as a legislative leader was slightly more than $100,000, Madigan's retirement check would be the deal that keeps on giving. And like all retirees, Madigan stood to get 3 percent pension increases each subsequent year.[53]

One of the few things that can stop pension spigots once they start flowing for lawmakers are convictions tied to corruption during their public service. And often they'll try to negotiate a plea deal for a misdemeanor unrelated to their legislative post or some other criminal charge that would let them keep their pension.

Some ex-lawmakers demonstrated extreme levels of creativity to boost their pensions, including former state Representative Bob Molaro, a stalwart Madigan ally. Molaro managed to nearly double his annual state legislative pension by writing a nineteen-page white paper for Fourteenth Ward Alderman Ed Burke, the City Council's Finance Committee chairman. Burke paid Molaro $12,000 for a one-month stint. That let Molaro annualize the $12,000-a-month rate to boost his $64,000-a-year legislative pension to more than $120,000. It was legal for Molaro, who died in 2020, but the average taxpayer doesn't think a deal like that for an ex-lawmaker is anywhere close to fair. That type of boost is being phased out as old-timers retire from the House and Senate.[54]

To many lawmakers, the Illinois Supreme Court's unanimous ruling that struck down the 2013 pension overhaul set back the effort to cut out-of-control costs. But the high court's decision did not automatically translate into a crushing political loss for Madigan in Springfield. Voting for a pension plan took the sizzling topic off of the legislature's immediate agenda and quieted outside "good-government" critics. Lawmakers initially could tell constituents that the legislature voted for a pension fix rather than have it hanging as an unresolved campaign issue. As the pension law moved through the courts, the heat on lawmakers to fix the problem cooled. Once the court ruled, the momentum for massive reform started to fade. The failure to come up with a new solution caused the pension hole to grow bigger, and every taxpayer suffered. But the Madigan machine kept humming.

Democratic Committeeman Michael Madigan of the Thirteenth Ward speaks before the park board in Chicago on July 28, 1970. (Photo credit: Alton Kaste/*Chicago Tribune*/TNS)

House Speaker Michael Madigan, left, and Governor James Thompson meet with groups in Madigan's Springfield office to work on a school reform package in 1988, the year the two teamed up to save the White Sox. (Photo credit: Chuck Berman/*Chicago Tribune*/TNS)

Governor Rod Blagojevich, left, Chicago Mayor Richard M. Daley, and House Speaker Michael Madigan, right, enjoy a Democratic rally on Governor's Day at the Illinois State Fair, August 16, 2006. (Photo credit: Charles Osgood/*Chicago Tribune*/TNS)

House Speaker Michael Madigan listens closely in a House committee on January 7, 2007, regarding a rate hike proposed by ComEd. (Photo credit: Jose More/*Chicago Tribune*/TNS)

Attorney General Lisa Madigan is sworn in while accompanied by husband Pat Byrnes, left; daughters, Rebecca, 5, and Lucy, 2; mother, Shirley; and father, Speaker Michael Madigan, on January 10, 2011, in Springfield. (Photo credit: Michael Tercha/*Chicago Tribune*/TNS)

House Speaker Michael Madigan lightheartedly points to Governor Bruce Rauner as Senate President John Cullerton smiles before the governor's budget address to the General Assembly in the House chambers on February 17, 2016. (Photo credit: Antonio Perez/*Chicago Tribune*/TNS)

House Speaker Michael Madigan supports gay marriage bill on November 5, 2013, saying, "For those that just happen to be gay—living in a very harmonious, productive relationship but illegal—who am I to judge that they should be illegal?" (Photo credit: Antonio Perez/*Chicago Tribune*/TNS)

House Speaker Michael Madigan and Chicago Mayor Rahm Emanuel chat before testifying at a House committee in support of funding for a Barack Obama presidential center in Chicago on April 17, 2014. (Photo credit: Antonio Perez/*Chicago Tribune*/TNS)

House Speaker Michael Madigan, chair of the state Democratic Party, confers with Cook County Assessor Joe Berrios, chair of the Cook County Democratic Party, at a political event at Chicago's Erie Cafe on October 23, 2015. (Photo credit: Antonio Perez/*Chicago Tribune*/TNS)

President Barack Obama, left, greets Illinois House Speaker Michael Madigan, center, and Senate President John Cullerton as he prepares to speak in the House chamber of the state Capitol on February 10, 2016. (Photo credit: Terrence Antonio James/*Chicago Tribune*/TNS)

Proud of his Irish roots, Illinois House Speaker Michael Madigan, center, takes his spot before marching in the Chicago St. Patrick's Day Parade on March 12, 2016. (Photo credit: John J. Kim/*Chicago Tribune*/TNS)

House Speaker Michael Madigan speaks after a House Democratic caucus on November 12, 2019, at the state Capitol. Two weeks earlier he told reporters asking about federal investigations, "I'm not a target of anything." (Photo credit: Zbigniew Bzdak/*Chicago Tribune*/TNS)

House Speaker Michael Madigan stares across the House chamber before Governor J. B. Pritzker's first budget address to a joint session of the Illinois House and Senate on February 20, 2019. (Photo credit: E. Jason Wambsgans/Chicago Tribune/TNS)

Near the end of his reign, House Speaker Michael Madigan, wearing a mask during the COVID-19 pandemic, appears as the House convenes, for safety reasons, at an expansive convention center in Springfield on January 8, 2021. (Photo credit: E. Jason Wambsgans/*Chicago Tribune*/TNS)

PART III

A CAREER POLITICAL LEADER

8

A PATRONAGE ARMY

"You can understand that there are
many people that are involved with me
and campaigns and community service.
Among these many people, some are
better than others."
—Speaker Michael Madigan, 2014

For decades, federal judges have sought to rein in patronage in Illinois, but it's remarkable how often people tied to Madigan managed to get government jobs, promotions, and pay raises. It's even more remarkable how many folks who walk his precincts managed to collect government checks. In Chicago, though, there is a simple, unspoken axiom in ward politics: power comes not just from what the people can do for you; it's what you can do for the people who walk your precincts.

Every once in a while, the public gets an insider explanation of how ward politics works—and, in rare cases, in Madigan's own words. That was the case in 2013 and 2014 when a scandal at Chicago's commuter rail system, Metra, erupted over whether Madigan went a step too far in trying to exert his clout.

Nobody had to explain patronage to Madigan, of course. And nobody had to explain clout to him either. A straight line can be drawn from patronage king Richard J. Daley to the speaker himself. As a law student at Loyola University in the mid-1960s, Madigan landed a job as a clerk in the city law department with the help of his father, a longtime friend of Daley the First. It didn't hurt that Madigan's father was the superintendent of the Thirteenth Ward and that he and Daley had worked together under County Clerk Michael Flynn, once the Thirteenth Ward committeeman. It also didn't hurt that the father told his son to introduce himself to the mayor, particularly since the young law student and the mayor both held memberships at the Lake Shore Club, an athletic association then along Michigan Avenue. Once nicely embedded in the law clerk position, Madigan made the best of it. After all, he hadn't been flung into a remote corner of the city. The law clerk's City Hall office happened to be down the hallway from Hizzoner's office, and the young Madigan and the nation's most powerful mayor would bump into each other from time to time. When Madigan's father died in October 1966, the mayor then remembered the son of the Thirteenth Ward superintendent and former colleague in the county clerk's office. Thanks to Daley and his connections with Democrats running state government, Michael Madigan, fresh out of law school, started a state job working as a hearing examiner at the Illinois Commerce Commission.[1]

By the summer of 1969, one year after the whole world was watching the Democratic National Convention debacle unfold amid billy clubs and violence on Chicago's streets, Madigan became the Thirteenth Ward's new committeeman. The previous committeeman had died, leaving an opening, and precinct captains gathered to choose a successor. It was not a landslide, but Madigan showed that he had learned early on how to round up votes. The late ward superintendent's son, an up-and-coming Daley protégé, won 49–31. The eighteen-vote margin launched Madigan's career as a committeeman that has lasted more than half a century. The Thirteenth Ward had a strong Republican committeeman. Madigan knew the mayor would appreciate a Democratic committeeman who could galvanize the disparate interests of the Polish, Italian, Irish, and Lithuanian clans of the Southwest Side neighborhood into a strong organization, one where precinct captains acted as agents for both Madigan and Daley, with the mayor's wishes always taking priority. In those early days, Madigan taught the precinct workers to be salespeople, getting them to push for a particular vote or a sample ballot as if they were selling encyclopedias door to door. "They wanted a job in the patronage system," Madigan told interviewers for the Richard J. Daley Oral History Collection at the University of Illinois at Chicago. "I would tell them, 'Yes, we can put you in a job. But you're going to work for the Democratic Party.'"[2]

As the decades rolled along, Madigan persisted in advancing people he favored. A task force arising from the Metra scandal said Madigan was a "prominent participant" in patronage hiring at the commuter agency. He did more than recommend people for positions, according to the task force report, which former U.S. Attorney Patrick Fitzgerald had a hand in writing.[3] "The records, fairly read, show that in some cases he did not recommend people to be hired—he in effect decided they were hired," the report said.[4] Madigan's patronage proficiency was so highly regarded in some quarters that pockets of government ended up with nicknames in his honor. One of those was the city's Streets and Sanitation Department's Bureau of Electricity, where Madigan enjoyed such success in placing people that the agency became known as "Madigan Electric." The bureau, along with its nickname, received a prominent mention in the 2009 federal trial of Al Sanchez, the Hispanic Democratic Organization honcho and former Streets and Sanitation director convicted of illegal political hiring under Mayor Richard M. Daley.[5] But Madigan was just a side note, not a defendant. The reference to "Madigan Electric" just enhanced his reputation among admirers and prompted more grumbling from detractors.

Administrators around the state and local governments became familiar with calls from Madigan pushing a job candidate. But requests at Metra put him at the center of a fiery dispute in the summer of 2013. The commuter train system that connects Chicago and the suburbs had a fairly new CEO: Alex Clifford, an ex-Marine brought in from California to clean up the system. His predecessor, Phil Pagano, jumped in front of a train after he was caught taking $475,000 in unauthorized vacation pay to cover costs of extramarital affairs, among other things.[6] Metra folks likely didn't figure they'd have monumental worries about the newly hired military-trained Clifford. What they may not have realized is that Clifford wasn't keen on showing deference to Madigan. The issue simmered and eventually erupted. In the end, Clifford walked away with a severance package worth up to $871,000.[7] What prompted even bigger gasps than the cash giveaway, though, was an eight-page confidential memo Clifford left behind.

Tribune reporters Richard Wronski, a veteran of the transit beat, and Stacy St. Clair, a star in her own right, obtained the Clifford memo and splashed it across the front page. They called the memo the scandal's "proverbial smoking gun." Clifford wrote that his "refusal to capitulate" to Madigan's patronage demands irritated some of Metra's board members and led to the Metra chief's demise. Clifford contended that two Metra members—then Chairman Brad O'Halloran and former Chairman Larry Huggins—"conspired" to get him out of his job—charges they would deny. Clifford said they chided him for not accommodating lawmakers, worrying that shutting down Madigan could be a setback for the agency.[8] After all, Madigan could make critical decisions influencing the use of transit operating and construction funds for the Regional Transportation Authority, which oversees Metra.

The patronage dispute might have been written off as forgettable compared to Pagano's one-way ticket out, but the cost of the settlement—one that roiled lawmakers—and the whiff of Madigan's involvement meant the story would not go away quickly. What's more, it showed the kind of granular detail Madigan paid attention to when he helped a loyal political worker. Records show that Madigan's part of the saga started out low-key. He gave a message to a trusted ally, Metra contract lobbyist Tom Cullen, a political savant who had worked on the speaker's legislative staff for years and remained one of his go-to campaign strategists even after he left government to become a lobbyist. Madigan wanted Metra to give a raise to Thirteenth Ward acolyte Patrick Ward, a labor relations specialist, and to give a job to another person, who was not identified, according to Clifford.[9]

In the history of Chicago, that's clearly not much of a request, but Clifford's response might well be viewed as somewhat historic: Rather than falling over himself like the legions of pols who sought to curry favor with Madigan, Clifford's reaction left politicos at Metra aghast. He didn't dispatch officials to carry out the speaker's wishes. Instead, he told his staff to ignore the speaker's requests. Old hands at Illinois politics might say the smarter play would have been to give Madigan what he wanted— a suggestion that would make the regular citizenry cringe. But what an average family might think is a reasonable reaction to Madigan's request may be anathema in Chicago politics. Folks with little power want to please the big political bosses, hoping to bask in the reflected glory and mooch a few partisan crumbs. As a result, Clifford's order to ignore Madigan did not go unchallenged. Clifford explained that the query resurfaced when Huggins brought it up a few months later, sparking an argument and illustrating again how much officials didn't like to disappoint the speaker.[10]

The descriptions in Clifford's memo provided insight into the insular world of Madigan's politics—or at least the way his actions can be perceived. Clifford recounted asking Ward why the pressure to give a Metra worker a raise was coming from the speaker of the House, and the explanation that Clifford wrote down could have come right out of Richard J. Daley's playbook from fifty years earlier. "Mr. Ward said that his family had supported Mr. Madigan for many years and worked on his political campaigns," the memo said. "He said that he had discussed his Metra employment with Mr. Madigan at a Madigan political event, where he told Mr. Madigan that he felt underpaid." Reporters at the time made a simple check of records: Ward made fifty-seven thousand dollars a year. He had worked for multiple Madigan campaigns. He also contributed seventeen thousand dollars to political committees controlled by the speaker or his daughter, Lisa Madigan, the former state senator who became attorney general.[11]

At first the contents of the Clifford memo only trickled out. The memo's existence, including Madigan's involvement, had remained a secret, part of a confidentiality agreement that Metra officials were relying on to keep the contents under wraps. But as details began to emerge, former Republican Senator Jack Schaffer of Crystal Lake, an outspoken Metra board member who voted against the severance package, lashed out: "This is $250,000 in severance and $500,000 in hush money." His remarks were made before the Illinois House Mass Transit Committee chaired by Representative Deb Mell, the daughter of Dick Mell, the longtime alderman and leader of the North Side's influential Thirty-Third Ward. Metra officials denied the allegations, and Metra's outside counsel, Joseph Gagliardo, denied Schaffer's "hush money" charge, saying Clifford wanted confidentiality as he went out to find another job.[12]

But as the issue of Clifford's severance package gained political traction, state lawmakers had more questions. The Mell hearings started another Madigan subchapter. Even before Mell's committee could dig in, Madigan sought to diffuse criticism. He revealed he had recommended to Metra in March 2012 that Ward, the labor relations specialist, should get more money based on his education and job performance. Ward hadn't had a raise for three years, and his responsibilities had increased, the speaker explained. But Clifford was aware of a freeze on salary increases for non-contractual employees. And when Clifford raised concerns about the speaker's meddling, Madigan backed away. Getting this explanation out before Mell's hearing gave Madigan a chance to get ahead of the story and might have saved him from a more negative spin had he waited for lawmakers to pry it loose during a public hearing. But the issue would not go away. Clifford had contended that his contract was not being renewed because Metra board leaders worried about his refusal to comply with "'Madigan's requests for politically motivated employment actions.'"[13] Clifford said he inquired about renewing his contract but that O'Halloran said he first had to assess the damage of denying Madigan's requests.[14] The tale illustrates how Madigan managed to get into people's heads. Helping out Ward may have been a small request, but fear of merely the potential for major blowback over rebuffing the speaker? Once that level of worry took hold, Madigan had already won.

The episode meant Clifford had put his finger on one of the great conundrums in Illinois politics. At a Regional Transportation Authority hearing, Clifford testified he did not believe Madigan broke any laws—not a surprise for folks who long have watched the speaker inch up to the boundary between legal and illegal but not step over the line. Legions of people who worked with him swear he had a strong code of ethics that required strict adherence to the rules. But Clifford had a different take about the speaker's attempt to intervene in salary adjustments or other job actions: "I thought it was an ethical and moral character flaw."[15]

Republicans—long outhustled, outwitted, and outworked by Madigan and his Democrats—loved it. They had tried for years to tarnish the Madigan brand. Now, with questions about his actions lingering, Madigan asked Legislative Inspector General Thomas Homer to look into whether the speaker had overstepped his authority. Homer is a former state's attorney from Fulton County, where downstate Canton is located just south of Peoria. He also served as a Democrat in the House under Madigan and later as an appellate court justice. Following his time on the court, Homer accepted the part-time gig as legislative inspector general (IG). He had a reputation as a straight-shooter. He was not a hotdogger looking for a populist cause to make a name for himself, but the former prosecutor wasn't shy about immersing himself in controversial issues. This would be the biggest he would handle in a little over a decade as the legislative IG.

At the heart of the issue facing Homer was whether Madigan had created pressure that helped push Clifford out of his job—a point Madigan denied. But as Homer leaned into the matter, there were other questions:

What did it mean when Metra's chairperson came to the speaker's Capitol office to chat about issues involving the suburban transit line and then left with a yellow Post-It note that bore the names of two transit workers the speaker wanted to see promoted? Or what did it mean when Cullen, the Metra lobbyist and loyal political strategist for Madigan, left the speaker's office with two resumes? Or what did it mean when Madigan rang up the cell phone of a precinct captain to let him know about a state job? Even when the answers look obvious, motivation isn't always easy to nail down.

Illinois being Illinois, of course, the legislative IG examination was cloaked in secrecy. Along with Madigan, Homer interviewed a string of witnesses, but the transcripts were secret. And when Homer filed his report? Yes, that was also secret. On a busy afternoon in April 2014, an announcement from the speaker's office said the report was completed. Writing what we could get, our *Tribune* story reflected the few details we gathered on deadline and attributed the conclusions to Madigan's team: "An investigation by the Illinois legislative inspector general into allegations of political pressure at Metra found that House Speaker Michael Madigan did not violate the state's ethics act, Madigan's office said today."[16]

Only three months earlier, in January 2014, the *Tribune* rolled out its own attempt to measure the breadth and depth of Madigan's patronage army. The Metra blowup provided fuel for the project, led by David Kidwell, John Chase, and Alex Richards. Using a conservative count, they tallied more than four hundred government employees or retirees who had worked elections for Madigan, donated regularly to his campaign funds, registered voters, walked precincts, or circulated candidate petitions for him. The speaker kept working to connect them with jobs, land them raises, and help them move up the ladder. Many of these folks turn out when Madigan needs to rack up votes in House races throughout Illinois. For that story, Madigan issued a statement: "The individuals who assist in community projects and campaigns have a strong interest in politics and government, just like the supporters and volunteers of any other public official. They share my belief in fairness for working middle-class families, strong and safe neighborhoods, and civic responsibility."[17]

One thing made clear in Madigan's press release about the Metra investigation was that the IG "found no violation." Homer didn't have much to add, given there's very little to say when the report itself is secret. Even so, Homer delivered a note of caution: "A decision to close an investigation based on insufficient evidence does not constitute a Good Housekeeping seal of approval or a best practices award."[18]

A statement like Homer's means one thing to a reporter: There's more to the story. But Homer's hands were tied. He reported to the Legislative Ethics Commission, consisting of eight lawmakers—two from each of the four partisan caucuses. Lawmakers decided which reports went public, and the evenly divided partisan split on the commission could keep reports sealed, such as in matters like the Madigan report, where allegations of wrongdoing were deemed unfounded. At least five out of eight members of the commission—which is divided evenly between Republicans and Democrats—are needed to release a report. But that bar is impossible to clear when the commission is stacked with enough loyalists from both parties to block even a mild admonishment from being released to the public.

Just because a document is secret, though, doesn't mean it will stay secret. The Madigan Metra report took three months to pry out, verify, and get into print. Finally, a story ran across the top of page 1 of the *Tribune*—and it revealed that Homer delivered a harsh assessment:

> A secret report put together by the legislature's watchdog in the wake of last summer's Metra scandal offers new insight into how Democratic House Speaker Michael Madigan navigates the intersection of public business and ward-style patronage through his Southwest Side office and Illinois Capitol suite.
>
> The analysis by then–Inspector General Thomas Homer—based on interviews with Madigan's political allies, government officials and the speaker himself—presents those methods in an unflattering fashion.[19]

For one thing, Madigan's interview involved giving his views on getting people jobs, raises, and promotions. The exchange with Homer was enlightening to all of the Madigan watchers—the people who love him, hate him, and outright worship him. In an interview with Homer, Madigan not only touted the work-related credentials of Patrick Ward, the Thirteenth Ward foot soldier, but he also talked about the political experience of Ward, whom Madigan supported for the Metra raise. The speaker said he was "generally trying to help Pat Ward get a promotion" by making the "request to Metra." According to the Homer interview, Madigan also affirmed that he was making the request to Metra through Marty Quinn, the speaker's handpicked Thirteenth Ward alderman, and Cullen, the

Metra lobbyist. Homer's interview netted one of the more revealing comments from Madigan, who guards his words as carefully as the first Mayor Daley taught him. "You can understand that there are many people that are involved with me and campaigns and community service," Madigan said in an interview with Homer. "Among these many people, some are better than others. [He] happens to be one of those who is better than others."[20]

Homer's analysis took a dim view of Madigan's coziness between his politics and the way he pushed government jobs for his political friends. Homer called it "naïve to believe" that Madigan "was not primarily motivated by Ward's longtime service to the 13th Ward and status as a campaign contributor" when the speaker pressed Metra on Ward's behalf. Homer provided another example of how Madigan stuck by his man. Once Clifford and Ward spoke about why Madigan would involve himself in a Metra worker's job, Ward left Metra and called Alderman Quinn in November 2012. One day a couple of months later, Madigan called Ward on his cell phone. There was an opening at the Illinois Department of Central Management Services. In January 2013 Madigan met with the agency's director of labor relations, and the speaker brought up Ward's name once the briefing on state matters had concluded. The agency spokesperson, Anjali Julka, explained, "After the meeting, the speaker recommended a candidate for any openings in the labor relations bureau and provided a resume." Ward got the job, one with an annual salary of seventy thousand dollars.[21]

In his report, Homer also outlined two other examples of concern. One dealt with then Metra Chair Carole Doris. Clifford recalled that he and Doris met with Madigan in his Springfield office in January 2011. Clifford left and Doris stayed. But Clifford recalled that Doris exited the speaker's office moments later with a "look of concern." Doris recalled carrying a yellow Post-It note with the names of two people Madigan wanted promoted. Years later, she could not recall whether Madigan actually wanted promotions for the two people on her tiny slip of paper or just to "put in a good word for them." Homer said that Doris took no action regarding the two. The second case involved Cullen, the Metra lobbyist. Clifford recalled Cullen coming out of a Madigan meeting at the Capitol with two resumes in hand. In his interview with Homer, Cullen did not remember Madigan handing the lobbyist two resumes but acknowledged "he may have."[22]

Homer made a point in his report about "proximity." Madigan would have a discussion with Metra officials about official government matters. And then there would be his questions about people and jobs. Homer underscored Madigan's chats with Metra officials about their government issues and the speaker's mentions of his favored Metra employees. Homer said that proximity "created the impression among Metra officials that the speaker's support for Metra's legislative initiatives may be linked."[23]

"While this may not have been the speaker's intention," Homer wrote, "the natural inferences to be drawn by Metra officials should have been obvious. Moreover, when the requested promotions were not immediately forthcoming, the follow-up inquiries by the speaker or his agents created additional angst at Metra and contributed to the controversy."[24]

Wholesale patronage that used to be commonplace has slowed considerably from the heyday of Mayor Richard J. Daley. Attorney Michael Shakman is responsible for launching the federal court fight to wring politics out of public employment decisions. Far-reaching antipatronage court orders—commonly known as "Shakman decrees"—dating to 1972 prohibit taking public employment actions such as hirings, firings, and promotions based on political factors. There are exceptions for policy-making positions; top-level jobs like chiefs of staff, agency directors, and others with key roles focused on confidential matters; or carrying out the wishes of the top boss. Federal court oversight is put in place when a judge determines that a government has failed to free itself from politics when making government personnel decisions. Judges have assigned monitors to serve as watchdogs to report on progress or failures. Once a judge determines that a particular government office is in compliance with antipatronage orders, then the federal court oversight is ended. Federal monitors helped both Chicago Mayor Rahm Emanuel and Cook County Sheriff Tom Dart resolve Shakman cases. Emanuel inherited a federal monitor in the mayor's office, and Dart embraced the idea of installing a monitor when he became sheriff. Cook County Board President Toni Preckwinkle, in her first two terms, convinced a judge to end federal oversight, because she professionalized personnel practices in a government long known as a patronage haven. Because she did have the leeway to use politics in employment moves in a limited number of positions, however, the *Tribune* found dozens of employees tied to clout masters like Madigan, Mayor Richard M. Daley, and Secretary of State Jesse White among her ranks.[25]

Though Shakman has focused on the top government offices in Chicago and Cook County, he has expanded to win court oversight of the Illinois Department of Transportation. It was fueled by an investigation by Executive Inspector General Ricardo Meza that found hundreds of people were hired into a special "staff assistant" position without following rules to keep politics away from most state hiring decisions.[26]

"Patronage costs the public money," Shakman explained in an interview with WLS-AM 890's Bill Cameron, long the dean of the press corps at Chicago's City Hall:

> It's inefficient. People get hired for government jobs because they work their precincts, not because they work for the public. And the result is you don't get good public service when you hire on a political basis. Number two, it distorts the election process. The incumbents who control the jobs have a chance of getting elected that's much better than the chance of anybody else to get elected. So it effectively skews the Democratic process. And number three, jobs are important, and . . . fair access to jobs are important to people. There are a lot of people who would like the jobs that the state, for example, hands out on a patronage basis. They should have a right to compete for those jobs on an even playing field, and if they're qualified, more qualified than the patronage-sponsored employee, they should get the job.[27]

Patronage in Illinois state government also changed in 1990, the last full year that Governor Jim Thompson served during his fourteen-year tenure. Attorney Mary Lee Leahy, like Madigan a Con-Con delegate, won a sweeping antipatronage case before the U.S. Supreme Court known as the Rutan decision on behalf of lead plaintiff Cynthia Rutan. Under the high court's ruling, there are protected jobs in which there should be no political connection in hiring, promoting, transferring, or firing and a higher-echelon level of jobs where politics plays a role.

There are basically three major types of employees, with varying levels of protection. One is covered by a collective bargaining agreement, which usually handles discipline through arbitration. The second category is called "merit compensation employees," who are not in collective bargaining units but can be disciplined for good cause once they complete probation. The third group is known as "exempt employees," who serve at the will of an agency director or the governor.[28]

Rewarding lawmakers for loyalty and longevity was part of Madigan's playbook in running the House. He would decide who would get committee chairmanships—and the more than ten thousand dollars that went with the job. But he had his own guidelines, and he could create as many committees and chairmanships as he wanted to fit his needs. "We have a policy that before someone can be appointed as the chair of a committee and get the stipend, they have to have completed two terms. They have to have been elected to three terms—excuse me—appointed or elected to three terms," Madigan said in a 2018 deposition. "And then they enter an eligible class of people that can be appointed as chairs of committees."[29] It was one more way he could exert a measure of control.

Besides state and local patronage jobs, Madigan had a successful track record of placing judges in the Cook County courts. *Tribune* reporters Jeff Coen and Todd Lighty wrote about what sitting judges called "Madigan's List," the lawyers whom the speaker named in brief letters to members of the judiciary when associate judge positions were open. "Dear Judge," Madigan wrote on General Assembly stationery, "I believe that these people would be excellent members of the judiciary."[30] Associate judges are chosen by the elected full circuit judges, many of whom were elected with the backing of the Cook County Democratic Party, where Madigan held sway, and Fourteenth Ward Alderman Ed Burke long ran the judicial slating committee. Burke's wife, Anne Burke, became an Illinois Supreme Court justice with family and party help. In one stretch from 2003 through early 2011, Madigan recommended thirty-seven lawyers to become associate judges, and twenty-five were selected outright, according to a review of documents and interviews by Coen and Lighty. Others landed appointments to the bench. Madigan issued a statement for the story, saying he made recommendations for judicial openings free of political influence or self-interest and "because I believe I am an experienced evaluator of those who seek to serve in the judiciary."[31]

While Madigan's property tax–appeal firm practice included going before some judges who received a boost from Democrats, the speaker said his "personal code of conduct" prohibited any conflict of interest. "Over a number of years, various people have asked for my support in their bid to be elected associate judge," Madigan wrote to the reporters. "My comments in reaction to those requests concerning the election of associate judges are not made on behalf or in connection with my law firm, public or political positions."[32] The story reinforced the reality that it's not hard to find a lawyer who didn't make Madigan's list. Or a lawyer with a tale about a judge getting a call from Madigan with the names of judicial candidates he preferred.

Madigan did not always get his way. As a young ward committee member, he blew the whistle on a political rival who held the Thirteenth Ward superintendent position—the position Madigan's father once held—because the rival was known to duck out of his city job to work a side gig at a funeral home. "The guy was a political nuisance," Madigan recalled in an oral history about the first Mayor Daley. The rival got moved out of the ward to desk duty downtown—until he pulled his own strings with the mayor, who clasped his hands together and told the young Madigan to bring people together rather than pull them apart. "I went in to see the mayor," Madigan recalled.

> I pleaded my case. I got nowhere. At the end of the conversation—people have told you that at the end of a meeting, he'd rise out of his chair, he'd extend his hand, you were out the door. . . . So he rose out of his chair, and he just told me, "Well, you may not like it, but I'm the boss and this is the way that it's going to be." So me being me, I said, "Okay, you're right. You're the boss. But do you know what? I'm going to prove you wrong." I spun on my heels and I walked out of his office. Well, I got my say in. But I didn't get to see him for about nine months.

Did the patronage stop? "I didn't get to see him, but he didn't cut off the patronage. That was the big thing—the patronage jobs. They would come out of City Hall. So in terms of what the Thirteenth Ward would have, we would get our share. He wasn't going to cut me off, but he wasn't going to waste his time with me for a while."[33]

Later on, Madigan had a public spat with Mayor Jane Byrne that cost him legal business. When Mayor Michael Bilandic lost to Mayor Jane Byrne and the horse-drawn sleigh that she rode when he couldn't clear the streets of snow in 1979, Madigan said he was "on my own" in representing Chicago at the state Capitol. But Byrne didn't take that suggestion lightly. She ended the twenty thousand dollars in annual city legal business that Daley had bestowed on Madigan's law firm and threatened to fire two of his political allies from city jobs. As *Tribune* reporter John Camper once put it, "Madigan quickly fell into line, saving his friends' jobs but never recovering the legal work. He continued to coexist with Byrne, while he set in motion the legislative maneuvering that would ensure his power for the next decade."[34]

In a 2018 deposition, Madigan outlined what goes into his thinking when recommending someone, such as a precinct captain, for a job and gave a glimpse into his job-placing skill. "You can understand that many people come to me asking for recommendations for employment, and I render recommendations for employment in both the private and the public sector. I do it in both. But there's a test that people have to meet," he said. "They have to be, to my knowledge, they have to be honest, hardworking people with integrity. And if they are, I'll recommend to a potential employer the best of my knowledge and my experience with this person, this would be a good worker for your office, a good worker for your business whatever it may be." Madigan knew his recommendations so well that when asked about a policy analyst at city hall, he corrected the attorney interviewing him in the deposition, saying the person referenced now worked for the Chicago Housing Authority. "I recommended him to the CHA," Madigan testified, adding, "He was hired."[35]

When Alderman Mike Zalewski of the neighboring Twenty-Third Ward left the City Council, Madigan said he recommended state Representative Silvana Tabares, a Chicago Democrat who had worked to help the speaker's political organization. She was appointed to the ward seat. Madigan was asked who had received his recommendation, and the speaker didn't hesitate to mention the mayor who had the appointment power: "Rahm Emanuel."[36]

Though Madigan was aggressive in placing people into state, county, and city government jobs, he developed a separate patronage-style system over the years in the private sector. Madigan's practice of hooking up allies and precinct workers with jobs would become part of the ComEd federal investigation that ultimately helped loosen his grip on the speaker's gavel. The 2020 ComEd case tied him to jobs and contracts the utility company gave to his allies, ranging from former council members, such as Zalewski, to his favored foot soldiers. Prosecutors alleged that Madigan's activities went from placing people into meter reader jobs, to putting as many as a dozen interns into the company's summer program, to landing a person on the ComEd board.

When Madigan responded to lawmakers about the ComEd scandal, there were echoes of Metra, echoes of ward politics, echoes of the Daley days. The Madigan response, of course, was not as memorable as Daley's tirade to criticism in 1973 when he tossed some city insurance business to a firm with ties to one of his sons: "If I can't help my sons, then they can kiss my ass," he said, according to folks who witnessed his outburst. Over the years, Daley's words have been soft-brushed into "kiss my mistletoe."[37]

Madigan's written response to lawmakers about the ComEd scandal would not be as vivid. He wrote that "helping people find jobs is not a crime." Nor is it "ethically improper," he said, for public officials to recommend people for jobs. "To the contrary, I believe that it is part of my duties as a community and political leader to help good people find work—from potential executives to college interns, and more."[38]

9

MADIGAN AND MADIGAN

"She knew."
—Speaker Michael Madigan,
    August 7, 2013

The terse answer rolled off Speaker Madigan's tongue on that summer day in 2013, the high point of a long-term drama that played out on the public stage between the speaker and his daughter, Lisa. As attorney general (AG), she had been raising money at a pace that made people think she would challenge incumbent Democratic Governor Pat Quinn in the 2014 primary race. She had more money in her political war chest and was raising it faster than Quinn in early 2013. Her ascension had long looked inevitable, and she'd done little to discourage speculation that this would be the time to seize her destiny as the state's first woman governor.[1]

For months she wouldn't rule out a run, throwing the political chattering class into overdrive at the possibility. Intentionally or not, both Madigans had done their part to fuel the political buzz. But then one day in July 2013, without warning, she ended the discussion with an email. "I feel strongly that the state would not be well served by having a governor and speaker of the House from the same family and have never planned to run for governor if that would be the case," Lisa Madigan said. "With Speaker Madigan planning to continue in office, I will not run for governor."[2]

The reaction? Shock. But a second, slow read of the announcement brought a more profound realization. Her statement looked a lot like a hard political swing at her father. She had backers who wondered why the speaker wouldn't step down and clear the path for her. But the speaker's insiders immediately jumped to his defense, likening his daughter's words to a cheap shot and showing a lack of respect for the man to whom she owed so much. In Springfield the speaker could always count on a chorus of defenders on any topic, whether he deserved it or not. Lisa Madigan pointed out in her statement that she'd given serious thought to seeking a higher step on the political ladder. "I considered running for governor because of the need for effective management from that office and the frustration so many of us feel about the current lack of progress on critical issues facing Illinois," she said, taking a clear shot at Quinn. "Ultimately, however, there has always been another consideration that impacts my decision."[3]

At least to some degree, Lisa Madigan's race for a fourth term as AG instead of governor mostly tamped down voter concerns about too much power being concentrated in the hands of one family. That was always an undercurrent as she held the job of attorney general and her father remained speaker and Illinois Democratic Party chair. How would she, as governor, handle telling the speaker no when he really wanted something? How would the speaker handle his daughter as governor when she turned him down? Those are questions raised by academics and barstool philosophers, a category of political observers that is never in short supply in Illinois. So when she made her announcement that she would run for reelection, the question that raged in the political world was what to make of her sharp comment about her father—and, of course: What does the speaker think?

Because Lisa Madigan chose to release a statement rather than face questions in a news conference, her written words would carry the day. The idea that she took a pass on the governor's race was one thing. But the political calculation was difficult. It's a tall order to run against an incumbent, even if that incumbent is considered weak. It's an even taller order to take on an incumbent from your own party. No doubt the speaker remembered the 1976 primary in which Mayor Richard J. Daley backed Democratic Secretary of State Michael Howlett against incumbent Democratic Governor Dan Walker, who repeatedly feuded with the mayor and Democrats in the legislature. Howlett won the primary, but he was weakened from the fight and lost the general election to Republican Jim Thompson. Governor Thompson went on to hold the office for a record four straight terms. That dynamic is part of any discussion about a Democrat taking on an incumbent Democrat in a statewide race, but the issue is more than an interesting story in the Madigan household. The speaker actually lived through it.

Speaker Madigan also lived through what it took to rise up and consolidate his own power. Winning the position of attorney general is a fine accomplishment, but the speaker held the most important job in the family franchise, and he made it clear that, despite her hints of running for governor, he had not planned to walk away. Weeks went by before reporters could ask the speaker in person. But they caught up with him on his way into a speech at the Union League Club of Chicago, and he let it be known that his daughter should not have been surprised by his plans to keep his post. "Lisa and I had spoken about that on several occasions, and she knew very well that I did not plan to retire," the elder Madigan said. "She knew what my position was. She knew."[4]

Madigan often prefers to speak little and clarify less. *Tribune* reporter Monique Garcia explained his comment this way: "It was unclear, as is often the case when political questions and the Madigans intersect, whether the speaker was offering a public brushback to his daughter, who a month earlier had laid much of the blame at his feet for deciding not to run for governor."[5] In Illinois there's always a couple of extra layers of context. Right before Lisa Madigan announced her decision, the speaker had been under fire for his involvement in the Metra scandal, in which ex-CEO Alex Clifford alleged that he was muscled out when he refused to give in to the speaker's patronage requests. Republicans, always looking for a way to do political damage to the speaker, fanned the flames. But even if Metra were not a factor in her decision, the easiest political path for the attorney general was to run for a fourth term.

How did she get to that point? Despite the odd public statements between the speaker and his daughter, their relationship was strong. Lisa was in elementary school when her mother, Shirley, married Michael Madigan. Shirley, a former airline flight attendant, had met Mike while she worked as a receptionist at a Chicago law firm. Lisa kept the last name Murray until she turned eighteen, a time when she could decide for herself whether she wanted to use the Madigan name. Michael Madigan made her adoption official not long thereafter, though people close to his family say he had long before embraced her as his daughter. In her younger days, she traveled with him once school was out in the summer to see Springfield firsthand, sitting in his chair on the House floor, listening to debate, or working as a House page—sometimes popping over to the press box on the Democratic side and talking to reporters about what was going on. She went to Georgetown University, served a short stint for U.S. Senator Paul Simon, the well-regarded Democrat from Southern Illinois, and went off to South Africa, where she lived in a convent and taught Zulu girls English, algebra, and other subjects.[6]

By 1998, when she first ran for state Senate, Lisa Madigan was an aggressive and ambitious rising political star. She took on incumbent Democratic Senator Bruce Farley for a seat on Chicago's North Side when he was indicted in a federal ghost-payrolling scheme. Previously a member of the House, Farley had been an ally of the speaker, even giving a nominating speech for Madigan as he sought his fifth term running the House. "All of the people of the State of Illinois certainly appreciate . . . his idea of compassion. His attitude of compassion," Farley said then. But Farley's thoughts would change when the new-generation Madigan took aim at the old-school pol.[7] The speaker wasn't that gung-ho initially about his daughter getting into the political game and sent her to a series of political friends to talk about it. She came back more determined, telling her father, "You've shown me you can make a difference." He got on board with her mission to defeat Farley, throwing his political weight and resources behind his daughter.[8] Farley, in turn, would plead guilty and be sentenced to prison. Lisa Madigan got a glimpse during that race of how difficult it would be to break away from the shadow of her father, an issue that would ring true throughout her life in public office. "I knew people were going to hear the name and assume we're the same even though we come at it from different angles. But I know it's going to continue to be a challenge," she said.[9]

Her father's political stature would be something she would have to address again in her run for attorney general only four years into her Senate career, but it would be amplified on a much bigger stage. She was a thirty-five-year-old, first-term state senator eight years out of law school, yet her political advantages were extraordinary. Lisa Madigan became adept at dismissing references to the political baggage generated by the ever-present anti-Madigan crowd, a combination of regular moderate Republicans, hard-right zealots, and assorted critics, who saw the speaker as the reason Illinois was losing its luster as the once-proud "Land of Lincoln." Once again, friends say, the speaker was momentarily hesitant about her statewide plans but quickly went all in. Losing was not an option. She and her father had a zeal to win. It became infectious among ardent supporters, firing up longtime precinct soldiers, patronage workers, and high-level political operatives who had long carried an undying loyalty to the speaker. They wanted what the speaker wanted, and the biggest test came in her victories in 2002.

In telling about Lisa Madigan's 2002 statewide primary race, *Tribune* political writer Rick Pearson wrote a classic piece about how the speaker immersed himself into her attorney general campaign: "When the telephone rang in the home of a Cook County elected official last month, both the caller and the question he posed were completely unexpected. 'This is Mike Madigan,' the caller said. 'May I have a copy of your wedding invitation list?'" The speaker spent months calling Democrats, advocates, elected officials, and friends to build lists of potential givers for a fund-raising juggernaut the speaker called "Friends and Family." Pearson explained:

> Madigan is calling in every favor and asking for support from the lowliest Democratic precinct captain to the biggest labor unions. Madigan . . . has spent decades consolidating his political power and perfecting the art of arm-twisting. He has hoarded campaign cash and used it as a cudgel to threaten and reward Democrats. He holds life or death control over the political careers of hundreds of party loyalists and those who work for them, and he can grease or squelch the pet legislation of interest groups depending on whether they play along. He has never been shy about using that clout, but he also has never put it to use in such an aggressive and personal way.[10]

Steve Brown, the speaker's spokesman, flatly denied that Madigan exerted pressure to support to his daughter: "If somebody thinks that pressure is being applied, they either don't exist or they have no experience with this office." Not everyone saw it that way. One political operative summed it up to Pearson like this: "We're biting our tongue, swallowing the blood and endorsing daddy's little girl."[11]

A talented and competitive campaigner, Lisa Madigan could whip up a crowd at Democratic gatherings. Her spirited political rhetoric was as energetic as her father's was subdued. She would raise her arms, clench her fists, and point a forefinger skyward to generate cheers from a state fair crowd, whereas the speaker, even in front of a friendly fair crowd, once gave a self-conscious half grin when he slowly waved a broom above his head to call for a Democratic sweep in the next election. Of course, people cheered wildly for him anyway. Lisa Madigan said she is "blessed" with her mother's personality. "I love my father dearly," she said, "but he's not Mr. Personality."[12]

In her 2002 primary, Lisa Madigan would handily dispatch opponent John Schmidt, a former high-ranking official in the U.S. Justice Department, just as the speaker had predicted in an interview with *Tribune* columnist John Kass. "The last few weeks have been busy, and difficult, because there have been a lot of unfounded and negative charges hurled at my daughter's campaign," Madigan said shortly before Election Day. "But I think she'll win the primary election. I think voters are intelligent people. They'll consider the tone of the campaign. And they're going to disregard much of the negative advertising."[13] To almost no one's surprise, the speaker was right. She won. Schmidt offered his own analysis: "I think I was up against every ounce of power and money and muscle that the Democratic organization could bring to bear. And in the end, they won."[14]

The big test came in the 2002 general election against DuPage County State's Attorney Joe Birkett, a Republican. He represented an aggressive prosecutor from one of the most Republican counties in America. On her side, Lisa Madigan had the reenergized remnants of the Chicago political machine. Chicago Democrats formed a major confluence of the various city power bases in 2002: On the Southwest Side, the speaker's Thirteenth Ward sphere of influence generated big votes for Lisa Madigan in the race for AG, and former Illinois Senate President and Cook County Assessor Thomas Hynes's Nineteenth Ward came out for his son, state Comptroller Dan Hynes. On the Northwest Side, Alderman Dick Mell's Thirty-Third Ward backed his son-in-law, U.S. Representative Rod Blagojevich, for governor. And, of course, there was incumbent Secretary of State Jesse White, the popular Black former state legislator who brought enormous statewide appeal. For Democrats, especially in Chicago, the stars could not have been aligned much better: The city's political warlords held together long enough to back each other's relatives, and Democratic votes overwhelmingly rolled in from African American wards. Democrats controlled a new Madigan-drawn legislative map through the latest redistricting, giving them an incentive to take back the Senate and bolster Speaker Madigan's majority. Tie in big labor's desire to put a Democrat in the governor's mansion for the first time in twenty-six years, and the party formed the closest thing to an old-fashioned Chicago juggernaut.

Birkett suffered from Lisa Madigan's relentless campaign questions about his role in the prosecution of Rolando Cruz for the murder of ten-year-old Jeanine Nicarico of Naperville in 1983. Cruz would be one of three men convicted and later exonerated. One of Madigan's late campaign ads said, "Rolando Cruz spent seven years on Death Row despite overwhelming evidence of his innocence. But Joe Birkett? He continued to prosecute Cruz using coerced testimony."[15] Birkett has steadfastly countered her description as being "100 percent false."[16] In election coverage, the *Tribune* reported that Birkett refused "to personally acknowledge the innocence" of Cruz, who was sentenced twice to Death Row but found not guilty at a third trial. Birkett did not have a role in the first two cases.[17] He worked on the third go-around but said he did not take part in the trial itself.

Birkett also committed unforced political errors, such as accepting a ten-thousand-dollar campaign loan from the political fund of a sitting judge in a DuPage courthouse. Birkett said there was nothing improper, because no regulations banned the loan, that the two were longtime friends from when he had supervised and mentored the judge while he served as a prosecutor. An ethics expert still whistled foul. Steven Lubet, a law professor at Northwestern University, said the "relationship between a judge and a state's attorney should be limited to the courtroom. They shouldn't have financial entanglements."[18]

At the annual late-summer fund-raiser for the speaker's Thirteenth Ward, the patronage workers and blue-collar crew of his political operation came out in force for Lisa Madigan's first statewide run. She shook hands at the event site's doorway, with the speaker on a visitor's left and the daughter on the right. Lisa Madigan campaign stickers sat on tables for visitors to grab in between their beer, smoked sausages, mini sandwiches, and batter-fried hot peppers. A big sign said it all: "Welcome Mike & Lisa Madigan and friends."[19]

The state's 2002 campaign records show that Lisa Madigan won generous backing from workers on state, city, county, and other local government payrolls who had given to the Thirteenth Ward. When the *Tribune* checked the numbers, at least eighty-two public employees who had contributed to the Thirteenth Ward Democratic operation poured nearly $125,000 into her campaign fund over three years. Nearly half of the public servants who contributed to Lisa Madigan lived in her father's ward. Caulkers, truck drivers, laborers, and electricians often gave between 2 and 3 percent of their annual salaries to the Madigans, a *Tribune* analysis showed.[20]

As well as the donations from Thirteenth Ward foot soldiers, a few of Lisa Madigan's contributions drew questions—including a twenty-five-thousand-dollar contribution from a performer associated with music that promoted white power, hatred of religion, and violence toward women. The contributing musician was one of two sons of Sheldon Harris, then an appointed Cook County judge. Each son gave twenty-five-thousand dollars to her, for a total of fifty thousand dollars. Harris defended his sons, saying they were trust fund millionaires. Harris said that "they felt very appreciative" of the speaker's support for their father's candidacy for a full term on the bench and that they became "enthralled" by Lisa Madigan at a political event. Once the *Tribune* pointed out the issue, Madigan announced that her campaign would give the twenty-five-thousand dollars from the musician brother to an anti-bigotry organization. Judge Harris said the speaker did not solicit cash for his daughter.[21]

The general election was a tight race, but Lisa Madigan won with 50.39 percent of the vote; Birkett got 47.1 percent, and Libertarian Gary Shilts drew 2.51 percent.[22] She never faced a major threat in her next three AG races. After the hard-hitting stories about her during the campaign, however, the speaker substantially scaled back his availability to the press.

When Obama won the presidency in 2008, Lisa Madigan's name briefly came up as a potential replacement for him in the U.S. Senate seat he had vacated. Governor Rod Blagojevich had the appointment power to fill the Obama vacancy. At trial Blagojevich raised the idea that he had planned to appoint Lisa Madigan to the U.S. Senate as a way to win the speaker's support for the governor's agenda. But few put much stock in the idea that appointing her to the Senate could win peace with the speaker in the ongoing legislative battles with the governor. Blagojevich was arrested the month after Obama became president and appointed former Attorney General Roland Burris to the Senate before the governor was impeached. At that time, Lisa Madigan also said she didn't seek that Senate appointment. "I've never asked to be considered for the Senate seat," she said in an interview shortly after the FBI arrested Blagojevich. "And one of my issues always was with Governor Blagojevich. . . . If I would get an appointment, he'd be able to appoint the attorney general, and I never had any faith that he would appoint somebody of integrity."[23]

Because Pat Quinn was a rookie governor who had moved up when Blagojevich was kicked out of office, Lisa Madigan would be seen as a potential challenger in 2010. But she took a pass on the chance to run for either governor or U.S. Senate, choosing to run for her third term as AG. At a Chicago news conference, she explained her difficult choice and made it clear that she liked her career path. "There was plenty of agonizing over my decision," she said. "I have a job that I love right now, and I also have a family that I love, and I plan on continuing to serve as your attorney general because I think it's absolutely vital to have an independent advocate in that office," she said.[24]

Most interesting to political junkies was the difference in how she had answered in 2009 when asked whether her father's position played a role in her decision to stay on as attorney general rather than go for governor. "No, I made a decision about what was best for me, and what was best for my family, and what I ultimately thought was best for the state at this point," she said.[25] At the height of her appeal, Lisa Madigan remained a sought-after candidate for U.S. Senate, especially among Democrats in Washington who wanted her to run when Burris finished the Obama term. She got courted to run by President Obama, who had served in Springfield with her in the Illinois Senate. With Obama in the White House, there was even speculation that she could end up on the U.S. Supreme Court.

The speculation about Lisa Madigan's political future became less intense when she decided in 2018 that she would not run for a fifth term as attorney general. But such conjecture never goes away completely. She avoided a 2018 race with the Republican candidate, former Miss America Erika Harold, a Harvard law graduate. Governor Bruce Rauner, who backed Harold and was waging war daily against the speaker, would have pummeled the Madigans in an effort to help Harold. The campaign could have tarnished Lisa Madigan even if she had run and won big. When Madigan announced her decision on 2018, Harold thanked her for her service. But the Illinois Republican Party, reflecting the Rauner fight with the speaker, was less than gracious: "Thanks to her father, Lisa Madigan knew her days as Attorney General were numbered. The Madigan brand is toxic for every single Illinois Democrat. This should be the beginning of the end of the Madigan Family's disastrous reign over Illinois." The speaker avoided the political noise and delivered a straightforward statement of praise. "It has been my privilege to watch her fight for the people of Illinois and do the right thing every day," he said. "No father could be prouder of his daughter's personal and professional accomplishments, and I look forward to watching her continue her commitment to helping people in a new capacity."[26]

As attorney general, Lisa Madigan won credit for sinking a proposal for a casino in Rosemont when she outlined alleged connections between Mayor Donald Stephens and others to organized crime—charges the longtime mayor denied.[27] She investigated problems with hiring under the Blagojevich administration and turned over her files to U.S. Attorney Patrick Fitzgerald. His office cited "allegations of endemic hiring fraud," but he eventually sent the governor to prison over the attempted sale of the Obama seat and other widespread corruption.[28] Once Blagojevich was arrested, Lisa Madigan searched for ways to remove him from office immediately. She even sought an Illinois Supreme Court ruling that Blagojevich was unfit to govern, but that effort was unsuccessful.[29]

Lisa Madigan also embraced the AG role as a consumer watchdog. She argued against giving ComEd the lucrative legislative deals that have come under federal scrutiny, saying they were not good enough for consumers. Her father eventually sided with the company even when she remained opposed. Her successes in the office included going after phony online colleges, nursing home deficiencies, and payday loan practices that hurt the little guy. She sued Trump International Hotel and Tower Chicago, alleging that it endangered fish when it siphoned water from the Chicago River and pumped it back out thirty-five degrees hotter. She also went after big banks for substandard loan practices that contributed to the Great Recession.

In seeking to improve openness in government, she created a public access counselor position to help citizens and the press shake loose public records from recalcitrant government officials. At times very helpful and at other times siding with state agency officials who dream up worst-case scenarios to block the release of public records, the office has fallen short of what is needed, but it is a step forward. Many pockets of government in Illinois still carry a culture of secrecy instead of a four-square commitment to openness. But Lisa Madigan delivered a major victory for transparency when she determined that public officials should release copies of subpoenas in criminal investigations when reporters file for them under the Freedom of Information Act, a position that Blagojevich long resisted.[30] The Better Government Association followed up with a lawsuit and the courts agreed that subpoenas should be released.[31]

As election cycles come and go, questions still linger about her now that she has a ranking post at a major law firm: What might have been had she stayed in the game? And will she come back? The political class is left with a new twist on an old question: What does Lisa Madigan think? One of her last acts in January 2019 as outgoing attorney general was swearing in her father to his eighteenth term as speaker. While he still had his right hand raised, she concluded with a comment that said it all: "Congratulations, you're the speaker again."[32] It would be his last term as speaker.

10
THE POLITICS OF MONEY

"My first obligation is to win the House."
—Speaker Michael Madigan,
    October 16, 1998

Every spring for decades, the "Evening on the Lake" became the don't-miss Springfield event, the most important kiss-the-ring moment for everybody who wanted to be somebody, where the wannabes and never-wills rubbed shoulders with the big-shot lobbyists and, of course, the most powerful politician in Illinois. They drove nearly ten miles south of the Capitol to a community college parking lot and then boarded shuttle buses that zigzagged past policemen who waved them through. They deboarded directly into a line at the entrance of the Island Bay Yacht Club, where Speaker Michael Madigan shook their hands as they walked in. The greeting would be brisk, the hors d'oeuvres plentiful, the cocktails cold.

Year after year, Madigan put out a House calendar that scheduled no session day on an early Monday in May. The state banned fund-raisers in Sangamon County, where Springfield is, during session days, but the speaker managed a workaround. Lobbyists knew to mark down the open Monday for the speaker's event, an evening that set the stage for the final burst of legislative action in the closing weeks of the spring session. Many of the same contributors would seek his favor on legislation back at the Capitol. When done appropriately, there was nothing illegal. Madigan and his campaign contributors routinely insisted there was no connection between his official government acts and political donations. But there's no doubt that it was cozy.

Springfield revolves around money. The control of both political and public money increases a politician's power and enables him or her to dominate the agenda. And many Illinois leaders have made corrupt bargains to acquire and maintain that power. During Madigan's long tenure, Illinoisans saw Republican Governor George Ryan go to prison over a corruption rooted in selling licenses to supplement his political coffers while he was secretary of state and Democratic Governor Rod Blagojevich accused of attempting to raise campaign cash in exchange for routine government business, a practice called pay-to-play.

But Madigan's story is like no other. He was an expert at using money to reward legislators who were loyal to him and to defeat those who weren't. And he was proficient at exploiting legal loopholes for raising and spending campaign cash. The Evening on the Lake is just one small example of his political reach—overseer of the legislature, big money raiser, lord over lobbyists, and leader of loyalists who work for him in state government and live to play politics for him too.[1]

Lines, of course, have been drawn over the years to clamp down on some of Illinois' special brand of coziness. The ban on Sangamon County fund-raisers on legislative session days is a nod to a bygone era when a lobbyist could buy tickets to a lawmaker's breakfast fund-raiser and hope for a favorable vote in the lawmaker's committee before lunch. Or when a gambling lobbyist could make headlines for passing out campaign checks to lawmakers just steps from the House chamber. Or when a young Democratic state senator named Paul Simon could write for *Harper's* magazine in 1965 of the "sometimes sinister" lobbyist-legislator alliance, saying, "Cold cash passes directly from one hand to another." His colleagues responded by giving him a "Benedict Arnold Award."[2]

Still, over the years, legislative leaders managed to consolidate their power over rank-and-file lawmakers through control of fund-raising and control over which competitive legislative races they favored with the most campaign funds. But through longevity and hard work, command of a strong political organization, and a sheer will to keep his speakership, Madigan usually outperformed all comers. With his tightly drawn House rules, he controlled what legislation moved in the Capitol, giving him leverage over House and Senate lawmakers, the governor, and powerful interest groups that wanted public money appropriated for pet projects. Madigan also controlled information, his staff, and the resources to rank-and-file lawmakers and committee chairs, positioning them as weaker and pushing interest groups to deal with him directly. Political scientist Kent

Redfield, a campaign finance expert and longtime Madigan watcher, explained the impact of this consolidation: "Power in Springfield helps the leaders raise money for elections, and power in elections translates into electing more members with loyalty to the leaders, which makes the leaders more powerful in Springfield."[3]

Madigan's political money machine in the 2020 election cycle outpaced the fund-raising of the other three House and Senate partisan caucuses combined. The four campaign funds Madigan controlled raised nearly $28.2 million; the other three legislative leaders generated a total of just under $23.8 million. Compared to the House Republican tally of $6.7 million, Madigan was positioned to spend $4.00 for every buck raised by House GOP leader Jim Durkin of Western Springs. Laborers, lawyers, operating engineers, Teamsters, teachers, and pipe fitters poured donations worth six and seven figures into the Madigan-controlled funds.[4] The Madigan money advantage and the anti-Trump turnout in key corners of the state had Democrats hoping they could increase their modern-day record of a 74–44 House majority. They pumped up little-known suburban Democratic candidates with a relentless stream of costly television commercials on major Chicago stations. In the end, though, Madigan's House Democrats lost a seat in the 2020 election, a sign to many detractors that his political baggage had begun to weigh on his party.

The always-powerful strength of legislative leaders had grown in the 1990s, along with their longevity. At the time, Madigan was part of a quartet of legislative leaders—Republican Senate President James "Pate" Philip of Wood Dale, Senate Minority Leader Emil Jones of Chicago, and Lee Daniels, who served as minority leader as well as speaker in the two years that Republicans gained control of the House.[5] These four played enormous roles in shaping as many as two dozen targeted races in each election cycle that both parties believed they had a shot to win. While most districts are gerrymandered so that they are deemed "safe" for one party or the other, the targeted races are the ones where the sizes of the legislative majorities and minorities are determined. And they are expensive. In the 1980s the races cost in the low six figures for each candidate in the general election. In the last three election cycles through 2020, they cost between $1 million and $2 million for each candidate. To fund these types of races, a candidate usually needs help from the legislative leaders. And that gives the leaders even more leverage on individual lawmakers.[6]

Spending in statewide races has become eye-popping over the last few election cycles, but lawmakers knew they needed to make changes following the aggressive pay-to-play politics of Governor Rod Blagojevich. They passed a ban on a practice that allowed big campaign contributors to land lucrative state contracts from the statewide politicians who pass out the business. Additional post-Blagojevich limits have gone into place over the years, yet limits in Illinois seem made to be broken. Madigan and the three other legislative leaders learned to get around spending limits by exploiting a loophole in state law. Reporters Sandy Bergo and Chuck Neubauer revealed the flaws of state law, which was first sold as a way to give candidates with average financial means a way to fight ultra-wealthy opponents whose self-funding was not restricted by spending limits.

Once a candidate in a race puts more than $100,000 of his or her own money into a campaign—or gets that much support from a separate, friendly super PAC—the contribution limits are lifted for everyone in the race. What occurred, though, is that legislative leaders turned the law inside out. Instead of a defensive shield against wealthy candidates, they started using it as an offensive weapon. They put in more than $100,000 themselves—or, in the case of Durkin, money that was spent by friendly, supportive super PACs or independent committees on his behalf—to break the caps automatically so that their own supporters would be free of restrictive contribution limits. In their 2020 story for the nonpartisan Better Government Association, Bergo and Neubauer reported that Madigan took advantage of the loophole after Durkin had used it to raise millions of extra dollars in the prior election. In October 2016 an independent political committee called Turnaround Illinois allied with Durkin spent $101,843 on radio ads supporting his reelection. It was funded by Rauner, then the GOP governor, and billionaire investor and former *Chicago Tribune* executive Sam Zell in order to support General Assembly candidates who aligned with Rauner. Durkin got around the limits again in 2018 when the Republican State Leadership Committee broke the cap. The Washington-based committee spent $105,000 in support of Durkin's candidacy.[7]

But when Madigan went in, of course, he took the maneuver to another level. He pumped $100,000 plus one dollar into his campaign kitty and announced he was "self-funding" his 2018 race for his House seat. He made the move even though he was unopposed in the race. The maneuver allowed him to raise "nearly $12 million more than normally allowed, records showed. He sent $5.9 million to the Democratic Party of Illinois and the Democratic Majority, two campaign funds he also controls and uses to distribute cash to favored Democratic legislative candidates. He also spent more than $2.1 million on payroll and other office expenses for his political organization," Bergo and Neubauer reported. "The influx of cash apparently worked. Democrats gained seven House seats in 2018, restoring Madigan's 'supermajority'."[8] Both Madigan and Durkin used their methodologies to break the caps for the 2020 election season. New speaker Emanuel "Chris" Welch followed suit in September 2021 with a $100,000 loan to his own fund.

While Madigan's Lake Springfield fund-raiser would draw the most attention at the Capitol, rank-and-file legislators aggressively tap the captive statehouse crowds for contributions—even in years packed with partisan competition for campaign money. The crunch for campaign cash is a behind-the-scenes dynamic that is ever-present background noise. In 2012, running in newly drawn district boundaries that Madigan oversaw, more than twenty legislative fund-raisers were held on just one Monday night only days before the March primaries. "I referred to this as Super Tuesday," said Richard Guidice, a former Chicago lawmaker and longtime lobbyist whose clients ranged from road builders, to horse-racing tracks, to the movie industry. "We're seeing a whole bunch of folks all at one time." With fund-raisers for Democrats and Republicans overlapping on that frenzied night, lobbyists carried homemade spreadsheets with the time and place of the events. They trudged through parties hosted at downtown Springfield eateries, a lobbyist's apartment, a nineteenth-century bed-and-breakfast known as the Pasfield House, a smoke shop, union offices, and more—most within blocks of the Illinois Capitol. "When you're a legislator, you never quit campaigning," said then Senator Gary Forby, a Southern Illinois Democrat whose contests in Madigan's House would cost more than $1 million and twice as much when he ran for Senate. "You never quit raising money. It just takes a lot of money. It seems like every year it takes more money."[9]

In the spring of 2021, legislators passed a proposal to ban fund-raisers from being held anywhere in the state on legislative session days as well as the days before session—an attempt to eliminate closely timed events like Madigan's Evening on the Lake or Super Tuesdays for the rank and file.

Political money often came easy when Madigan held the speakership. Some contributors gave because they loved him, some because they wanted him to love them, some because they owed him, and some because they hoped giving a donation would keep him from hurting their cause. When you are the speaker, you don't always have to throw your own fund-raisers. Special interest groups are happy to do it for you. Some are more upscale than others, some sponsors are more thankful than others, and some folks are greedier than others.

When Commonwealth Edison would throw a Madigan bash, for instance, the leaders of the power company would put together a downtown soiree. It became an annual event, generating upward of two hundred thousand dollars, according to people with knowledge of the events. The speaker would speak, the corporate suits would cheer and express gratitude with words and checks. Madigan initially held this special celebration exclusively to raise money for Democrats—until the other three partisan caucuses caught on and stuck out their hands. Commonwealth Edison went along, but the amounts they raised were less for the other caucuses and the parties were smaller, according to sources.[10]

Commonwealth Edison and its parent company, Exelon, made sure to spread the wealth around in an effort to keep a line of communication open with lawmakers, especially when they had legislation under consideration. Records show that over five elections, starting in the 2010 election cycle and ending in that of 2018—a period that encompasses the 2011 and 2016 laws that have come under federal scrutiny—ComEd and Exelon poured $5.2 million into Illinois House and Senate races through legislators and candidates, legislative leaders and party committees, state parties, and statewide officers and candidates. The contributions tilted toward the majority Democrats every cycle. The only two companies that gave more money to state candidates, legislative leaders, and legislative caucus party committees in that same period were downstate power company Ameren, which benefited from ComEd legislation and gave about $5.9 million in donations, and AT&T, another regulated company, which gave $5.3 million in donations. All three had prominent Madigan staff alumni among their ranks.[11]

ComEd alone gave 173 donations, mostly to the rank and file, in the 2015–2016 election cycle, when the utility won a 2016 law it promoted as saving thousands of jobs, keeping some nuclear plants open and bumping up costs to customers. The utility gave 155 donations to the rank and file in the 2011–2012 election cycle,[12] a period when critics charged that legislators approved a law that boosted ComEd's bottom line but fell short on promises to help customers.[13] Lawmakers come and go during a two-year term, but ComEd's attempt to put money in the campaign kitties of almost every rank-and-file member of the General Assembly eased access to legislators—even opponents—when legislation important to the company was in play. Following word that ComEd and Exelon had received federal subpoenas in 2019, their giving tailed off. Redfield estimated that the two companies had dropped from a combined high-water mark of donating $1.3 million to state political funds in the two-year 2018 election cycle to about $265,000 in the two-year 2020 cycle.[14] But throughout Madigan's tenure, money-raising helped pave the way to Madigan's rise.

Madigan's role as chairman of the Illinois Democratic Party had expanded exponentially since he first took over in 1998. But in the weeks before he would start as chair, Madigan showed how creative he could be at it. U.S. Representative Glenn Poshard, a former state senator from Southern Illinois, won the Democratic primary for governor with Madigan's backing, but it took an effort to get him over the hump. Wanting to be viewed as a politician unbought by big money, Poshard made campaign finance reform a priority in his primary contest. He imposed a contribution limit of two thousand dollars from individuals and twenty-five thousand dollars from a politician's campaign fund. He pledged not to take money from political action committees and corporations. But when Madigan saw Poshard's campaign contributions waning in the primary, the speaker figured out a quick way to build up the congressman's coffers while pressing Poshard's promise to the limits. Madigan turned to his rank-and-file House Democrats.

"One by one," wrote Rick Pearson, the *Tribune* reporter who broke the story, "several Downstate lawmakers were summoned into a room in the Springfield headquarters of the state's largest labor organization. They each received an empty envelope with an amount scrawled on it—up to $25,000," which they were urged to contribute from their own campaign funds. Three lawmakers recalled how Madigan stood alongside Poshard and asked them a direct question: "Can you help?" Poshard said his restrictions on contributions were designed to maintain his independence and prevent the appearance of special interest influence. But appearing with Madigan to make a special request of lawmakers in Springfield prompted questions about Poshard's independence and his commitment to the spirit of his contribution limits. "Madigan's not strong-arming anybody," Poshard said, explaining instead that the speaker "encouraged them to help me. And what's wrong with that?"[15]

Poshard's limits did not work as well for him in the general election against Republican opponent George Ryan. While attempting to demonstrate his commitment to reform, Poshard had unilaterally disarmed himself. He doubled individual contribution limits to four thousand dollars, and Madigan and special interest groups figured out ways to get around them. But the Ryan money machine raked in cash at a fast pace.

Was Madigan's embrace of Poshard merely another attempt to put a Democrat in the governor's office when it came time to redraw the district boundaries? No doubt, Madigan wanted a Democratic governor during a redistricting fight. But Madigan also saw Poshard as a candidate whose conservative stances could help Democrats running in districts that were far less liberal than many Chicago neighborhoods. That was critically important to the speaker. He held a precarious 60–58 majority, the slimmest of his career. Four years earlier, he had lost the Illinois House in the 1994 nationwide Republican wave that propelled DuPage County Republican Lee Daniels into the speakership and bounced Madigan back into the minority leader position. Madigan retook the House two years later on the strength of flipping six seats in Chicago's southern and southwest suburbs. The thinking was that the conservative Democrats in those southern suburbs—a bungalow belt then loaded with Reagan Democrats—could relate to Poshard's deep roots in Southern Illinois' conservative Democratic politics.

To strengthen his hand, Madigan quietly rented a small space in suburban Evergreen Park at taxpayer expense for a one-of-a-kind government satellite office to help the south suburban six develop all-important constituent services. As the 1998 campaign season heated up, the speaker shifted payments for that lease—which cost the state just over seven thousand dollars across two years—from taxpayer funds to his political fund and used the site as a staging ground for Democratic campaign activities.[16] If Poshard could spark a better turnout where Madigan's incumbent House Democrats needed a boost, the speaker's main goal of holding the majority would be easier to achieve. "My first obligation is to win the House," Madigan said.[17] Poshard lost, but Madigan would pick up two seats to push his majority to 62–56.

Madigan also showed Illinoisans in that campaign for governor that he knew how to play hardball. He authorized a searing television ad that attempted to tie the deaths of six children in a minivan crash in Wisconsin to a festering licenses-for-bribes scandal in Republican governor candidate

George Ryan's secretary of state office. The accident was caused when a metal part fell from a semitrailer truck driven by a man who prosecutors eventually would say got his license with a bribe. The ad, paid for by the Democratic Party, showed a black-and-white picture of the charred minivan, with a narrator saying, "Six children are dead. His office riddled with corruption, and George Ryan wants to be our governor?"[18] Ryan condemned the ad, as did Republican Governor Jim Edgar, a former secretary of state; Poshard supporter Phil Rock, the ex-Senate president and a former Democratic Party chair; and former U.S. Senator Paul Simon, a Democrat.[19]

Days later, three former secretary of state workers were among five people indicted in a federal racketeering, extortion, and mail fraud case that alleged $150,000 in bribes were traded for truck licenses and that tens of thousands of dollars ended up in Ryan's campaign fund. At that time, U.S. Attorney Scott Lassar said Ryan was not a subject of the probe— undermining Democratic efforts to take full advantage of the scandal dubbed "Operation Safe Road."[20]

Madigan explained that he knew the federal government was planning indictments tied to the license-selling scandal and had learned about telling discoveries made by a longtime ally, attorney Joseph Power Jr., who represented the Reverend Duane "Scott" Willis and his wife, Janet, in a civil suit over their six children's deaths. "We gave it a great deal of thought and consideration because it was a dramatic ad," Madigan said. "My decision to go forward with the ad was with what I knew would develop from the federal action involving mismanagement of the office." Madigan saw running the ad as part of the politics of the moment: "This is election time, and you have to expect that."[21, 22]

When Ryan won the election, Madigan proved he could be practical as well, especially with public money available in a flush state treasury. He and the new governor put the campaign behind them and got down to business—grilling up thousands of pork-barrel projects to distribute around the state and burning through a cash surplus Edgar had built up. Ryan, Madigan, and the three other legislative leaders—Daniels, Philip, and Jones—put together a secretive $1.5 billion taxpayer-funded spending machine from a combination of general funds and borrowed money. When political leaders deliver legislative district projects, they build loyalty. Lawmaker projects ranged from good sewers, clean water, smooth roads, and better schools to tutus for youth dancers in McHenry County and a Jack Benny statue for Waukegan, where the comedian grew up.[23]

They also swept up plenty of "spork"—soccer fields, ice rinks, baseball dia-monds, and football bleachers—initiatives inspired by lawmakers' love of both sports and pork. Lawmakers would wind up with a positive afterglow for passing out pork that was worth as much as a campaign donation but paid for with taxpayer dollars. One lawmaker wound up awarded with the key to a city. And House Republican leader Lee Daniels was honored with a polar bear named Lee at Lincoln Park Zoo.[24]

Former Governor Jim Edgar, who had left more than a billion dollars in the state's operating kitty after inheriting early 1990s recession-era budget problems, remained taken aback by the aggressive spending when interviewed in 2021: "I never dreamed, after what we went through in the early 1990s, that the legislature . . . would go back on a spending spree like that." Edgar recalled Madigan as a "fiscally conservative speaker" when they worked together, and he decided to ask Madigan what happened. Madigan's response, Edgar said, was that he still would work with the governor in office and "this is what the [new] governor wants to do."[25]

As a faltering economy spiraled downward faster following the Sep-tember 11, 2001, terrorist attacks, state funds got tighter. But Madigan defended making the pork-barrel deals in flush times and keeping the promised funds flowing when budgets got tighter. The speaker said, "A member of the Legislature is entitled to this spending." He brushed aside criticism of lawmakers bringing home the bacon even when the budget is tight: "If a person is a member of the Legislature, and they cannot initiate a spending item, then why are they here? Why do they seek election? Why do they come to the Capitol and represent their voters if they are not able to initiate spending items? Why serve? Why?"[26] At times, the distribution of pork-barrel projects caused old-timers in safe seats to grumble. Law-makers in more politically vulnerable targeted races sometimes received more public money to pass out for pork-barrel projects, a way to give an incumbent in a tight legislative contest a political boost. It's an example of how the political benefit of public money weighed heavily into who got what.

Madigan knew how to use crafty ways to make sure public funds kept flowing into his district. In the last year of Governor Pat Quinn's admin-istration, Madigan took extra steps to protect $35 million he designated for a handful of schools in Chicago, including in his Southwest Side leg-islative district. In that 2014 campaign year, it was unclear whether Quinn would be able to win another term as governor or if the big-spending

Republican challenger, Bruce Rauner, might be the chief executive come January 2015. Money was tight again, and Rauner did not support keeping a temporary income tax hike in place if he won. Madigan's move proved prescient. When he beat Quinn and took office, Rauner froze spending and cut the budget. Many grants were halted, including $40 million for downstate schools that had been allocated to the Illinois State Board of Education for distribution. But because of an unusual legislative maneuver, Madigan and fellow Democrats had placed the specially designated $35 million for Chicago schools into the office of Democratic Secretary of State Jesse White. The money was secure with White because his office is independent and separate from the governor's office. The state constitution did not give the governor the ability to reach into White's office unilaterally to sweep the money away for another purpose or freeze it.[27]

White sent the money to the Chicago Public Schools. His office said he had no authority to do otherwise. The biggest single chunk of the $35 million Madigan grant—$13 million—went to a middle school under construction in the speaker's Southwest Side district to relieve overcrowding as the Hispanic population boomed in local schools. A school in the nearby district of Chicago Democratic Representative Dan Burke received $6.5 million, and a school in House Majority Leader Barbara Flynn Currie's South Side District received $5.5 million. The rest was designated for installing air conditioning in schools throughout the city.[28]

When Madigan wrote the legislation to put the money in White's office, he knew that he and Quinn often clashed. And Rauner, the challenger, was still an unknown. Madigan spokesperson Steve Brown said the decision to allocate the money through White was "just a way of safeguarding that spending decision—made by the legislature, signed into law." In short, it represented a way to prevent that particular $35 million from being frozen or rechanneled to pay other bills. "You see hijinks from the governors' offices all the time—regardless of party, regardless of time," Brown said. The Chicago Public Schools maintained that the money went to critical needs to relieve overcrowding—not just because senior lawmakers wanted the money. One Republican senator, Matt Murphy of Palatine, grumbled that other areas of the state took "real cuts so that pork like this could be spent" in Madigan's district. But Representative Frank Mautino, the Spring Valley Democrat who later became auditor general, thought about the $40 million for downstate school grants that disappeared and wondered whether giving that money to the Illinois State

Board of Education had been the right move. "Maybe I wish I'd put the grants in Jesse's office," Mautino said.[29]

Madigan's use of campaign cash sometimes baffled onlookers even if his political moves fit within his standard playbook. Take the case of Chicago Democratic Representative Derrick Smith, who performed the rare feat of getting arrested on federal bribery charges shortly after he was appointed to fill a vacancy in a House seat. He took a seven-thousand-dollar cash bribe in exchange for supporting a fifty-thousand-dollar state grant for a day-care center the government created for an undercover sting. Smith fell for it. He was caught on tape specifically requesting cash, saying, "I don't want no trace of it."[30]

Despite the notorious start to his career, Smith won the primary a week later with nearly 77 percent of the vote. He ignored pleas from fellow Democrats who asked him to resign from the House and give up his spot on the ballot in the general election. So Madigan took action to dump him. With the speaker in the chair, the House expelled Smith on a 100–6 vote. He became the first House lawmaker to be tossed out over perceived misdeeds in 107 years—a period nearly as long as the Cubs' drought between World Series championships.[31]

But the strange saga didn't end. Smith kept his name on the general election ballot. And five months later, as Barack Obama celebrated his 2012 reelection at Chicago's giant McCormick Place convention center, Smith won back the West Side district located only miles away from the president's event. He was sworn in for the new term he won while still facing the federal charges. Two years later, Smith ran again. Despite once overseeing Smith's expulsion, Madigan decided to back him. The speaker poured more than seventy-two thousand dollars into campaign brochures, mailing costs, and staffers to help Smith in the 2014 primary. It didn't faze Steve Brown when asked about the oddity of the speaker backing Smith in the primary despite his high-profile role in expelling Smith. "We're backing incumbents," Brown said.[32]

There was another factor in play. By supporting Smith for reelection, Madigan also won kudos from some of the rookie lawmaker's fellow Black caucus colleagues—an important bloc among the speaker's House Democrats—who felt Smith should be supported because he was innocent until proven guilty. Smith ended up losing his primary, losing his trial, and, after weeping in the courtroom, being sentenced to five months in prison.[33]

The charge of bribery might not have stopped Madigan from contributing campaign money to a reliable Democratic vote like Smith. But the speaker somewhat subtly deviated from the notion of backing incumbents when it came to a rogue House Democrat who angered him over legislative and party politics. In what currently stands as the state's most expensive legislative primary, more than $6 million was spent in the 2016 contest that pitted South Side Democratic Representative Ken Dunkin against challenger Julianna Stratton.[34] The House District 5 primary became a proxy fight between Madigan and Republican Governor Bruce Rauner. Dunkin had repeatedly broken from Madigan in favor of Rauner on key votes, including when the speaker and labor unions needed him. Neither Madigan nor Rauner preferred to be directly linked to their positions even though everybody viewed them as the main players. So Madigan's allies—including eleven House Democrats contributing most of a $560,000 chunk from incumbents' campaign committees—sent their money directly to the Stratton campaign rather than through Madigan-controlled committees. Rauner's allies did something similar.[35]

The political gymnastics did little to convince anyone that their fingerprints were not on the race. And the leader of the free world, Barack Obama, making a rare endorsement in a state legislative race as a sitting president, cut a commercial for Stratton, who crushed Dunkin. Seeing Dunkin defeated was a major win for Madigan, because it gave him a supermajority of seventy-four more predictable Democrats, three above what is needed to pass key pieces of legislation and override a governor's veto.

Stratton didn't stay long in the seat. During the next election, governor candidate J. B. Pritzker tabbed her as his Democratic running mate, and the House District 5 seat opened up again. Madigan needed a new candidate. And he needed to staff up. Turns out that a woman who didn't get a job in that new campaign would send shockwaves through Madigan's government and political operation. She gave a simple reason why she wasn't picked: retaliation.

PART IV

CRACKS IN THE SYSTEM

11

TURNING POINT

"In November, a courageous woman made
me aware that a high-ranking individual
within my political operation had
previously made unwanted advances and
sent her inappropriate text messages."
—Speaker Michael Madigan,
   February 12, 2018

The Thirteenth Ward was buzzing: What's up with Kevin? Where's Kevin?
Precinct captains knew something had happened. Staff had received an
email. But what they all learned came as a surprise: Kevin Quinn, the guy
they had talked to for twenty years in the Thirteenth Ward headquarters, was out. Not just gone for the day or the week. He was out of the
organization. How could that be? Kevin Quinn, the brother of Chicago
Alderman Marty Quinn? Gone? About the time the questions hit a fever
pitch, Speaker Madigan decided to say something publicly. He rolled out
an unusual statement on a Monday morning, February 12, 2018, a state
holiday when workers were given the day off in honor of Abraham Lincoln's birthday. It looked like a good day to drop what appeared on the
surface to be a one-day story. Few officials were available for details, reaction, and records on a holiday. Madigan's statement gave him a chance
to control the spin, get ahead of it all. But the story didn't stop with the
speaker's statement. The story was only beginning.

For Madigan, 2018 would become a year of reckoning, the year the
#MeToo movement caught up with Springfield. Sure, he would remain

a winner in political fights against Governor Bruce Rauner and pick up Democratic seats in the fall election. But he faced the prospect of having to recalibrate a way to address the concerns of women in politics. No one could have predicted how the Kevin Quinn matter would rattle the House that Madigan built. But Quinn would become a major #MeToo flashpoint in Illinois politics, a symbol of ward-style patronage and nepotism gone bad. Madigan would be knocked back on his heels, defending his efforts to address conduct by underlings but then admitting publicly and explaining repeatedly that he had failed to do enough and needed to do more. Before the year was half over, Madigan would need to sever political ties with a lobbyist—a former House Democratic staffer—accused of abusive behavior in campaigns. A veteran House Democrat would step down from his leadership position following sexual harassment accusations from a marijuana advocate. And the speaker's chief of staff would leave under pressure when faced with sexual harassment allegations from a mid-level clerk. Madigan would meet with staffers of every rank within his office. He would allow an outside investigation that criticized his insular style, a style that gave too much leeway to the power-tripping staffers who wrongly used their freedom to bully and sexually harass the lower-ranked workers.

Over the years, reporters scrutinized Madigan through vast troves of public records and reported on his high-stakes political and government maneuvers: pork-barrel projects, private property tax appeals, campaign spending, legislative proposals, and wide-open clashes with other public officials. Undeterred, he brought home the bacon, won big tax breaks for his law firm's clients, pushed patronage, and wielded extraordinary political clout. But news stories about those activities usually saw the Madigan organization from only the outside looking in. Rare was the chance for the public to view the Madigan organization from the inside looking out. The view from inside the speaker's political machine offered a turning point in the narrative of the state's most powerful politician. Fissures began to form in the Madigan Mystique.

In early February 2018, a few phone calls started coming into the Tribune Tower. There was scant detail at first. But a sexual harassment case was brewing inside Madigan's ward, and a woman might be ready to talk.

A tip like that is tough to gauge over the phone. A story about harassment is difficult to prove, and sexual harassment is extremely tough. But it is not impossible. A year earlier, I wrote a story about sexual harassment allegations lodged against the head of security for O'Hare and

Midway airports during the period when he served in his previous job at the Illinois Tollway. He was fired within a week. The month after that, another City Hall scandal began to unfold; this time racist, sexist, and homophobic emails in the city's water department toppled the head of the agency and several others, including the son of a former alderman. Two state workers linked to the scandal also lost their jobs, including the son of a former state lawmaker. Society was at the beginning of a cathartic moment about what should be left unsaid and what should be aired out. Across the nation, the #MeToo movement was taking hold.

In Illinois more than two hundred people had signed an open letter in late 2017 from "The Women Who Make Illinois Run" that outlined Springfield's demeaning culture. "Every industry has its own version of the casting couch," the letter said. "Illinois politics is no exception." The letter made clear that women had had enough: "The time has come for us to raise our collective voices, share our stories, and say #NoMore."

Without naming names, the group detailed how women had to endure the crude jokes and untoward advances at a popular Springfield bar, the overtures of a male legislator—identified only as a "chamber leader"—who asked out a young female staffer under the guise of mentoring and then explained he has an "open marriage." They told of the candidate who "slides his hands across the body of his fund-raising consultant," calls and texts in the middle of the night, and then balks at paying her for actual work because she refuses his advances. "We see it. We live it. We power through it. Every day," the letter said.[1]

Shortly after the letter came out, Madigan said, "We can and should do more to ensure no individual is the target of sexual harassment in the Capitol or anywhere else." The speaker put forward a proposal, including a provision calling for sexual harassment training for government employees and lobbyists.[2] But in a hearing on Madigan's bill, a surprise witness stepped out of the audience and took over the story line. Denise Rotheimer, an activist for victims of violent crime, testified that Democratic Senator Ira Silverstein of Chicago had repeatedly made unwanted comments to her, sending hundreds of Facebook messages, calling her late at night, and telling her she was "intoxicating."[3]

She had taken her complaint more than a year earlier to Senate president John Cullerton's office, where senior staff talked to Silverstein and forwarded the matter to the legislative inspector general, according to an aide. But there was a problem: the IG post had been vacant for nearly three years.[4] Other than an interim IG for six months, no permanent replacement had taken over for Tom Homer when he left the post in 2014 shortly after finishing the Metra patronage report critical of Madigan. Complaints languished.[5]

A week after Rotheimer's testimony, the General Assembly used its fall session to approve a ban on sexual harassment among state officials, start annual training to address the issue, and create a task force to develop more proposals to reduce sexual harassment. Lawmakers also appointed an interim legislative inspector general, former federal prosecutor Julie Porter, who concluded in late January 2018 that Silverstein's dealings with Rotheimer did not amount to sexual harassment. Instead, Porter said, the veteran senator behaved "in a manner unbecoming of a legislator" and should receive counseling. Rotheimer called the process "rigged" and warned that other women would hesitate to report misconduct.[6]

The revelations proved costly to Silverstein, the husband of Chicago's Fiftieth Ward Alderman Deb Silverstein. He would first lose his post on the Senate Democratic leadership team and then lose a primary for his Senate seat. Yet the Silverstein episode represented only a prelude to what a whistleblower from inside the Madigan organization was about to tell. The *Tribune* had begun exploring the tips about that potential case of sexual harassment. Was there documentation? Is it verifiable? Is it credible? Will the woman go on the record? Negotiations had begun with a go-between.

In a carefully arranged meeting at a neutral spot not far from Tribune Tower, I went with *Tribune* photojournalist Stacey Wescott to speak with Alaina Hampton for the first time. It was late on February 11, 2018, a Sunday night. "I basically lost everything I worked for because some guy could not control himself," Hampton told us.[7]

Detail by detail, the twenty-eight-year-old Hampton, who grew up in the small central Illinois town of Pleasant Plains, just west of Springfield, told how she once poured her heart into working for Madigan and his political team. She said she had worked occasionally in Madigan's Thirteenth Ward headquarters. She then worked as a legislative aide in a nearby district office for state Democratic Representative Silvana Tabares of Chicago, but Hampton reported weekly to Marty Quinn, the Thirteenth Ward alderman who doubled as Madigan's political general. Hampton viewed Quinn as a mentor as she knocked on doors and drummed up support for Democratic incumbents and candidates in House races, particularly where the speaker's endorsed candidates could be in trouble or needed boots on the ground.

Hampton recalled her role as a campaign manager for Julianna Stratton in the March 2016 Democratic primary for the South Side's Illinois House District 5, an intensive proxy fight between Madigan and Governor Rauner. And Stratton won. Beating incumbent Ken Dunkin was sweet for Madigan, especially since a primary win is tantamount to success in the general election in the Democratic stronghold of Chicago.

Shortly after the big win, Hampton dropped into the Thirteenth Ward headquarters, and Marty Quinn waved her into his office. She recalled Quinn asking her if she wanted a nine-to-five job to pick up a salary but still have time to perform political work for the Madigan organization. She said she was open to it and that he asked for her resume. A few weeks passed. She said she next found herself interviewing for a job at the Chicago Heights Economic Development Corporation, where friends of the Quinn and Madigan family worked. She got the job. During her off hours, Hampton said, she also spent twenty-five to thirty hours a week campaigning for Democrats in contested races outside Chicago.

That's when Hampton said she started getting more directives from Kevin Quinn, the alderman's brother. She checked with Marty Quinn about his brother's role but said she was told that Kevin was within his rights to give directives and coordinate with her. After a while, though, Kevin crossed the line between professional and personal. And he would not let up, sending a relentless string of texts seeking to go out with her. "When the messages began, I started cutting back on going to the ward office," she said. "I used to go there about once a week. I just didn't feel comfortable seeing him, Kevin."[8]

Kevin Quinn wrote a text to Hampton, telling her that he saw her in a bikini in a Facebook picture. He texted that she was "smoking hot." She tried to laugh him off, but he kept pressing. She responded that she wanted to maintain a professional relationship. Quinn persisted over the next few months, telling her, "U really do not know me. I will not brag or flaunt. But I am the best dude you will meet. . . . No bullshit."

In a Hampton response only weeks before the November election, she again wrote Quinn a stern message: "I need you to stop. I have dedicated a lot of time to this election cycle, and I will continue to do so, but I need to be able to do my work without you contacting me like this. I'm not interested. I just want to do my work."[9]

By February 2017, Hampton reported Kevin Quinn's activities to his brother, the alderman. Both Marty Quinn and Hampton said the harassment stopped once Marty contacted his brother. But she recalled a question in her meeting with Alderman Quinn that made her wonder about her future with the organization. Marty Quinn, she said, asked her if she'd like to be a precinct captain in the Thirteenth Ward—part of Madigan's elite political army. In recounting the moment, she said she worried that Kevin Quinn would be going to the same precinct meetings. "I was going to be expected to continue to work with someone that was obsessed with me," she recalled. "I think I knew at that point that I was not—I wasn't going to come back. I was scared. I was terrified to be there."[10]

About two months later, Hampton left the Madigan organization and signed up for the Marie Newman congressional primary campaign against U.S. Representative Dan Lipinski, whose alliance with Madigan dated back to the congressman's father, himself a former congressman.[11] Joining up with a Lipinski foe did not win Hampton any accolades from the Thirteenth Ward organization. But she later left the Newman campaign for reasons sealed in a nondisclosure agreement. When asked about the departure, the Newman campaign only praised Hampton for playing a "critical role" in helping the candidate get her race launched and wished her well in her "fight for justice."[12]

Hampton stayed in the political game as a consultant. She worked on a Cook County commissioner race and others. But then she decided to reach out to Madigan himself. In November 2017, Hampton sent a letter to Madigan's home to explain why she had left his organization. "I do not want to hurt any of you—I care very deeply about people involved. I only needed to tell you because it has been very painful to experience alone," she wrote.[13]

The speaker reached out to trusted attorney Heather Wier Vaught, a former chief legal counsel on his House staff who took on special assignments for him. Wier Vaught and Hampton met at a downtown coffee shop. They hugged at the end of their discussion, but they left with far different opinions about how the meeting went.[14]

In an interview later, Wier Vaught said her impression was that Hampton "got closure by notifying the speaker, and what happened to Kevin Quinn as a result of that did not matter to her." Hampton contended Wier Vaught was insensitive to the sexual harassment allegations, saying the attorney had jokingly asked if Hampton were seeking a twenty-five-thousand-dollar payout or a front-page story in the *Chicago Tribune*.[15]

Wier Vaught said in an interview that Hampton's characterization "surprised" her.[16] The attorney acknowledged mentioning the *Tribune* but did not remember raising a dollar figure. They couldn't agree on whether Kevin Quinn actually was Hampton's supervisor. They also disagreed on whether Hampton told Alderman Quinn that she didn't want his brother fired. "I would never say that," Hampton said.[17]

One of Hampton's desires was to work on the House District 5 campaign of a Democrat running for the House to replace Stratton, who was chosen as J. B. Pritzker's running mate. Hampton inquired and thought she had the job, but it went to someone else. She felt she had been blackballed, retaliated against for complaining about the harassment. She said she had spent her twenties working for the Madigan political organization and that her experience was "literally stolen from me." She said she wanted to "make sure they're not able to do this to anyone else."[18]

Walking into the chill winds of a February night after that first downtown interview, Hampton looked back over her shoulder, and Stacey Wescott snapped her most telling picture—one that would be worthy of a spot on the paper's front page. But as Stacey and I trudged northward across the Michigan Avenue bridge toward the Tribune Tower, the biggest issue hanging was not how quickly the story could be turned around. It was what else we needed to nail down before the story could be published. Hampton had made strong allegations. Her story sounded credible. Importantly, she had kept the text messages and let us copy them. But it all had to be strength tested. One question was how to get a response from Madigan's office. Typically tight-lipped, Madigan's team could play cat and mouse. Chasing down all of the pieces could take weeks. But fairness demanded getting the other side of the story. The first step—getting the interview, pictures, and video on the record—was complete. As I pored over my notes and then left the Tribune Tower at 1:15 a.m. on February 12, Michigan Avenue was silent, street sounds muffled by a blanket of snow. What would come next?

Within hours the story shifted into overdrive. An email arrived midmorning from Madigan's team. In a press release, the speaker issued a public statement that filled in the missing pieces and provided much of their side of the story. Madigan did not mention Hampton by name, but he let it be known that Kevin Quinn was out of the organization and his state job with the speaker because of improper behavior. "In November, a courageous woman made me aware that a high-ranking individual within my political operation had previously made unwanted advances and sent her inappropriate text messages," the statement said.[19] This had the feel of a classic example of the speaker getting ahead of a story he knew was coming, but Madigan aides said they did not know Hampton had spoken to the *Tribune*. Now, only hours after the Hampton interview, the prospects of telling a fuller version of the story changed almost immediately. Instead of wondering how long it would take to run the story to ground, the question became: How quickly could we get it done?

Madigan's statement explained that Wier Vaught had "conducted numerous interviews, reviewed the evidence and recently came to the conclusion that the individual engaged in inappropriate conduct and failed to exercise the professional judgment I expect of those affiliated with my political organizations and the office of the speaker."[20]

There was another factor involved in the decision to dump Kevin Quinn. Madigan pointed out that Quinn had recently pleaded guilty to misdemeanor disorderly conduct, an issue arising from a run-in with the wife he was divorcing. Madigan said he and Alderman Quinn "decided that Kevin should no longer be affiliated with the political organization."[21]

Madigan's Monday morning announcement moved instantly into a top spot in Chicago's competitive news cycle. Yet no news outlet—TV, radio, or newspapers—immediately mentioned Hampton's name. Like its competitors, the *Tribune* initially posted the basics on the internet. A team of reporters jumped in to track down Kevin Quinn's payments from Madigan-controlled political committees and other details. There was always a chance that a competitor could figure out Hampton's name, post it on a website at any time, and be first to tell her story. The *Tribune* now had the Hampton interview, the text messages, and Madigan's statement. Kevin Quinn was not responding to attempts to get his comments. By late Monday afternoon, another important piece of the equation came in: Hampton filed a complaint with the U.S. Equal Employment Opportunity Commission, including copies of the text messages. The *Tribune* got a copy, locking down more pieces of the puzzle. With allegations in the complaint aligning with the Hampton interview, the story could be tied together with context and detail. Once competitors' deadlines had passed, the *Tribune* rolled out video, photographs, and copies of Quinn's text messages along with the Hampton interview on its website. The Tuesday *Tribune* that landed on doorsteps presented an exclusive package, including Wescott's front-page photo of Hampton looking over her shoulder on Michigan Avenue.

Dueling press conferences quickly unfolded in Chicago and Springfield the day the story broke. In Chicago, Hampton stepped in front of a bank of microphones in a law firm's conference room packed with television cameras and reporters. She maintained there was a "cover-up," and when pressed about the people involved, she said "all of them."[22] At the state Capitol in Springfield, Madigan and Wier Vaught took questions. At age seventy-five, Madigan faced the generational issues of whether he had lost touch with what was happening in a world stirred by the #MeToo movement. Heavy criticism also came from Democratic candidates running for governor. Chris Kennedy, a scion of the iconic political clan, charged that Madigan should step down as the Democratic Party chair if he knew of the allegations and "chose to protect his machine political allies instead of the women who were abused by them." Senator Daniel Biss, an Evanston Democrat, said Madigan had been speaker for too long. Biss called the story "further evidence of the larger culture of misogyny that must be addressed and why the misuse of power and privilege must be stopped." Democratic candidate J. B. Pritzker, known for tempering his criticism of Madigan and now teamed with Stratton, stood by Hampton "in that fight" and called for a thorough investigation.[23]

The #MeToo reckoning signaled the beginning of a watershed moment for Madigan, a new challenge for the speaker to overcome. Madigan had no plans, of course, to relinquish the speakership or the party chairmanship. But by week's end he released a carefully crafted letter to House Democrats: "We must rethink the culture of politics if we are to move forward as an institution and as Democrats."[24]

The letter, along with missives to his party allies, would be reviewed carefully by Madigan's inner circle, a small cadre of top staffers, ex-staffers, and Mike McClain—the former ComEd lobbyist, ex-lawmaker, and longtime speaker pal. Their suggestions back and forth signified the seriousness of the moment. "We must provide a positive work environment free from any type of harassment, including sexual harassment and bullying. I recognize this starts at the top, which means it starts with me and with each of you," the Madigan letter said.

We cannot tolerate harassment or abuse of any kind. Every member, employee, contractor and intern is valued and necessary for the operation of the General Assembly, this caucus, and for the successful election of

Democratic candidates in Illinois. No one should be made to feel other-wise. Everyone has a right to work without fear of harassment, abuse or retaliation.

We haven't done enough. I take responsibility for that. I would never condone, sweep under the rug or refuse to take any step to ensure we did not eradicate any behavior of this kind.[25]

Madigan also referenced a phrase he had used before when telling people to knock off their bad behavior. "I understand the 'knock it off' mentality is not enough, and we must, and will, do better moving forward."[26]

Within two weeks, Madigan and Wier Vaught released a partial list of nine misconduct complaints the office had investigated in the previous five years. They involved harassment, sexual harassment, discrimination, and retaliation. Names were not given. The partial list did not include "un-resolved complaints" nor complaints tied to the speaker's political team. But Madigan's release of the list was unprecedented. The move sought to put him on higher ground than the other three legislative caucuses, none of which would follow up with their own lists. The nine included a female staffer who reported that a male staffer said he would ruin her career if she broke off their personal relationship. Another female on staff reported a lawmaker's inappropriate sexual comment. Still another incident involved inappropriate behavior of a lobbyist, who lost his job. Chicago Democratic Representative Kelly Cassidy, who pressed for an outside investigation into the speaker's state and political organizations, contended the nine complaints were "just the tip of the iceberg."[27]

The Hampton allegations would hang over the 2018 spring legisla-tive session. Shortly after Hampton went public, Madigan found himself jettisoning a top political lieutenant, Shaw Decremer, a former-staffer-turned-lobbyist, following a female lawmaker's allegations that he had abused his power as a Democratic volunteer while helping on legisla-tive campaigns. Though not accused of sexual harassment, Decremer allegedly engaged in "inappropriate behavior by a volunteer toward a candidate and staff."[28] Lawmakers spent countless hours negotiating over how to improve the laws dealing with sexual harassment; how to change the culture in Springfield; how to, as Madigan said, do better. But as the spring session hurtled to a close, the final two days provided the unusual kind of irony that happens in Illinois.

With one day left in the session, the Illinois House made history. After years of frustration, House lawmakers approved the long-delayed U.S.

Equal Rights Amendment (ERA), marking the first time both chambers voted for the national proposal in the same session, a landmark occasion decades in the making. Illinois is where Representative Thomas "Terrible Tommy" Hanrahan, a McHenry County Democrat with a carpenters' union background, gained notoriety in the 1970s when he condemned ERA advocates as "braless, brainless broads"; where then majority leader Madigan and Representative Corneal Davis, the chief sponsor and fellow Chicago Democrat, fell two votes short of passage during a 1978 arm-waving, shout-filled raucous roll call; where Wanda Brandstetter was convicted in 1980 of bribery over an unsuccessful offer of one thousand dollars to a lawmaker's campaign for a pro-ERA vote; and where ERA supporters squirted blood on the Capitol floor in front of Governor Jim Thompson's office when the amendment failed in 1982. And it's the state where anti-ERA icon Phyllis Schlafly led the opposition in the 1970s and 1980s and reemerged at an Illinois Senate committee hearing in 2003 with a clear warning: "I've come back."[29]

With the national #MeToo movement in full swing, Democratic Representative Lou Lang of Skokie grabbed the momentum and gave an impassioned plea to a House still divided. "It is never too late to give women the rights they ought to be due under the Constitution of the United States," Lang told colleagues. The state's long march to approving the ERA represented an achievement in determination as well as tardiness, but the often-mentioned argument that Illinois had missed the 1982 deadline to ratify the amendment was immaterial to elated supporters.[30] The House voted 72–45, a tally that included backing from a few Republicans whose votes were necessary to collect one more than the required three-fifths supermajority of seventy-one. The Senate already had approved the measure. So the House vote sparked pandemonium. Cameras captured knots of joyous lawmakers—many with Lang in the middle. At the time, only one more state was needed to reach the thirty-eight required to ratify the ERA nationwide—if the deadline ultimately is extended. At age sixty-eight, Lang had managed to reach a mountaintop moment. Virginia would become state thirty-eight in January 2020, queuing up the legal fight over the question of whether the Illinois and Virginia votes came too late and whether other states could rescind support.[31]

But Lang's exhilaration on the day of the ERA victory would be tempered. Waiting in the rotunda, I had questions on a different topic. The usually accessible Lang, who had dodged talking for hours, made a beeline across the marble floor to the speaker's suite of offices, saying "[he's] got a meeting right now." The timing was definitely awkward given his ERA success, but Lang attempted to cut off any inquiry. With the lawmaker about to slip behind the speaker's double wooden doors, I made it clear that a woman named Maryann Loncar might come out the next day with allegations that Lang had sexually harassed her. Lang said, "I have no comment about Maryann."[32] The next afternoon, on May 31, Lang would resign his coveted position on Madigan's leadership team. With television cameras rolling at a packed Capitol news conference, Loncar accused Lang of verbal abuse, "inappropriate behavior," and years of harassment.

With Rotheimer at her side, Loncar detailed her own complaints. She told reporters Lang had once placed a hand on her lower back and asked if her husband "knew how lucky he is to have a wife like you." She said Lang called her one night while she was out to dinner with family and told her that he would have joined her if she "weren't with her husband." She said she considered the touching and the dinner comments sexual harassment. But she said she did not report it. "Where was I going to go? Was I going to go to the speaker, who sits right next to Lou Lang?" she said. "Was I going to go to the ethics committee, with him sitting on it? Was I? Do any of you know what that feels like? To be humiliated? To not have anywhere to go?"[33]

Lang didn't wait for Loncar to finish. He lit up reporters' iPhones while Loncar was still talking. In an email statement, Lang said he would step down from his deputy majority leader role and give up his positions on a sensitive rules oversight panel and on the Legislative Ethics Commission, where the Madigan loyalist had once served as chair. Lang called on the legislative inspector general to investigate. He then held his own news conference with supporters crowded around him. "From beginning to end, the allegations are absurd," Lang said.[34]

Even so, Lang became the highest-ranking House lawmaker directly impacted by the new #MeToo atmosphere. Madigan responded with a statement that returned to the word "courage," the word he had used to address the Alaina Hampton matter. "I appreciate the courage it takes for individuals to come forward to share their experiences, and in doing so urge us all to do better," Madigan said.[35]

With pressure building, both houses approved legislation that, as explained in debate by House Majority Leader Barbara Currie, D-Chicago, "would allow the Legislative Inspector General to begin to initiate an investigation into claims of sexual harassment without the approval" of the Legislative Ethics Commission.[36] The legislation also made the auditor general the backup IG if the post remained vacant for more than six months, an attempt to avoid the paralyzing politics that had left the IG office inoperable and let complaints go unaddressed.[37]

In less than four months, Lang would declare himself "vindicated." Acting IG Julie Porter wrote to Lang: "Because a preponderance of evidence does not support Loncar's allegations that you engaged in misconduct, I am closing the matter." Porter said she tried to contact Loncar through email, mail, and Facebook, but Loncar "declined to respond to my overtures." In turn, Loncar echoed her fears about having no place to go where she thought she could get a fair shake. She issued a statement, calling the process a "joke."[38] Lang ran unopposed in the November election, winning a seventeenth term in the House. But he quit only days before he would have been sworn in for the new term and subsequently became a lobbyist.[39]

The Lang chapter served as a precursor to the swift ouster of Timothy Mapes, the man Madigan chose to be his chief of staff, clerk of the House, and executive director of the Illinois Democratic Party all at once. Less than a week after Lang resigned from Madigan's leadership team, Sherri Garrett stepped up to a microphone at a Chicago news conference and outlined a string of allegations that turned the establishment on its head.

Garrett worked with Mapes and for him. She helped with keeping track of the daily legislative action in a job known as a "minute clerk." Her duties included carrying the speaker's gavel to and from the podium during legislative session days. She made forty-two thousand dollars a year. But standing before a group of hard-edged Chicago reporters, the fifty-three-year-old woman from central Illinois had the aura of a person who had held back long enough. She accused Mapes of sexual harassment and a "culture of sexism, harassment and bullying that creates an extremely difficult working environment."[40]

Mapes had long flaunted his tight relationship with Madigan in ways big and small—to the point where he underscored his gatekeeper role for the speaker with a sign in his statehouse office that referenced the "Wizard of Oz." One political operative remembered it was pointed and direct: "Nobody gets in to see the wizard. Not nobody. Not no how."[41]

Calmly alleging a number of Mapes moments, Garrett told the news conference that she had "personally witnessed bullying and repeated harassment that was often sexual and sexist in nature." She alleged that Mapes had talked about her undergarments and made other comments that left her "stunned and uncomfortable." Garrett recounted once telling Mapes how Democratic Representative Ken Dunkin, while on the House floor, told her and another staffer he wanted to take both home to "see which of you will be the naughtiest." Garrett said she reported the incident, but Mapes's response "was that it would blow over." If left to Mapes's "sole discretion," she said, "the entire incident would have been swept under the rug."[42]

Only months after Alaina Hampton's revelations, Madigan acted quickly. In three short hours, Mapes was gone from his government jobs as clerk and chief of staff and his political post with the Madigan-run Illinois Democratic Party. Representative Cassidy, who had pressed for a full investigation into how the speaker dealt with sexual harassment and discrimination issues, showed up in support at the Garrett news conference. Cassidy later texted Garrett when they learned Mapes was out of power, "telling her what a badass she was today. . . . Just how strong."[43]

With pressure increasing, Madigan ordered an outside investigation of how he handled sexual harassment complaints, the workplace culture, and other issues. It took the heat off for only so long. The report wrapped up a year later, and Mapes received some of the harshest criticism in the 202-page probe led by Maggie Hickey, a former federal prosecutor and former state executive inspector general.

Hickey dispensed with Loncar's accusations against Lang in much the same way as the legislative IG did, saying there was "insufficient evidence to support" them. Loncar also chose not to cooperate with Hickey, Lang denied the allegations, and Hickey could not find corroboration for them in more than one hundred interviews during her overall investigation. "During her press conference, Ms. Loncar acknowledged that she was a neophyte in the political system, and many of her claims reflect that inexperience," Hickey wrote. "Ultimately, we did not find sufficient evidence to conclude that Ms. Loncar knowingly lied about her claims. Instead, we believe that it is more likely that she was wrong about her claims. While it is difficult to make this assessment without speaking to Ms. Loncar, Ms. Loncar had a right not to cooperate with the investigation, and her exercise of that right is not evidence that she lied."[44]

Hickey's investigation provided the added bonus of cracking open a door into the inner world of Madigan's government operations, where rank-and-file workers were discouraged from speaking freely, particularly to the press. Hickey interviewed the speaker himself along with more than a dozen Democratic lawmakers, more than eighty former staffers and other bureaucrats still on the payroll, as well as others involved in Illinois politics.

Hickey "found sufficient evidence to conclude" that Mapes did not discharge his duties as chief of staff and House clerk in a "courteous and efficient manner" when he made inappropriate comments to or around Garrett. Hickey chastised Mapes for mocking Garrett for "coming forward with serious concerns about potential sexual harassment." Garrett "no longer felt comfortable voicing her concerns about workplace harassment to him or others. This allowed Mr. Mapes's behavior to continue unchecked until Ms. Garrett's press conference, which led to the quick and unplanned resignation of Mr. Mapes."[45]

Hickey found criticism of Mapes's behavior was widely known. But his actions arose from a Capitol culture that never was held up as a paragon of political correctness: "People from across the Capitol workplace reported that they had witnessed or personally experienced what they described as inappropriate sexual conduct in the Capitol workplace. They described conduct that included inappropriate sexual comments and unwelcome sexual advances." But Hickey found "most workers across the speaker's office and across genders and positions said that they were more concerned with bullying than with inappropriate sexual conduct. What is more, the vast majority said that they would not have reported misconduct" under Mapes for several reasons.[46]

Mapes had served as Madigan's chief of staff since 1992, added the political role of executive director of the Madigan-run Democratic Party of Illinois in 1998, and added the role of House clerk in 2011. Hickey said that giving all of that power to Mapes had failed:

Mapes had discretion to affect their positions, opportunities, and benefits. In some cases, people believed that they were more replaceable than the subjects of their potential complaints. People were also concerned that making complaints would reflect negatively on them. Even though we identified only a few instances when the speaker's office terminated a worker's employment, workers commonly perceived that they could lose their jobs at any time and for any or no reason. In fact, most of the people interviewed—regardless of their views of Mr. Mapes—agreed that Mr. Mapes commonly threatened people's jobs or reminded them that they were dispensable. People believed that Mr. Mapes attempted to motivate workers through fear and that a few other supervisors throughout the years emulated this practice. Some people also raised the additional concern that, given Mr. Mapes's political ties, he could make or break their careers outside of the Speaker's office as well."[47]

Tim Mapes and Kevin Quinn would be criticized one more time in separate examinations. Carol Pope, the new legislative inspector general, issued reports in October 2019 recommending that the two Madigan aides should never be rehired as state employees or contractors. In her report, Pope reviewed how Quinn's text messages to Alaina Hampton became "increasingly personal." And when Quinn let her know he looked forward to working with her over the next two years, the report said, Hampton had a "panic attack."[48]

"Victims, like myself," Hampton wrote, "are shamed, labeled liars and considered by those in Speaker Madigan's organizations to be disloyal. In addition to being ostracized, we face retaliation and being blackballed while the perpetrators go unpunished and undeterred in their miscon-duct. For far too long in Illinois there has been no safe avenue, let alone any avenue, for redress. Hopefully now, in part because of this founded summary report, the systematic shaming of victims and the protection of powerful and high-ranking political operatives will end."[49]

Quinn filed a letter, where he apologized to Hampton; his wife, with whom he was in divorce proceedings; his former employer; and his former coworkers. "I take full responsibility for my behavior," Quinn said.[50] As for Garrett, Pope found her "entirely credible" and noted that she was "still traumatized by Mr. Mapes' inappropriate conduct over many years." Garrett retired before the report became public, but she "was trembling and emotionally wrought" when retelling the incidents, Pope reported.[51]

Mapes argued that Pope's decision should not be made public, con-tending in a letter from his attorney, James C. Pullos, that the "evidence of sexual harassment is grossly insufficient." He argued that the allegations in Pope's report "are baseless and untrue." Before going into a point-by-point rebuttal, Pullos argued that the longtime Madigan lieutenant handled issues

with a sense of urgency and always placed the needs of good government above all other concerns. It is undeniable that the many challenges fac-ing Illinois required hard work, determination and commitment. In his role as chief of staff, he held staff to the highest standards and demanded that staff members share these expectations to meet the many demands confronting our state on a daily basis. Mapes would not compromise his own expectations to improperly sexually harass Ms. Garrett. [Pope's] report improperly maligns Mapes' entire career with spurious allegations and disregards the honorable contributions that Mapes made on behalf of the state of Illinois.[52]

For his part, Madigan pointed to a package of sexual harassment legislation that further guards against harassment and discrimination to public- and private-sector workplaces statewide. "I have strengthened and improved protections for victims of harassment in both my office and across my political organizations," Madigan said in a statement. "These changes include instituting mandatory training on sexual harassment, intimidation, and other important workplace protections, and creating strong reporting mechanisms to report workplace complaints. I am committed to ensuring that anyone who reports a complaint is protected, they are treated fairly and that everyone has a safe and welcoming work environment."[53]

As Madigan addressed the Hickey report, however, the speaker and his political organization faced more questions about their way of doing business. Hampton had filed a suit in federal court alleging retaliation for reporting sexual harassment, a case that impacted his standing with anyone sympathetic to the plight of women working in and around government. One of Madigan's 2016 primary opponents alleged in another federal case that the speaker had placed sham candidates on the ballot to improve his chances of winning his House district. And the first signs of federal authorities taking an interest in Madigan began to surface.

12

UPS AND DOWNS

"We're not interested in a quick killing
here. We're interested in a long-term
relationship."
—Speaker Michael Madigan, May 2014

Going into 2019, Speaker Madigan was on top of his political world—
unaware of how much federal cases would shake the Democratic old
guard and, by extension, the speaker himself. After all, his nemesis, Republican Governor Bruce Rauner, had been swept out of office by billionaire Democrat J. B. Pritzker in the 2018 election, ending what the
speaker called an "epic struggle."[1] The House and the Senate remained
in Democratic hands. In fact, Madigan's House Democratic caucus held
a modern-day record 74–44 majority over Republicans. Madigan could
focus on building a good record for Democrats to run on as they sought
to undo the damage of a two-year budget stalemate with Rauner, start
to right the state's finances with money pouring in from the income tax
hike the speaker had cobbled together with Republican help, and, most
importantly, set his sights on the 2020 races. With Democrats in charge
of the governor's office and both chambers, Madigan only had to hang
on to the House and Senate in the 2020 elections. That way the speaker
could walk into the 2021 redistricting year while in control of everything
he needed to draw district boundaries that would favor Democrats up
to the 2032 elections. House and Senate Democrats could tweak their
district maps to ensure success, and the Democratic governor could sign
whatever they sent.

Most folks would see that as a pretty awesome way to start the new year, but Madigan was not one to let go of his bad memories from the Rauner years. The speaker delivered a good-riddance farewell during his inaugural speech to the newly sworn lawmakers. "Four long years of character assassination," Madigan said. "Four long years of personal vilification. Four long years of strident negotiating positions, also known as 'my way or the highway.'"[2] Rauner had pounded Madigan mercilessly, using a combination of the governor's bully pulpit and tens of millions of dollars in negative ads in hopes of undermining the speaker and driving Illinois into a right-to-work mentality and an antiunion state of mind. Madigan wouldn't let that happen. He had withstood the drip, drip, drip from the multitude of anti-Madigan ads, and he looked unconcerned that each drop might wear down his speakership like water pouring steadily on a rock. As Madigan stood on top of it all, he basked in victory. He looked at the new class of lawmakers and sought to use the Rauner years as a teaching moment. "Some might say, as we put an end to these last four years, 'Let's just close the book,'" Madigan said. "As we do move beyond these last four years, let's not just talk in terms of closing the book. Rather, let's think in terms of closing one chapter of the book, [and] take lessons from that chapter so we can move to a new chapter where people work with people."[3]

Working together should generally be a lot easier when your own party holds the governorship and majorities in the House and the Senate. That's not always the case, given how Madigan and other Democrats clashed with Dan Walker and Rod Blagojevich—two Democratic governors who eventually went to prison—and Pat Quinn, whose populist style consistently rubbed Madigan the wrong way. Pritzker's even-keel approach to legislative relations changed the political dynamics overnight. He lifted political roadblocks that had stymied key initiatives for years.

Madigan and Senate President John Cullerton quickly queued up a pro-worker victory for Pritzker. With only dwindling numbers of Republicans left to resist, the two Democratic leaders rushed through a hike in the state's $8.25-an-hour minimum wage. The Madigan-Cullerton juggernaut passed legislation to gradually increase the minimum to $15, and Pritzker, who called increasing the wage a priority, happily signed it. That launched a spring session lovefest with Pritzker, one that Madigan was happy to embrace and one that Cullerton stuck around to enjoy before making a surprise announcement in the fall that he would retire. They approved recreational marijuana, sports betting, and an expansion of casinos, including one for Chicago. They approved Pritzker's proposed constitutional amendment that was meant to allow the state to move from a flat-rate income tax to a graduated rate that would hit people with the biggest paychecks the hardest, setting up a contentious 2020 question for voters—a gamble they did not know would fail miserably once voters weighed in. And they approved the granddaddy of all pork-barrel bonanzas—a $45 billion construction program. There were big dollars for highways, bridges, and public transportation supported by higher state gas taxes and license plate fees.

A long list of other projects would be fueled by new money from the casino expansion, the new sports betting proceeds, and increased taxes on parking, smoking, and video poker. There was cash for goodies like baseball fields, pickleball courts, and dog parks. As usual, the speaker did more than okay: He secured $50 million for the Illinois Arts Council, which is chaired by his wife, Shirley. He scored $98 million in transportation-related funding to muffle intensely loud screeching sounds emanating from a Belt Railway Yard in Bedford Park. And he supported $31 million to build the Academy for Global Citizenship, a charter school in the district of freshman Democratic Representative Aaron Ortiz of Chicago, who had knocked out Representative Dan Burke, the brother of Fourteenth Ward Alderman Edward Burke.[4]

Yes, that spring of 2019 was a nice run for Democrats. Republicans even won a few business breaks. They all were happy that the Rauner-Madigan wars were over. But as this new era of good feelings took hold in Springfield, the federal courthouse in Chicago was filled with activity. And the more the FBI dug in, the more they provided another inside look at the biggest names among ruling Democratic regulars in the city of Chicago, including some of Madigan's well-known political allies.

Revving up at the beginning of the year, federal authorities filed the very first criminal complaint in January 2019 against Ed Burke, the dean of the City Council, whose ward neighbors Madigan's territory. Federal prosecutors would start building cases in ways once thought unfathomable. Burke, married to Illinois Supreme Court Chief Justice Anne Burke, faced a federal charge over two-bit shakedowns, the kind of allegations people wouldn't expect from a guy who wore dark pinstripe suits with flashy handkerchiefs stuffed in his breast pocket. He carried himself as if he were a cut above the dozens of colleagues he'd seen carted off to prison over his half century in office. The charges he faced officially alleged attempted extortion, but the details were pure Chicago.

Burke allegedly tried to pressure executives of a fast-food restaurant—a Burger King in his ward—to send his law firm their property tax business. He allegedly played hardball on city permits the restaurant needed in order to renovate. Prosecutors said Burke put in a stop-work order and sent a city inspector to issue tickets for failing to get a city permit for work on the Burger King driveway—even though that permit had been issued already. Burke, the complaint said, wanted assurances that the law business was coming his way before "we can expedite your permits." In a December 2017 meeting with two executives, Burke allegedly suggested they "get involved with other politicians in Chicago." Maybe that's a reasonable idea in Chicago's political universe, but Burke's proposal came with major political ramifications for Cook County Board President Toni Preckwinkle's 2019 race for mayor.[5]

Preckwinkle's political troubles had been telegraphed when federal authorities raided Burke's City Hall and ward offices on November 29, 2018, only weeks after she won her third term as county board president.[6] Preckwinkle scrambled to cleanse her campaign fund of nearly thirteen thousand dollars in Burke donations. She sent an equivalent amount to charities.[7] But when the feds added an attempted extortion count to Burke's case, Preckwinkle suffered even more. The charge alleged that Burke had squeezed one of the fast-food executives into giving ten thousand dollars to Preckwinkle's campaign fund. Compounding matters was that Preckwinkle had to amend her campaign reports. Her political fund had rejected the executive's ten-thousand-dollar donation because the amount was over the fifty-six-hundred-dollar limit for an individual, but her campaign didn't record the action properly. Struggling to gain attention in her own run for mayor, Lori Lightfoot seized the opportunity to highlight her anticorruption background as a federal prosecutor. "I think she's got to answer to the voters what exactly is the relationship between her and Ed Burke. Ed Burke never does anything without expecting a quid pro quo. He's a cunning and strategic person," Lightfoot said. "The fact he decided he was going to, as alleged in the complaint, strong-arm and extort a contribution for her said there's some kind of relationship, and he wanted to get something out of it. She's got to explain, what is the quid pro quo?"[8]

Lightfoot and other candidates further hounded Preckwinkle for refusing to give up $116,000 that she'd received during a fund-raiser at

Burke's house a year earlier, and Preckwinkle vowed to give it all back.[9] Her troubles then began to multiply. The *Tribune* broke a story that Preckwinkle had given Burke's son a six-figure county job when the younger Burke was under investigation while working for Sheriff Tom Dart. She faced increasing pressure to take action. Using her power as head of the Cook County Democratic Party, Preckwinkle ousted Ed Burke from his coveted chair of the party's judicial slating committee and demanded—unsuccessfully—that he resign from his posts as both Fourteenth Ward committeeman and alderman. She never completely recovered from the political damage before the mayoral election, eventually losing to Lightfoot in an April runoff. Burke won reelection to the City Council but later lost his post as Democratic committeeman.[10]

January 2019 did not close out quietly for Democratic regulars, courtesy of the *Sun-Times* and an extraordinary scoop involving Twenty-Fifth Ward Alderman Danny Solis, the City Council's zoning committee chair. Armed with what was supposed to be a sealed affidavit in support of getting a search warrant for Solis's property and offices, *Sun-Times* reporters Jon Seidel, Fran Spielman, Mark Brown, and Tim Novak told of how Solis spent more than two years cooperating in a federal investigation, including helping to record conversations with Burke. Salacious details poured out about Solis, that he was "deeply in debt and routinely on the prowl for sex, Viagra, campaign contributions and other favors." They quoted him as saying he liked Asian women and that he wanted a "good massage, with a nice ending."[11] Suddenly it became clear to everyone why Solis had announced a few weeks earlier that he was not seeking reelection. But once readers absorbed the details of Solis's sordid behavior, one more item drew everyone's attention: The feds had secretly recorded Michael Madigan.[12]

The mere mention that the cautious Madigan would be caught on a federal recording was enough to give highly competitive Chicago reporters at other news outlets a jolt, first kicking themselves for not having the story and then jumping into the fray to try to find new angles. The affidavit, written by FBI Special Agent Steven D. Noldin, offered his interpretation: "Solis has agreed to take action in his official capacity as an alderman for private benefits directed to Michael Madigan."[13] But the Madigan Mystique carried the story only so far. When the story broke, the recording of Madigan was nearly five years old. It was from August 2014. Madigan had hosted a meeting in his law office, the headquarters of his tax appeals business. Solis was there with a developer who represented a Chinese businessman also at the meeting. The businessman was attempting to have property in Chicago's Chinatown rezoned to allow for construction of a hotel. The developer would be revealed later as See Y. Wong, who wore the wire that captured Madigan.[14] Caught up in his own fraud scheme, Wong had started cooperating with federal authorities in May 2014 hoping to minimize potential punishment for alleged crimes that included lying to banks. Wong agreed to record Solis and, later, Solis and Madigan in the speaker's downtown private law office, according to a federal affidavit. Court records showed Madigan made a pitch for having his specialized property tax law firm represent the hotel in Chinatown—and other projects as well. "We're not interested in a quick killing here," Madigan allegedly said. "We're interested in a long-term relationship."[15]

As the meeting broke up, the affidavit said, Wong snapped pictures of the Chinese businessman, Madigan, and Solis. Madigan and Solis then allegedly met privately for four minutes. After leaving the office, the affidavit said, Wong told Solis the Chinese man would love to give the business to the speaker but the zoning change was "very critical." Solis replied, "Well, if he works with the speaker, he will get anything he needs for that hotel." Wong thanked Solis, who responded, "And he's going to benefit from being with the speaker . . . okay?" The federal agent, in his affidavit, interpreted that to mean that "by hiring Madigan's private firm," the Chinese businessman would "ensure that Solis and Madigan would take official action benefiting" the Chinese businessman "in their capacity as public officials." Wong told Solis that he would be going to a fund-raiser for the alderman on behalf of the Chinese businessman, who had "sent in money to be a vice chair" of the event. At the fund-raiser, Wong then provided a twenty-five-hundred-dollar check written by the businessman. Solis would oversee the zoning committee meeting that approved the zoning change.[16]

In the end, though, Noldin's affidavit, which was filed in May 2016, said there had been no agreement signed to hire Madigan's firm. Further, the hotel project did not move forward. As a result, the speaker's actions outlined in the affidavit looked to be intriguing, but it was hard to tell at that time if it were any more than that. Madigan's attorney, Heather Wier Vaught, said in a statement to the *Sun-Times*, "The speaker recalls attending several meetings with Ald. Solis over the past five years, including meetings with individuals in need of legal representation. If, indeed, some of his conversations were being recorded, the speaker did not know that, but he has no concern if they were. The speaker has no recollection of ever suggesting that he would take official action for a private law firm client or potential client. To our knowledge, neither the speaker nor his law firm is under investigation."[17]

As the *Sun-Times* stories began to hit, a polar vortex descended on Chicago. The *Tribune* and every other news outlet struggled to catch up. The affidavit, discovered in an open court file, had been sealed back up as soon as authorities knew it had been accidentally accessible long enough for the *Sun-Times* to grab it. Before persuading a federal court to reopen the file, the *Tribune* was forced to rely on its own sources and cite the *Sun-Times* to play catch-up. It's not a position any newspaper wants to be in against a direct competitor. *Tribune* reporters reminded readers that the Madigan disclosure spotlighted how he often danced around the intersection of his dual roles as speaker of the Illinois House and a major private tax appeals lawyer. Madigan always maintained he followed a strict personal code of ethics to avoid conflicts of interest.

The speaker had survived a variety of probes in the past, such as the state investigation into patronage hiring at Metra and federal allegations into mixing politics and state business. One federal investigation, for example, looked into three of the four legislative caucuses, including House Democrats, over allegations of paying government salaries to staffers doing political work in the 2000 campaign. But the only staffer from either side of the aisle who went to prison was Mike Tristano, the chief of staff to House Republican leader Lee Daniels of Elmhurst.[18] Madigan's team was cleared.

As the *Sun-Times* headed toward the end of the month rightly celebrating its hefty scoops, the polar vortex hit the deep freeze on January 31. The temperature fell to minus 21 degrees and the windchill dropped to minus 41. But while most of Chicago stayed home, the *Tribune* stayed the course and came back with its own major Madigan story online. The *Tribune* disclosed a set of depositions that gave readers one more inside-looking-out view of Madigan's secretive political machine. The centerpiece of the story was in what Madigan said was the first deposition he had ever given. The story delved into a lawsuit charging that Madigan and his political team had put up a couple of fake candidates to divide the anti-Madigan vote with a more serious challenger in the 2016 primary election.

As an old-school print guy, it irked me that we popped the story online shortly after noon on the day before it came out in the print version of the paper. The world of newspaper journalism is focused more and more on breaking news online rather than rolling out a major print story in the paper at the same time it hits the internet. The theory is that more people end up reading it, which is great, but it also gives the competition a chance to catch up faster by grabbing a piece of a story that took us weeks to put together.

The *Sun-Times* gave chase immediately after the *Tribune* story went online, allowing them to recover enough of the story that both newspapers had Madigan on their front pages the next day. The early release of the *Tribune* story, though, gave a glimpse into the logic of breaking news online. With most Chicagoans at home checking their computers and iPhones for cold-weather updates, the *Tribune* newsroom monitors that tracked which stories people were reading lit up immediately. The Madigan package, supplemented with numerous depositions from political operatives in his organization, became the most-read story on the *Tribune*'s website, and other news outlets started to cite the story we broke.[19] Madigan would stay the hottest topic in town.

13

SHAMS?

"We viewed this as a Republican Rauner
invasion of the Democrat primary."
—Speaker Michael Madigan,
September 13, 2018

In Chicago's Thirteenth Ward, which he'd controlled for half a century,
Speaker Michael Madigan should not have needed to worry about reelection to his Southwest Side district in the Illinois House. His precinct captains came off as almost fanatical about hitting the streets, knocking on
doors, working year-round to keep the king on the throne. He ran the
ward as much like a machine as Richard J. Daley would expect of his greatest disciple. But Madigan's 2016 primary race showed signs of a powerful
politician whose desire to win is aggressively and meticulously balanced by
making sure he does not lose. So state Representative Michael Madigan,
the record-setting boss of the Thirteenth Ward, boss of the Illinois Democratic Party, and boss of the Illinois House, demonstrated in the March
2016 Democratic primary that his organization was not one to take chances
when it came to tending to the most basic piece of his power base: his own
seat in the House of Representatives.

Madigan won that primary race with 65 percent of the vote, to no one's
surprise, but *how* he won became the heart of a federal lawsuit filed by
one of his challengers, Jason Gonzales, a political neophyte. When the
Tribune rolled out a veritable autopsy of that 2016 race on the paper's
website on January 31, 2019, it became a coda to Madigan's month of
political ups and downs.

The unusual cache of depositions arising from the lawsuit provided one of the rarest in-depth looks at a powerful big-city Democrat's political operations—a perspective from insiders who normally would never speak publicly about internal secrets. They also showed the extent to which the organization would go to avoid giving up too much information. Numerous depositions depicted lawyers and witnesses parrying over that ever-elusive question of how the speaker conducted his campaign. After the seventy-six-year-old Madigan swore to tell the truth, he confirmed that the September 13, 2018, deposition at a downtown law office was the first he had ever given—a noted accomplishment for a politician so intrinsically a part of state government but so practiced at keeping his fingerprints hidden. In many ways the question-and-answer session was classic Madigan: precise at times, vague at others; flashes of dry wit, signs of lingering resentment; tactical, careful, tight-lipped. "Taciturn" was an apt word an editor slipped into the copy to describe the speaker.[1] Despite his reputation for having a long memory, as the *Tribune* story noted, Madigan answered questions more than one hundred times with short phrases: "I don't recall," "I don't remember," "I don't know," and "I have no memory."[2]

Key to understanding Madigan's answers is reviewing the disdain he held for Rauner, whose time as chief executive already was fading fast when the speaker sat for his deposition. Less than two months before the November 2018 election, Rauner clearly looked like he would lose his reelection campaign against Madigan's man, Democratic billionaire J. B. Pritzker. But Madigan blamed the governor for putting Gonzales up against the speaker in his 2016 primary. "We viewed this as a Republican Rauner invasion of the Democratic primary," Madigan testified. Rauner and Gonzales both denied it, but the speaker called the race a "choice between Mike Madigan and Governor Rauner's surrogate."[3] Several Rauner contributors gave to Gonzales, ranging from the conservative Illinois Opportunity Project to Blair Hull, who had lost a 2004 Democratic primary for U.S. Senate to Barack Obama, who was then a state senator from the South Side. Hull had clashed with Madigan over the years. Gonzales said Hull also helped pay the legal bills for his lawyer, Tony Peraica, a former Republican Cook County commissioner.[4] Kent Redfield, the retired university professor who is also an Illinois campaign finance expert, noted that Hull was the primary source of $873,000 in independent expenditures from a committee called Illinois United for Change. That lends credence,

Redfield said, to Madigan's concern about Rauner trying to influence the speaker's House district race.[5]

Madigan buttressed his suspicions of a Republican invasion with a story about an early but disturbing tête-à-tête he had with Rauner, one that took place in February 2015 at the Executive Mansion only weeks after Rauner's inauguration.[6] Rauner outlined what he called the "Turnaround Agenda." He sought probusiness items such as limits on lawsuit awards, cheaper workers' compensation, and a local property tax freeze without a politically workable plan to make up for revenues lost. He also wanted antiunion measures such as abolishing a state law that mandates "prevailing" wages for construction workers on public works projects, and enacting right-to-work legislation that would ban union contracts from requiring covered workers to help pay union representation costs.[7]

As a starting point, he planned to encourage local governments, like counties and cities, to become "right-to-work" zones, an idea that Attorney General Lisa Madigan determined would run afoul of federal law.[8] Two other major items on Rauner's list effectively took aim at the nation's longest-tenured speaker: term limits for lawmakers and statewide elected officials, and changes in the highly partisan way legislative districts are redrawn every ten years—the redistricting process that Madigan had mastered.[9]

Rauner's top-down business approach, where the CEO dictates policy, did not sit well with the speaker. Rauner's tactic might have worked in states where Republicans ruled both chambers but not in Illinois, where both houses held strong Democratic majorities. Not in the state where the 1886 Haymarket Riot and the Pullman strike of 1894 still echo in the streets of Chicago. And not in a state where Madigan repeatedly had driven home the point that the General Assembly is a "co-equal" branch of government that will not take orders from the executive branch. Madigan recalled that he was unimpressed with Rauner's Turnaround Agenda. "I told him I wasn't going to support it," Madigan said in his deposition. "So you know what he said to me? 'Well, if you don't support my agenda, I'm just going to come after you,' and it was only a few weeks later that they spent $1 million on downstate TV defaming me. So if you're concerned about nastiness in politics, why don't you go over and talk to Bruce Rauner?"[10]

Madigan may have thought Rauner's remarks at the Executive Mansion extended beyond Springfield legislative issues and that the governor wanted to "go after" the speaker in his primary race. "I was concerned with all the money that Bruce Rauner was going to bring into the election, that's what I was concerned with," Madigan testified. Since that early run-in with the governor, the animosity between the two had grown. During the two-year budget stalemate, the governor had blanketed the state with TV ads attempting to drag down Madigan along with any Democratic candidates they could tie to him. Madigan testified he believed Rauner's plans in 2016 were to "employ the methods we are now familiar with to discredit me, in effect, defame me and my family name, including my daughter, the attorney general."[11]

In Jason Gonzales, Madigan had an opponent who was far from a typical challenger, from his resume on down to his chaotic home life growing up. Gonzales testified he had lived in the Little Village area of Chicago, moved with his family to Carpentersville, and went to schools in Barrington. His lawsuit said he had experienced behavioral disorders and had trouble in school. At seventeen he left home and told his father, "You will not make me miserable," the suit said. As a teen, he said, he spent seventy-one days behind bars for crimes involving forgery and illegal use of a credit card. Yet, he said, he still went on to garner degrees from Duke, MIT, and Harvard. In the waning hours of Governor Pat Quinn's administration, Gonzales secured a pardon for his convictions. But high-level degrees and a pardon from a governor are one thing. Taking on the speaker of the House when a challenger can be easily attacked is difficult to overcome.[12]

When Gonzales moved into Madigan's district in the last half of 2014, he landed in a world where he had not lived before. He had cousins, aunts, and uncles who had been there for thirty years, according to his deposition. But Madigan had been controlling a loyal crew of foot soldiers in his Southwest Side enclave since he seized the powerful committeeman post in July 1969. Madigan drew the legislative district in 2011 with a roughly 60 percent Hispanic population that had steadily increased, but he testified he has "broad and deep support among Hispanic voters. I live in a Hispanic neighborhood. I know my neighbors. I know how they feel about me."[13]

Gonzales saw the Hispanic demographics as an opportunity. "I looked for a Hispanic community where I felt I could be a leader and also a Hispanic community that I felt had been underrepresented, and that area happened to be the 22nd District of Illinois," Gonzales testified. "I decided on a district that I felt I could actually win based on the numbers." Madigan attorney Adam Vaught (who is married to Heather Wier Vaught, the speaker's former top lawyer in the House) pressed Gonzales about his motive for running against Madigan. Why not move into another district instead of taking on the speaker of the House? Gonzales said that picking a different district "wasn't worth it. . . . I didn't want to go into [the] state legislature and be beholden to Michael Madigan. Had I gone in for any other race and won, I wouldn't be free. I wouldn't be free to represent the interest of my people. I would basically be beholden to him, and that's one thing I knew I didn't want."[14]

Following Vaught, Madigan's longtime attorney Michael Kasper brought out the closest thing to a surprise. Insiders knew it, but Kasper drew out a rarely cited footnote: Gonzales acknowledged that he had walked into the Thirteenth Ward headquarters only about a week before he filed the paperwork in Springfield.

"I was considering dropping out of the race," Gonzales testified.

"In fact," Kasper said, "you told them you weren't going to run, didn't you?"

"My words to them were, 'I don't think I'm going to do this,'" Gonzales recalled. "And that's all I said, and, yeah, that was it."

"Why did you do that?" Kasper asked.

"Well, it was a number of things," Gonzales said, "but what really was bothering me at the time was the daunting task of taking on Michael Madigan. What could happen? Would my safety be in jeopardy? Would my livelihood be in jeopardy? I mean, really it was a risk-reward calculation. Did I have the support that I needed? And I didn't know if I did or not because, really, my campaign was launched on a shoestring. I mean, I had to loan my own campaign money in order to get it started. So I was at the point where I was going to withdraw."[15]

What made Gonzales go ahead? "I had some personal reckonings with myself and my goals, and I basically decided that I really had nothing to lose. But if I could win, which I believe I could have won, here would be obviously, a payoff. . . . As much as I don't want to do this, as much as I'm afraid to do it, I need to face my fears, and I need to step out and take a risk. If I fall on my face, I fall on my face."[16]

When he traveled to Springfield to file his paperwork to get on the 2016 Democratic primary ballot, Gonzales knew Madigan was the only candidate who had already filed in the race. Gonzales arrived at the State

Board of Elections a little before the 5:00 p.m. deadline in late November. The popular thought is that candidates like their names to be listed either first or last on a ballot. The rule of thumb is that those spots are worth a couple of extra percentage points over candidates whose names appear in between. Gonzales said he noticed Shaw Decremer, a former Madigan House-staffer-turned-lobbyist, hanging around the election office. Decremer was still on good paper before Madigan booted him from his organization during the next election cycle. As Gonzales prepared to file, Decremer spotted him. Gonzales saw Decremer grab a couple of bankers boxes, leave the room, make a phone call, and return with nominating petitions in hand. Gonzales recalled Decremer saying he thought Gonzales wasn't running. "I changed my mind," Gonzales said. As the clock ticked toward 5:00 p.m., Gonzales went over to see if any other candidates had filed in the race against Madigan. Gonzales still recalled an election board staffer's response: "'Yeah, there's two candidates that were just filed right after yours.'"[17]

With those words, the March 2016 Democratic primary took on new dimensions. Gonzales would argue during his campaign that the two last-minute candidates were shams—two people whom, he charged, were recruited by Madigan to draw votes from Gonzales, who saw himself as the only legitimate challenger. To well-seasoned Chicago voters, sham candidates are part of the fabric of elections. The idea that Madigan would have a sham or two running in his race produced more shrugs than outrage in a city that had seen it all. Madigan and other legislators had been accused of putting up shams in previous races. But what was most unusual this time is that somebody would make a federal case out of it. Five months after he lost the primary, Gonzales went to court with a long-shot theory. He wasn't trying to overturn the primary results. But he alleged the two extra candidates, who had Hispanic-sounding names, were indeed shams put up by Team Madigan to divide the Hispanic vote. Gonzales argued that diluting the vote represented a voting rights violation.[18]

As the depositions unfolded, Shaw Decremer acknowledged he had hauled to Springfield the nominating petitions for the two additional candidates in the race: Grasiela Rodriguez, a dispatcher for a ready-mix truck company, and Joe Barboza, a union construction laborer. Peraica, the Gonzales lawyer, pressed Decremer on why a Madigan loyalist would be handling paperwork for candidates who would challenge the boss:

"Why would you be bringing Grasiela Rodriguez's petitions—who is an opponent of Michael Madigan—to file for her?"

"Because someone asked me to," Decremer said.

"Who?" Peraica asked.

"I don't know. I don't recall," Decremer said.

Decremer also testified that he did not actually file the Rodriguez and Gonzales petitions.

"Who filed them?" Peraica asked.

"I don't recall," Decremer said.

Pressing Decremer, Peraica asked if the Madigan operative worried that people would see him as a "turncoat" for helping Madigan's opponents. Decremer answered, "No."[19]

When Peraica quizzed Madigan, the speaker acknowledged that his odds improve with more people in the race. "I study returns," Madigan said, "and you know that in my case, for certain, not every applicant for a ballot in the Democratic primary is going to vote for me. And, therefore, in a primary election it's advantageous to me to have multiple candidates."

Multiple Hispanic candidates? Peraica asked.

"Not Hispanic, just multiple candidates," Madigan said.[20]

Hoping to show a pattern, Peraica confirmed with Rodriguez that her husband, Mike, had run against Madigan in 2012. In that race, Madigan's major competition was twenty-five-year-old Michele Piszczor, who contended that she was the only "legitimate candidate" running against the speaker and standing up against the machine.[21] She did better than Mike Rodriguez and a fourth candidate, Olivia Trejo, but Madigan crushed them all with about 75 percent of the vote. At a suburban Bedford Park Holiday Inn, Madigan declared victory and commended his troops, saying, "We ran a real strong campaign."[22] Piszczor had received financial backing and support from conservative Republican businessman Jack Roeser, but she denied political allegations that she was a GOP plant.[23] "These rats are ruining the state," Roeser told WTTW-TV. "It's Madigan, he's the genius who screwed the whole thing up. I'll do every damn thing to help her that I can."[24]

In his deposition, Madigan had his own assessment: "2012 was another Republican invasion of the Democratic primary." The suggestion gave Peraica a chance to explore why one Rodriguez would run against Madigan in 2012 and the other in 2016. So Peraica asked the speaker if he knew the Rodriguezes had put a Madigan campaign sign in their front yard in 2016. Madigan's response was short: "I didn't know that."[25]

Peraica pushed for clarity from Grasiela Rodriguez. In her deposition, she acknowledged that beating the speaker would be difficult, but, she said, she believed she could defeat him: "I was motivated." Rodriguez said she sought help from Jennifer Solski in collecting signatures on nominating petitions that would be filed at the board of elections. She said she knew Solski from a neighborhood diner not far from Madigan's headquarters.[26] Solski, a precinct captain who Madigan said worked on constituent services in the ward, testified that she knew Rodriguez from passing out literature. But when asked if Rodriguez ever sought advice on how to run for office, Solski said, "I don't recall."[27]

As Grasiela Rodriguez defended her own case as a legitimate candidate in the 2016 primary, Peraica dug in. He sought to see what she knew about her own campaign. She answered that she didn't know two key people who collected signatures on her nominating petitions.[28] One of the circulators said he didn't know how his name got on her petitions. The other, Joseph Nasella, played so hard to get that a federal judge ordered U.S. marshals to go and find him. For months he had avoided process servers in Hammond, Indiana; Lansing, Illinois; and his mother's residence in Chicago's Tenth Ward. When he finally sat for his deposition, Nasella didn't give it up easily, stiff-arming lawyers even on basic questions about his life: "Where I live and who I f— is my business." Nasella is a mechanic. His work and political life have been through many highs and lows, including time spent with the Cicero Voters Alliance and the now-defunct Hispanic Democratic Organization, which tanked when the feds exposed a city job-rigging scandal—the one in which "Madigan Electric" received a cursory mention in court. He was terminated from a fleet management job at the city of Chicago in 2008, getting marked down in personnel files as a "discharge for cause." He wound up at a job in Cicero but said he left when he couldn't stand working for his supervisor. He later wandered into the Thirteenth Ward headquarters, where he asked Kevin Quinn, the alderman's brother, about getting into Madigan's operation. "I inquired, I knocked on the door, and I sold myself," Nasella said. Once in, Nasella recalled registering voters, canvassing, collecting signatures on petitions, and an array of political odds and ends. He spent time inside the Madigan headquarters, though the boss, not surprisingly, spoke very little. "Hello. Good morning. That's it. He was pretty tight-lipped," Nasclla said.[29]

In his own deposition, Madigan said he did not know Nasella and could not remember meeting him—again not unusual for a speaker who did not make it a daily habit to mingle with the rank-and-file troops. "If he were to walk in the room," Madigan testified, "I wouldn't recognize the guy."[30]

Nasella remembered one question in particular one day from Kevin Quinn. "It was strange," Nasella said. He explained that Quinn asked him to go out and collect signatures on nomination petitions for Grasiela Rodriguez. The request came complete with tools of the trade: a "walk list" of places to go for signatures and a clipboard. Curious about the game plan, Nasella had a question for Quinn: Why would the speaker's team want to collect signatures for a candidate running against Madigan for his own House district seat? "I couldn't get looked in the eye," Nasella said, saying Quinn responded with a "poker face." So Nasella did what was asked of him. Two months after Madigan's primary win, Nasella said, he got a job "in most likelihood" with the help of Kevin Quinn at an office run by Secretary of State Jesse White, a longtime Madigan ally. Nasella said he later got a job at a state park, which is overseen by the governor's office, but he said no one pulled any strings for him. As Nasella put it, "I didn't have no yank."[31]

Peraica and Stephen Boulton, a second Gonzales lawyer, wanted mysteries cleared up about two others involved in collecting signatures on nominating petitions for Rodriguez. One was sixty-two-year-old Michael Kuba, who testified that he read at a sixth-grade level. Kuba signed numerous petitions as the official "circulator." The man who accompanied Kuba was Eugene Pagois, who testified that he had been a Madigan precinct captain since 2012. Records showed Pagois had worked on Madigan's House staff, for the secretary of state, and at McCormick Place, where in 2018 he made $156,594. He also testified he is related to the late senator Frank Savickas, whose district once overlapped with Madigan's House district. The depositions showed that Kuba had once lived in Pagois's home. What Peraica and Boulton alleged is that Pagois took the lead on collecting signatures even though Kuba signed the petitions. The two attorneys alleged the move was done to obscure Pagois's ties to Madigan. But Vaught disagreed. He argued in a court hearing that Pagois helped out with collecting signatures because he realized that Kuba is "probably not the guy to go door to door." Kuba's own deposition raised doubts about his role. He testified he went with Pagois "to be a spotter to make sure it's not forged signatures." Kuba further testified, "I didn't do the talking." Instead, he said, "Gene did at the doors, you know, when we go see the people." Boulton seized on the Kuba remarks during Pagois's deposition, questioning why he had Kuba with him as they went door to door.[32]

"Because he was helping me," Pagois said.

Boulton pushed Pagois, asking, "Well, you were the precinct captain, and you were the one doing a lot of the talking; why did [Kuba] sign as the circulator and not you?"

"Because he was with me," Pagois testified.

"Why didn't you sign them?" Boulton asked.

"Just the way it turned out," Pagois said.[33]

Kevin Quinn also had a cameo in the candidacy of Joe Barboza, the other candidate who Gonzalez alleged to be a sham. Quinn testified that he had met Barboza at a Thirteenth Ward event. Quinn said his brother, Alderman Marty Quinn, green-lighted getting in touch with Charlie Hernandez, a longtime Cicero politician married to one of Madigan's House Democrats. "I had asked Charlie to see if Joe would be interested in running as a Democrat," Kevin Quinn testified. He said he never heard back. Madigan also remembered a "very short" conversation with Hernandez about Barboza and Gonzales. But the speaker said he did not ask Hernandez to ask Barboza about running. In his own deposition, Barboza testified that neither Madigan nor his associates asked him to run. Barboza said he decided to run after talking to friends in his neighborhood.[34]

Seeking a breakthrough, Peraica peppered Madigan with questions to see if he had ever coaxed political allies to stack the ballot with fake candidates.

"I don't remember that," Madigan said.

"Is it possible that you did?" Peraica asked.

"No," Madigan responded.

"So you're certain that you didn't?" Peraica asked.

"I don't remember," Madigan said.

Seeking to put the matter to rest, as we reported, Madigan attorney Michael Kasper went over the point again. This time Madigan said he did not direct anyone associated with him to recruit candidates to run against him, nor did he know of anyone connected to him who had done so.

"The answer is no," Madigan said.[35]

As a campaigner, Gonzales recalled knocking on eleven thousand doors in the district. A billboard with Gonzales's picture on it even shadowed the Madigan headquarters on Sixty-Fifth and Pulaski. But the message on the streets belonged to Madigan. Out campaigning, Gonzales didn't have to look far to find a man with a sign that read "Vote NO on convicted felon Jason Gonzales." Anti-Gonzales campaign mailers with grainy pictures of him blanketed the district telling voters that he pleaded guilty to "multiple felonies" and couldn't be trusted because of his record of deception and dishonesty. Television attack ads came complete with an image of a jail cell. There was fine print about his pardon in the varied attacks, but Gonzales felt that was not enough.[36]

Gonzales contended the pardon was equivalent to an acquittal, meaning he was not a felon. In politics, of course, that's a difficult argument to pull off. "Well, it's hardball tactics," Gonzales testified. "You know, it's Chicago politics. I suppose you have to expect that, especially in a race like this. So I knew he was going to hit me hard, but I believe that, again, some of the things that he and his affiliate organizations did during the campaign were defamatory." Gonzales maintained that he was drowned out by "Speaker Madigan's attacks three, four times a week through the mail, commercials, precinct captain letters that were telling people things that just weren't true."[37]

Madigan pointed to Rauner when asked if he ever suggested the brochures sent by the Friends of Michael Madigan campaign committee were too nasty: "Have you seen the TV ads put on by Rauner against me, which were running through that period of time? . . . I'm talking about the nastiness of the campaign. . . . And the defamation that's been performed on me and my family simply because we've got a governor that thinks he's a dictator, and he was supporting Gonzales. That's why Gonzales was there, to advance the Rauner agenda."[38]

In turn, Gonzales gave a grim assessment of his experience running against the speaker. "This guy's trying to destroy your soul," Gonzales said. "He just doesn't want to defeat you. He wants to make sure that you never come back again, that you leave this state or you do something. He just destroys you, not just politically, but spiritually and mentally."[39]

Gonzales, who identified himself as Mexican American, testified he would have won had the two other Hispanics not been in the race. But Kasper pointed out that Madigan had won again and again in heavily

Hispanic precincts, including where the population was 90 percent Hispanic. One example Kasper gave—the Forty-Fourth Precinct in the Thirteenth Ward on the district's east side—tallied 443 voters for Madigan, 26 votes for Gonzales, 6 for Rodriguez, and only 1 for Barboza. Seasoned Democratic committeepersons keep track of who is on their side and who isn't, who will likely vote their way and who won't. They categorize these voters as plusses and minuses. They register voters who they believe will be plusses. They get them to vote early by mail. They make sure they have the palm cards with the candidates the committee members support, and they drive individual voters to the polling places on Election Day. "We worked to identify our voters and get them voted," Madigan testified. "And our polling told us at the beginning that I had over 65 percent support. That's [what] I got on Election Day because we identify our voters."[40]

As the depositions wrapped up in the court case, the two sides looked to the judge for a ruling. The Gonzales team wanted to take the case to trial, saying a jury should get to weigh in on whether Madigan's folks conspired to stack the ballot with phony candidates. The Madigan team wanted the proceedings to be over, saying Gonzales "at best" alleged that the two additional candidates were spoilers, who would have served in office if elected but whose presence on the ballot made it harder for Gonzales to win outright. They argued there was no evidence the speaker had used his official state powers to deprive Gonzales of equal protection rights and no evidence of conspiracy. They also used a "dirty tricks" defense. Vaught explained it like this: "Complaints about campaign strategies, even 'dirty tricks' that successfully undermine candidates, are not actionable in federal court." Even if Gonzales's allegations were true, the argument went, the "purported conduct" of Madigan and the rest of the defendants "would be protected by the First Amendment."[41]

In the end, Madigan won again. U.S. District Judge Matthew Kennelly tossed out the suit on August 23, 2019, calling it "undisputed" that some Madigan loyalists worked on recruiting the two extra candidates. Kennelly also wrote the "evidence supports a reasonable inference that Madigan authorized or at least was aware of the recruitment effort." Kennelly ruled Gonzales made "deceptive tactics a central issue in his campaign" and received considerable news coverage about alleged shams on the ballot. The judge also determined that voters had a chance to weigh the sham allegations and throw Madigan out of office, but the speaker won anyway.[42]

"In reaching this conclusion, the court does not hold that there is no constitutional limit on election-related misconduct whenever that misconduct is publicly known before the votes are cast," Kennelly wrote. "In particular, the court is cognizant that there is evidence from which a reasonable jury could find that [Madigan and other defendants] engaged in a deliberate effort to interfere with voters' decision making. Such fraudulent interference in the form of sham candidates might, in an appropriate case, undermine the ability of the electorate to hold the offending candidate to account. But Gonzales has not pointed to evidence—or even alleged—that the defendants' fraud prevented the voters from punishing Madigan at the ballot box."[43]

Gonzales's lawyers quickly asked the judge to reconsider, suggesting his ruling was illogical. Boulton argued that Gonzales should not be penalized for telling voters two candidates were fakes, because the depositions showed that "Speaker Madigan and his agents were behind the sham candidacies." But Kennelly didn't change his mind. In a rare Saturday night decision, while Madigan was wrapping up the 2020 pandemic-shortened spring session in Springfield, Kennelly turned down the Gonzales team and ruled in the speaker's favor once more.[44]

Still unsatisfied, Peraica maintained that putting up shams is a basic fraud on the ballot that is fundamentally wrong and should be stopped. But the Seventh U.S. Circuit Court of Appeals was unmoved by the Gonzales argument that putting up allegedly fake candidates represented an excessive dirty trick.

Judge Frank Easterbrook called the "effort hardly necessary, since if every non-Madigan vote had gone to Gonzales, [Madigan] still would have won in a landslide." Writing for the three-judge appellate panel, Easterbrook said, "Gonzales smelled a rat from the start and made that known to the electorate, which swept Madigan back into office anyway." Further, Easterbrook wrote, "We mean no disrespect in recognizing that many false statements are made during political campaigns and that many a stratagem that one side deems clever will be seen by the opposition as a dirty trick. Opposing political figures may brand true statements as false and honest campaigning as a rotten subterfuge." Even so, Easterbrook said, "Voters rather than judges must decide when one side has gone overboard. The Constitution does not authorize the judiciary to upset that outcome or to penalize a politician for employing a shady strategy that voters tolerate." Peraica asked for the U.S. Supreme Court to make the messy matter one of the rare cases the high court's justices consider, but the justices declined in November 2021.[45]

No matter what the courts decided, though, a hard look at the raw numbers in Madigan's 2016 primary shows more than a highly effective political operation. Out of the 26,320 votes cast, Madigan got 17,155 votes, 65 percent; Gonzales got 7,124, for 27 percent; and the other two candidates together got 2,041, 8 percent. But the sham allegations were fast becoming just one of many politically troubling distractions arising from Madigan's Thirteenth Ward fiefdom. The willingness of the Thirteenth Ward to go to extraordinary lengths to win was even more evident the next time Madigan's handpicked Thirteenth Ward Alderman Marty Quinn ran for City Council.

14

MARTY'S CAMPAIGN

"I've never seen anything like this in 50 years of doing these cases. It's not just the volume but the level of recklessness I have not seen."

—Richard Means, former head of Cook County state's attorney's fraud investigations

Until 2019 Alderman Marty Quinn never had competition for the Thirteenth Ward City Council seat that Michael Madigan, head of the Thirteenth Ward's Democratic Committee, bestowed upon him. Quinn slipped into the City Council in 2011 following a Thirteenth Ward shuffle. He put his name on the ballot, and the sitting alderman, Frank Olivo, put his name on the ballot. The Thirteenth Ward political forces knocked all outsider candidates off the ballot, and then Olivo, a Madigan ally, withdrew from the race and conveniently landed a ComEd subcontract. Quinn stayed on the ballot, making him the only candidate, and he cruised into the council unopposed. When you make the right moves at the right time, it's a lesson that's only a slight twist on a popular phrase: Nobody gets in office that nobody sent. Madigan had a choice of one. The voters had a choice of one. And Madigan's choice won.[1]

Along came 2015, and nobody had to play any ballot games. No challengers filed against Quinn, and he ran unopposed for his second term. Candidates running without an opponent have time to work for allies who need help in their own races. That's especially helpful for guys like Marty

Quinn, who carried the far-reaching responsibilities of being Madigan's political general. But then came Quinn's 2019 race, where the impact of the Thirteenth Ward's fierce intensity can be no better illustrated than by the extraordinary lengths they went to win.

A college kid had the audacity to run in February 2019 for the seat owned by the Thirteenth Ward Democratic Organization. The nineteen-year-old DePaul University freshman, David Krupa, could easily be called overmatched. To collect signatures on his nominating petitions, Krupa needed help from his parents, grandmother, cousins, aunts, and uncles. Quinn, on the other hand, had Madigan's resources and ground troops at his command. What might be the most confounding issue of the whole campaign is that Quinn didn't simply ignore the youngster. Quinn's brother, Kevin, effectively had dragged Marty into the middle of the Alaina Hampton scandal. But that alone wouldn't have caused an upset in the Thirteenth Ward. Kevin was the one accused of sexual harassment and ousted, not Marty. Sure, Krupa was an annoyance. At worst, though, Quinn's record of running unopposed would be broken. Krupa was not a real threat. But what happened in the Quinn campaign drew the attention of a Cook County grand jury.[2]

Getting on the ballot in Illinois is one of the toughest parts of a political race. Candidates can fail to collect the minimum number of signatures required for the office they seek. The signatures could be collected outside of the district where the candidate is running and then be declared void. The addresses of the people who signed petitions could be wrong. There could be fake names, fake people, fake addresses, or all three. Instead of doing the hard work of collecting signatures by going door-to-door, lazy folks might gather around a table, sign a name, and pass the paperwork to another person who signs a name, who passes it to another who signs a name, who passes it to another, and so forth. In Chicago that's an old game called "round-tabling," passing petitions around a table to mix up the handwriting styles on different lines in the hope that nobody will catch on. To address the mistakes and fakes, an opponent can challenge the signatures, get them disqualified, and strike so many that the other candidate gets knocked out of the race. Every smart politician tries to win before Election Day, and one of the best ways to win is to bounce the opponents before they get on the ballot. Many candidates don't survive this process in Chicago. Petition challenges are common for offices around the state. Inevitably, legal fights play out before hearing officers in small, stuffy rooms downtown. Some might call the election lawyer business a specialty; others, a cottage industry. The losers in the process raise questions about the fairness of ballot access. They argue there are too many hurdles.

Few people argue that rules should be so loose that ballots become packed with candidates who are not serious. When Arnold Schwarzenegger won in the 2003 governor's recall election in California, for example, the top 10 finishers among 135 candidates included porn king Larry Flynt, former child star Gary Coleman, and porn star Mary Carey.[3] The 2021 California recall effort brought Caitlyn Jenner and radio host Larry Elder, adding another dash of celebrity to that political sideshow.

Illinois voters generally understand the need for basic requirements to get onto the ballot, but having too many hurdles is another thing altogether. Having lots of rules is an advantage to the political pros. They write the rules into law, have experience following them, and line up the best attorneys to use the rules to pick off opponents before the ballots are printed.

Barack Obama hired a good lawyer and played the Chicago game to his advantage in his first race for the Illinois Senate, clearing the ballot of four opponents until only his name was left. One of those, respected Chicago Senator Alice Palmer, who rushed to collect signatures in the state race once she lost in a special election for Congress, pulled out once Obama had her on the verge of elimination. The fairness of this process is a topic that bubbles up when would-be candidates start getting bumped from their races. Obama, a lawyer, community organizer, and leader of a voter registration drive, actually considered the more cerebral philosophies surrounding ballot access before he moved forward with challenges. He said he recognized "there's a legitimate argument to be made that you shouldn't create barriers to people getting on the ballot." But Obama determined that challenging flawed petitions of opponents was "just abiding by the rules that had been set up." Reflecting back to that state Senate race as he ran for president years later, Obama said in a *Tribune* interview that he "gave some thought to" the question of "should people be on the ballot even if they didn't meet the requirements? My conclusion was that, if you couldn't run a successful petition drive, then that raised questions in terms of how effective a representative you were going to be." Just the notion that Obama actually weighed what's fair or unfair is atypical in Chicago, where winning is what counts and winning big matters even more.[4]

In Marty Quinn's February 2019 contest against the young David Krupa, the Thirteenth Ward came down on the side of winning big. They pushed to the extreme a quirk in the law—perhaps to the point of redefining the metaphor of taking a hammer to an ant. The pro-Quinn forces prepared the usual challenges to signatures on petitions, the standard type of Chicago-style battle where politicians send in a team to pore over the paperwork their opponents filed to run, pick out the flawed signatures, and go in for the kill. But another phase of the attack on Krupa's candidacy began before he filed his nominating petitions, one that left both admirers and detractors of Madigan and Quinn slack-jawed.

Attorney Michael Dorf, who represented Krupa, said he had received a telephone tip from another lawyer about "this crazy thing going on in the 13th Ward." What Dorf learned that Friday night, just a week before the filing deadline, was nothing like anything he'd come across before. Quinn's team of door knockers had been going through neighborhoods for weeks asking people to sign an unusual document. They asked these voters to sign sworn affidavits that they had put their signatures on Krupa's nominating petitions but now wanted to rescind them. In most cases, this is legal. But the Quinn team put the law to the test. One theory behind the provision in the law is that people make real mistakes and might wish to scratch their names off of petitions they accidentally signed. Maybe they thought they were signing to support somebody else; maybe the errors were innocent. As a result, experts generally see only a handful of rescinded signatures in a single city political race. It may be more typical in nasty neighborhood fights over local referendums, such as whether a precinct should be voted dry or wet. But Dorf said he had "never seen an organized campaign" to round up a massive number of affidavits from voters wishing to remove their signatures from a candidate's petition.[5]

A longtime election lawyer, Dorf couldn't get it out of his mind. He also was one of the lawyers working on Lori Lightfoot's breakthrough campaign for mayor, but he decided he had better file a Freedom of Information (FOI) Act request over the weekend with the Chicago Board of Election Commissioners to look into the Quinn team's moves. Dorf's FOI request asked for copies of the affidavits that people filed to remove their signatures from Krupa's petitions. The law itself is a mind-bender of sorts. Voters wanting to withdraw their signatures had to notify election authorities before the candidate actually filed the petitions that had their signatures on them. A voter can't withdraw a signature once the candidate files. There is a bit of logic to the madness. If a signature could be withdrawn after a candidate's petitions are filed, opponents could see who signed and pressure those people to pull their names. Candidates who thought they had plenty of signatures when they filed could end up disqualified if a herd of voters suddenly rescinded their signatures. That would be chaos.

Instead, Dorf and Krupa confronted chaos of a different kind. With the deadline to file for City Council less than a week away, a city election lawyer called Dorf with a basic question about that FOI he had filed: Would Dorf like paper copies of his response or a thumb drive showing all of the affidavits from voters wishing to rescind signatures from Krupa's petitions? "I said, 'Why would I need a thumb drive?' And he said, 'Because I've got 2,500 of these,'" Dorf said. He thought the number would be exponentially smaller. "I was amazed," Dorf said. In comparison, he said, three or four people generally seek to rescind signatures on a candidate's petitions in a basic city election. Given that Quinn forces were still out collecting more affidavits, Dorf and Krupa decided they needed to slam the door. Krupa filed his petitions a couple of days sooner than he had planned.[6]

Dorf found the adventure became even stranger. Krupa needed only 473 valid signatures, but he submitted 1,729 to protect himself from losing some through typical post-filing challenges. And then came the shocker: Quinn forces had already filed 2,796 affidavits from people who completed sworn statements saying they had signed Krupa's nominating petitions and now wanted their names rescinded. In short, the Thirteenth Ward army collected more than a thousand signatures from people wanting to remove their signatures from Krupa's petitions than the actual number of signatures Krupa collected and filed in the first place. The bizarreness of the discovery made veteran election lawyers take notice. Election board spokesman Jim Allen said there "absolutely" had never been that many requests to rescind signatures in one race.[7]

One other statistic is even odder: only 187 of the 2,796 affidavits the pro-Quinn crew submitted actually matched the names of people who had signed Krupa's petitions. How did this happen? The Thirteenth Ward troops stormed neighborhoods and asked residents to sign sworn affidavits without always knowing whether these voters had put their signatures on Krupa's petitions. In kind of an elaborate hit-or-miss search, they collected as many signatures as they could. The head-scratching result?

Upward of 2,600 people who swore they wanted to rescind signatures on Krupa's petitions likely didn't sign them. "I've never seen anything like this in 50 years of doing these cases," said veteran election attorney Richard Means, whose experience ranged from heading election fraud investigations under Republican Cook County State's Attorney Bernard Carey to helping Democratic Mayor Harold Washington's campaign. "It's not just the volume but the level of recklessness I have not seen."[8]

The full story needed old-fashioned street reporting. So *Tribune* City Hall reporter Gregory Pratt and I hit the Thirteenth Ward for a few days of walk and knock. Going into the Thirteenth Ward is an experience like few others in Chicago. Pratt would later describe on Twitter that the adventure felt much like a trip in time back to the 1950s. Rows of brick houses, wooden porches, concrete stoops, manicured yards, well-paved streets, small unbroken sidewalks, apartments—plus a ubiquitous safety upgrade of electronic doorbells that recorded images of visitors. In dozens of interviews, ward residents acknowledged they felt pressure to sign pro-Quinn affidavits—sometimes not even knowing what they were signing.

Nikki Kiernicki, then forty-one, told how she refused to sign a sworn affidavit when a ward worker came by her home. She didn't have the same political philosophies as Krupa. So she doubted she had signed a Krupa petition. But she remembered how the ward heeler increased pressure on her, saying, "You need to sign this." She disagreed and recalled how the man got upset and raised his voice. At that point, she recounted to the *Tribune*, she told him to "get off my porch."[9]

Most residents we talked to wanted anonymity when they discussed the Madigan-Quinn machine. One woman described how two Thirteenth Ward political workers rushed her as she drove up to the curb in front of her house. When a clipboard was stuck under her nose, she signed the affidavit. She said she apologized to Krupa later. Still another woman told how a precinct worker who came around regularly started yelling at her when she refused to sign. She slammed the door on him. She declined to let reporters use her name, saying the proliferation of Quinn yard signs in her neighborhood reflected his powerful presence. "He's got so much muscle in this neighborhood. You know what I'm saying? I'm scared," she said. "I don't want no one to know I said anything."[10]

The drama at one home unfolded when a woman said she repeatedly dodged a pair of precinct visitors for weeks. She sent her husband to the door to fend them off and make up excuses for her absence. "They kept coming and coming and coming to my house," she said. "Three times a day for a very long time." But she couldn't avoid them forever. "Just when she thought it was safe to answer the door," as we wrote in the *Tribune*, "they were on her porch again."[11] She signed so they'd stop coming. She also didn't want people to know her name, saying she feared she'd lose city services if she went public.

One city worker said he turned back precinct workers one week. They returned eight times the next. He didn't respond. Then they started leaving voicemail messages. He said he did not sign the affidavit, and he wanted to remain anonymous. But he slipped us a great picture of the two political workers standing on his porch. The picture came straight from his doorbell camera.[12]

On a Saturday in December 2018, Dorf prepared to square off over the affidavits against Madigan's chief legal warrior, Michael Kasper. When Rahm Emanuel battled with opponents who argued he didn't meet the residency requirement to run for mayor because he'd been in Washington serving as Obama's chief of staff, he turned to Mike Kasper. Reporters showed up to record the Saturday showdown over the Quinn maneuvers. But without warning, Kasper dropped the challenge against Krupa. Kasper sent an email before the hearing got started. Dorf was prepared to subpoena Quinn, Madigan, and various Thirteenth Ward operatives, but that never happened when Kasper pulled the plug. Krupa would remain on the ballot.[13]

Dorf left that day with one other card on the table. He wanted Cook County State's Attorney Kim Foxx to review the matter for potential criminal violations. City election officials sent the records to both Foxx and the U.S. attorney's office. Krupa also had another line of attack. He filed a federal civil lawsuit against Quinn, his political committee, Madigan, and the Thirteenth Ward Democratic Organization. Krupa alleged that all of them were behind "literally thousands of false statements" and a "sheer fraud." Krupa alleged that felonies had been committed, including pushing people into perjury when they signed sworn affidavits. Krupa's federal court attorney was Tony Peraica, the same lawyer who represented Jason Gonzales, the candidate who lost to Madigan in the 2016 House race. Once again, attorney Adam Vaught stood on the Madigan-Quinn side of the case. Vaught didn't hold back. He filed a brief that charged Krupa's suit was "generally false, often defamatory, and periodically delusional."[14]

The pro-Quinn effort still makes experienced campaign workers shake their heads over the full-court effort to get Krupa tossed. One of those campaign veterans was Louis Rexing, a notary public who worked for Krupa. Rexing said Cook County state's attorney investigators had interviewed him about the case. Looking back, though, he wondered why Quinn even bothered to acknowledge Krupa was on the ballot. "There wasn't a doubt in my mind that Dave didn't have a real shooting chance," Rexing said, "because he really didn't have the time or the money to put together a big crew to go out there and compete against the machine." He took notice of the overkill.[15]

"Had they just sat here and done nothing, [Krupa's] name wouldn't have been anywhere," Rexing said. "But by the time they got done doing the stuff they were doing, the papers had picked up on it, the TV shows had picked up on it, and all of a sudden Dave has some name recognition that he wouldn't have had if it wasn't for these guys with their idiot attack on him."[16]

When the vote counting was finished, Marty Quinn won with more than 86 percent. Declining an interview about the extraordinary effort, Quinn offered a brief written statement. "I dropped the petition challenge nearly a year ago because my relationship with my constituents is paramount, and I didn't want anything to damage that," Quinn said. "Residents of the 13th Ward spoke resoundingly at the ballot box, and I think it's time to move on."[17]

At Madigan's Thirteenth Ward power base, the less scrutiny the better. Yet not everybody was ready to move on. The scrutiny on Madigan and his organization was growing.

PART V

THE FALL

15

HIMSELF

"I'm not a target of anything."
—Speaker Michael Madigan,
    October 29, 2019

From statewide officials and government staffers to legislators and lobbyists, Capitol denizens knew that Speaker Madigan and lobbyist Michael McClain shared a special bond. McClain could often be found sitting on a padded bench just outside the speaker's third-floor suite, chatting on his cell phone or holding court with a favored circle of lobbyists—the ex-lawmakers and former House Democratic staffers who shared the goal of keeping Madigan speaker.

Madigan and McClain forged a friendship as young lawmakers on the rise in the 1970s and early1980s. When Madigan became minority leader in 1981, he put McClain on his leadership team. But when Madigan won his first term as speaker in 1983, McClain had to find a job. He'd lost his election, a victim of the cutback amendment that squeezed the size of the House from 177 lawmakers to 118. Eventually, though, McClain returned to Springfield as a lobbyist, keeping his friendship and often dining out with Madigan, helping the speaker devise political strategy and picking up a golden lineup of clients who valued his access to the speaker. Those clients included Commonwealth Edison and its parent company, Exelon. They both sought—and won—lucrative changes in state law. One big win was a 2011 smart-grid modernization law pitched as a way to improve power reliability and delivery but criticized as too profitable for the company. The 2011 law gave ComEd the right to use a formula to set delivery rates, boosting yearly earnings to $638 million in 2020 from $379 million in 2012.[1] Another major victory, in 2016, kept some nuclear plants open and saved thousands of jobs but added costs to consumer bills. With that one last conquest, McClain retired from lobbying. Madigan hailed McClain for outstanding careers as a legislator and as a lobbyist, saying he operated "with complete honesty and integrity."[2] McClain couldn't hide his affection for the speaker: "I feel like I'm very close to him, and I love him like a brother, and I'm loyal to him."[3]

A little over two years later, the feds sought to put that loyalty to the test. By the time Madigan escorted Governor J. B. Pritzker onto the House floor to praise the rookie governor for his spring session success in June 2019, federal authorities had already raided the homes of three of the speaker's allies. The *Tribune* reported the raids at the home of McClain, the speaker's confidant, and Kevin Quinn, the longtime Madigan aide who had been booted over inappropriate behavior. The Better Government Association and WBEZ-FM uncovered the raid at the third home, that of former Chicago Alderman Mike Zalewski, who represented the Twenty-Third Ward, which had been run for decades by former U.S. Representative William Lipinski, a Madigan ally and the ward's longtime committeeman. The report showed the Zalewski angle centered on an attempt to get work for the retired alderman and the interactions between Madigan, Zalewski, and McClain. ComEd also confirmed receipt of a federal grand jury subpoena about its lobbying activities in the state of Illinois.[4]

Within weeks the *Tribune* found evidence of the newsroom adage that everything in Chicago is one big story. Federal courts reporter Jason Meisner and I teamed up to reveal that McClain and Kevin Quinn stood at the center of a remarkable confluence of the #MeToo scandal and the ComEd investigation. McClain, always eager to do favors for people, was among five active and former ComEd lobbyists linked to sending Quinn thousands of dollars in checks after Madigan cut him loose, according to interviews and bank records. Along with McClain, the checks could be tied to lobbyists Will Cousineau, whose bio with Washington-based Cornerstone Government Affairs called him Madigan's longest-serving political director; Tom Cullen, a previous Madigan political director and longtime party strategist ensconced in the speaker's organization for decades; former Democratic State Representative John Bradley of Marion, once part of Madigan's leadership team; and Mike Alvarez, a former Metropolitan Water Reclamation District commissioner. Cousineau and Bradley lobbied in Springfield for ComEd; Cullen had once lobbied the Capitol for ComEd but switched to Ameren; and Alvarez had lobbied for ComEd at City Hall. Cousineau's Cornerstone group confirmed it had been subpoenaed about Quinn's work as an independent contractor to do research and monitor legislative committee hearings at the rate of one thousand dollars a month for six months. A source with knowledge of the probe said the FBI was looking into the lobbyists' checks as part of its ongoing investigation.[5]

Timing, as we all know, can be everything in politics, and the timing of the checks didn't help the political optics for Madigan. Bank records the *Tribune* obtained showed the checks started flowing to Quinn in September 2018, which happened to be the same month Madigan authored an op-ed in the *Tribune* vowing strong reforms in the way his office would handle sexual harassment. "I have made it a personal mission to take this issue head-on and correct past mistakes," Madigan wrote. "I wish I would have done so sooner."[6]

Throughout the year, federal authorities kept cranking out public corruption cases that stretched from Chicago City Hall, to the city's southwest suburbs, to the statehouse. Democratic Senator Martin Sandoval, who embraced the nickname "Perro Grande," or "Big Dog," saw federal agents raid his Chicago home and Capitol office. ComEd and its parent, Exelon, also received new subpoenas seeking communication between the companies and Sandoval. He later pleaded guilty to taking more than a quarter of a million dollars in a bribery-related speed-camera case. But he died from COVID-19 while cooperating with authorities.[7] After he died, the feds dismissed the case against him.[8] Sandoval was the senator of the district that overlapped with Madigan's legislative turf. Their relationship was off and on, though, with Sandoval often joking how the speaker wanted to implant a computer chip in his head that would make him think as robotically as a Thirteenth Ward loyalist.

In October, Exelon Utilities CEO Anne Pramaggiore suddenly retired, catching off guard a phalanx of major business leaders who admired her smarts. Coming less than a week after ComEd and Exelon acknowledged they had received the second subpoena seeking communications with Sandoval, Pramaggiore's departure drew headline coverage. The company put out a vanilla statement thanking her for her "valuable service." But what put Pramaggiore in the middle of a growing whirlwind was that, according to a *Tribune* source, she was a focus of the ongoing federal probe. Pramaggiore played a major role in ComEd's legislative victories. As she worked from the highest echelons of Exelon and ComEd, she employed a huge phalanx of lobbyists tied to the speaker and shepherded by McClain. Before Pramaggiore moved up the ladder with Exelon, she had served as president and chief executive of ComEd.[9]

Already reeling, Illinois Democrats—and by extension, Madigan—suffered another blow from federal prosecutors. The feds accused Democratic Representative Luis Arroyo of Chicago of agreeing to pay twenty-five hundred dollars a month in kickbacks to Senator Terry Link, a Lake County Democrat who, sources said, had recorded Arroyo seeking support for sweepstakes gambling legislation and paying the first of the payments at a Skokie restaurant. Link, who was cooperating with authorities, had his own problems, later resigning and pleading guilty to a count of tax evasion. Staking out higher ground, Madigan called for Arroyo's resignation and issued a statement saying the state needed stronger ethics and lobbying laws. As he left a House Democratic caucus in Springfield, however, Madigan had to field a reporter's question about developments in the ComEd investigation. His answer was concise: "I'm not a target of anything."[10] A week later Arroyo stepped down as the House prepared to start hearings on whether to expel him. Madigan said the allegations lodged against Arroyo "go beyond anything that could be considered a lapse of judgment or minor indiscretion."[11]

By mid-November, one more major story broke through the clutter as Madigan and lawmakers gathered in Springfield for the fall session: two sources with knowledge of the probe said federal authorities had recorded McClain's phone calls as part of the investigation. One source said the recordings came from an FBI wiretap on McClain's cell phone. Teaming up with Meisner again, we pushed the story onto the *Tribune*'s website the night of November 12, a Tuesday, when the Springfield bars were loaded with lawmakers, lobbyists, government staffers, and reporters. People in those bars later said that conversation stopped momentarily as customers stared at the story popping up on their iPhones and Twitter accounts. Rich Miller's Capitol Fax, the all-statehouse-all-the-time website, posted the story that night, as usual, but he reposted it at the top of his page the next day with a note: "(This Tuesday night post has been bumped up for visibility.)"

Still hanging was whether the ever-cautious Madigan had been recorded on any of those McClain calls. But Meisner knew that explaining an important piece of context in our story would convey the seriousness of the development:

> Wiretaps are treated by the courts as an investigative method of last resort and require proof not only that a specific crime was being committed but also that the target was using a particular phone to do so. They must be signed off on by a deputy attorney general assigned to the U.S. Department of Justice in Washington before going before the chief federal judge for final approval.
>
> Once agents are up and listening in on a phone, they are required to provide meticulous details to the chief judge every 10 days that they are indeed gathering evidence of criminal activity [in order] to keep the recording ongoing.[12]

Before Capitol insiders got used to the idea that their friend Mike McClain's phone was tapped, his role in the #MeToo check scandal came into sharper focus. A deeper *Tribune* examination of more bank records and emails found that McClain had orchestrated the effort to send at least thirty-one thousand dollars to Quinn to soften his landing. Given the politically explosive ramifications of Madigan loyalists helping a top political lieutenant whom the speaker ousted in a major sexual harassment case, McClain recognized the sensitivity of the matter. He sent an email to the lobbyists, saying, "This is obviously confidential." But McClain gave Quinn a more explicit warning: "I cannot tell you how important it is to keep all of this confidential. These men are sticking their necks out knowing full well if it goes public before you are exonerated they will get the full blast from the 'MeToo' movement." He then explained how contracts could be written up for Quinn. Madigan spokesperson Eileen Boyce immediately sought to place distance between the speaker and McClain and the other lobbyists: "If a group of people were attempting to help Kevin Quinn, the speaker was not a part of it."[13]

Additional private emails we acquired illustrated McClain's deep involvement in Madigan's political organization. From a group of go-to fund-raisers whom McClain called the "Most Trusted of the Trusted," he requested help for a "secret project" to increase spending for House Democrats in competitive contests, known as "target" races, before the November 2018 general election.[14]

In asking for contributions, McClain didn't bother to use Madigan's name in emails to these trusted givers. Instead he slipped in a fond nickname for the speaker: "Himself," a term with Irish-Gaelic origins that refers to the head of the house. With chipper prose, McClain wrote, "We always called you the 'Most Trusted of the Trusted.' So, again, on behalf of Himself, I thank you for ALL your work to help him and the Caucus." McClain explained that he had reviewed the "magic Excel sheet" of contributors and made a plea: "Although many people are contributing to the 19 targets . . . [and/or] some of HIMSELF's Committees, there are some gaping holes too. So, anything you can do to ramp up your wonderful efforts would be appreciated!!!!!" Wrapping it up, McClain wrote, "We know you have millions of things to do and your 'special' effort here goes a long way in helping the Caucus and HIMSELF."[15]

In a world where Democrats hesitated to tangle with the powerful speaker, Madigan drew little public criticism over the checks to his former aide. But Senator Iris Martinez, a Chicago Democrat on the party's state central committee, shifted the public narrative when she called for the speaker to give a fuller explanation. While a Madigan spokesperson stood by the statement that the speaker was not part of any effort to send checks to Quinn, Martinez questioned whether Madigan was sincere about addressing sexual harassment if his "cronies paid the harasser."[16] She called for Madigan to tell "what he knew and when he knew" about the checks or resign as chairman of the Illinois Democratic Party. "Give us some answers or step down," Martinez said. Politically, she had more to gain and little to lose given that she was snubbed by Madigan and party slate makers in her four-way primary race for circuit clerk. But her outrage over the checks—which she insisted was not over prior feuds with Madigan—came as many female lawmakers stayed silent. Not only would she go on to beat three men in the Democratic primary and later win the circuit clerk post, but calling out Madigan came at a critical moment.[17]

Only days later, Madigan's team quietly reached a settlement in the federal lawsuit brought by Alaina Hampton, who contended she had been blackballed by his organization for calling out Quinn over sexual harassment. Word trickled out on the Friday night after Thanksgiving—a time when politicians try to bury negative news—that Hampton received $75,000 of a $275,000 settlement, and the rest went to pay legal fees. The four Madigan-controlled committees that reached the settlement with Hampton were the Democratic Party of Illinois, the Democratic

Majority, the Thirteenth Ward Democratic Organization, and Friends of Michael J. Madigan, the speaker's personal political committee. In a statement, Hampton said she had seen "positive changes" since she spoke out, including legislation to address sexual harassment. "A space has been created for an open and honest dialogue about sexism and abuse in the workplace that I'm confident will continue," Hampton said. A Madigan spokesperson issued a statement saying that Madigan and the state Democratic Party had made creating a "fair and welcoming workplace" a priority: "Speaker Madigan remains committed to protecting employees, volunteers and candidates who care about working families and the rights of women, minorities and others whose voices are often silenced. . . . Over the last two years, the speaker and the party have made significant changes to strengthen training, policies and reporting procedures for staff and volunteers to ensure their rights are protected." As in most settlements, the Madigan-controlled political committees did not admit liability nor wrongdoing. Both sides agreed not to disparage the other.[18]

With the Hampton settlement behind him, Madigan's 2019 political roller-coaster ride looked like it was almost over. But more phone calls and face-to-face interviews led to a front-page story showing that federal investigators had made inquiries about the speaker himself. Four people confirmed to the *Tribune* that federal authorities had asked questions about Madigan and his political operation. None of the sources would give permission to use their names, but the story explained that FBI agents and prosecutors asked about connections between ComEd lobbyists and Madigan; lobbyists giving contracts to people tied to the speaker; and city, state, and suburban government jobs held by his associates. While the breadth of the investigation was still hard to pinpoint, one of the most intriguing elements of the story was that numerous questions centered on the speaker's relationship and dealings with Michael McClain, the former ComEd lobbyist. Indeed, the most compelling quote from one source telegraphed the extent to which federal authorities had homed in on Madigan and McClain: "These were the people they were most focused on."[19]

16

PUBLIC OFFICIAL A

"If there was credible evidence that I had engaged in criminal misconduct, which I most certainly did not, I would be charged with a crime."

—Speaker Michael Madigan,
    November 19, 2020

Everyone will remember the year 2020 for the tragedies brought on by the raging coronavirus that affected almost every aspect of life. In Illinois alone, COVID-19 killed thousands, challenged Governor J. B. Pritzker to respond to a pandemic like no other, and turned the legislative session into a mini-camp that lasted only a few days. But as the world struggled to find a vaccine to overcome the unremitting infection, federal prosecutors in Chicago presented Illinoisans with a diagnosis of a homegrown political pandemic, one that ultimately stood to end Speaker Madigan's grip on the House.

U.S. Attorney John Lausch announced in July that ComEd had admitted to a years-long bribery scheme designed to "influence and reward" Madigan by giving contracts, jobs, and money to the speaker's political associates while the utility lobbied for legislation worth at least $150 million. The ComEd effort allegedly lasted from 2011 through 2019, a period that encompassed ComEd's heralded smart-grid overhaul as well as the salvation of Exelon's money-losing nuclear power plants and the jobs that went with them. ComEd agreed to pay a $200 million fine. Lausch agreed to defer prosecuting ComEd on a bribery charge for three years, giving the company time to cooperate as the investigation played out. If ComEd fulfilled its obligation, prosecutors would drop the bribery charge. Lausch warned that the case was ongoing: "It's vibrant, and it will continue."[1]

Though he was referenced throughout the court documents, Madigan was not charged, and he emphatically denied wrongdoing. In fact, the ComEd case did not mention Madigan by name, a common move used by prosecutors, but this time they took the uncommon step of specifically identifying him by his title: Speaker of the House of Representatives. It was here, in court documents, that prosecutors also bestowed upon Madigan an ignominious moniker: Public Official A.[2]

Madigan's prominence in the case signaled political problems for the chairman of the Democratic Party of Illinois. In the middle of an election year, when he hoped Democrats would rack up big wins, the speaker drew harsh rhetoric from members of both parties and the usually respectful Democratic Governor J. B. Pritzker. The governor said he was "deeply troubled and frankly I'm furious." Madigan "has a lot that he needs to answer for—to authorities, to investigators and most importantly to the people of Illinois," Pritzker said. "If these allegations of wrongdoing by the speaker are true, there is no question that he will have betrayed the public trust and he must resign."[3]

Pritzker already was fighting to convince Illinoisans to vote, in less than four months, for a constitutional amendment that would let the state tax people with the greatest incomes at a higher rate than the rest of its citizens—a graduated tax rate versus the state's current flat rate. Yet the ComEd case made the already difficult task of winning approval of the tax amendment tougher because Madigan backed it. The political plight of the House speaker, who helped shape Pritzker's proposed tax amendment, provided Republicans with political ammunition to use against the governor's signature proposal.

On top of the revelations in the ComEd agreement, federal officials cast a wider net across Madigan's sphere of influence. They subpoenaed Madigan's office in search of information about AT&T, Walgreens, and Rush University Medical Center, all places where politically savvy Madigan allies have held sway. The subpoena also sought records related to Madigan's political organization, his law firm, and various state and local politicians, including Thirteenth Ward Alderman Marty Quinn. Perhaps looking to breathe new life into a past line of inquiry, federal authorities also sought records involving ex-Alderman Danny Solis, whose meeting with Madigan, a developer and a businessman, had been recorded years earlier when the speaker pitched his law firm to do tax business for property in Chinatown.

Prosecutors said ComEd's bribes-for-favors scheme dated to 2011, when ComEd contract lobbyist Michael McClain and ComEd staff lobbyist John T. Hooker devised a plan to pay two Madigan associates as subcontractors to a consultant but allow them to do little or no work. ComEd also allegedly granted the Thirteenth Ward a hefty number of interns hired for summer jobs while they were home from college. A closer look into the case found ComEd money funneled to a "roster" of Madigan associates: retiring Twenty-Third Ward Alderman Mike Zalewski, whose home had been raided a year earlier; ex-Alderman Frank Olivo, who once represented Madigan's Thirteenth Ward; and Cook County Recorder of Deeds Ed Moody, a longtime Madigan precinct worker with legendary door-knocking skills.[4]

Citing one high-level maneuver, prosecutors described a frenzied push to place former McPier convention place executive Juan Ochoa onto ComEd's board of directors. In 2017 Madigan allegedly sought the Ochoa appointment through McClain, who no longer lobbied but still worked with the utility. McClain took it up with Anne Pramaggiore, who was then CEO of ComEd. Prosecutors said she met inside resistance and came up with a counteroffer. She allegedly asked McClain if Madigan would settle for giving Ochoa a seventy-eight-thousand-dollar part-time job instead. McClain, records showed, replied that Madigan would appreciate if Pramaggiore would "keep pressing." Pramaggiore eventually became CEO of Exelon Utilities and oversaw ComEd. She allegedly told McClain, "You take good care of me and so does our friend, and I will do the best that I can to take care of you." Nobody had to guess whom she meant when she said "our friend." In April 2019, Ochoa was appointed to the ComEd board, but he was gone by the time the company agreed to pay the $200 million fine in July 2020.[5]

Giving a glimpse into how clout translates to the private sector, the case detailed a McClain conversation in which he explained to a ComEd official in 2018 that a valuable Madigan associate on the utility payroll was "one of the top three precinct captains" who "trains people how to go door to door . . . so just to give you an idea how important this guy is."[6]

In the heat of the 2020 campaign, House Republican leader Jim Durkin of Western Springs, using Madigan's own House rules against him, sought immediately to increase scrutiny on the speaker. Durkin petitioned to hold hearings on whether Madigan's ties to ComEd should be considered conduct unbecoming a lawmaker and worthy of discipline that could, though considered a long shot, get the speaker removed from office. Madigan fired off a letter in which he refused to appear before the committee, calling Durkin's move a "politically motivated stunt motivated by a transparent political agenda using his government office and government resources to earn free media for himself and his political candidates." Durkin shot back: "Speaker Madigan continues to take the path that his own House rules apply to all except him."[7]

As we noted in the *Tribune*, there were a few things Madigan didn't mention in his letter to lawmakers—particularly that patronage jobs are the "lifeblood of Madigan's political organization," that the patronage workers often become foot soldiers who help Democratic legislative candidates get elected and vote to keep Madigan as the speaker, and that his powerful position in the House helps him generate business as the rainmaker for his private law firm, which wins major property tax reductions for numerous Chicago skyscrapers.[8]

In the end, Representative Emanuel "Chris" Welch, the Hillside Democrat who chaired the committee, ultimately stifled efforts to bring Madigan, McClain, and others to testify. Along the way, Welch sought to shift the blame onto Durkin based on an email trail that suggested he had urged ComEd to hire a GOP lobbyist. The what-about-ism argument gained little traction, yet Welch managed to protect Madigan from a deeper examination that he condemned as a Republican ploy. The hearings adjourned without taking action against the speaker, but Republicans had succeeded in using the process to muddy Madigan further.[9]

In late September, prosecutors added to the growing anguish in Democratic circles. Fidel Marquez, a former ComEd senior vice president who oversaw the company's lobbying, pleaded guilty to a charge of bribery conspiracy, making his first conviction in the sprawling utility case. He pledged to cooperate and expected leniency in return. Records showed McClain had advised Marquez in 2019 how to explain the various contract provisions to other ComEd officials: "I would say to you, don't put anything in writing. All it can do is hurt ya." One additional conversation cited in the case quoted Jay Doherty, a ComEd consultant and lobbyist who once headed the respected City Club of Chicago. Doherty allegedly told Marquez that the payments to Madigan associates were to keep the speaker "happy," according to ComEd's agreement with prosecutors.[10]

Citing Madigan's ties to the ComEd case, Democratic Representative Stephanie Kifowit of Oswego had seen enough. With the general election just a month away, she announced she would challenge Madigan for the speakership in the new term in January. Kifowit, a Marine Corps veteran, stood among a handful of House Democrats who had called for Madigan's resignation once he became Public Official A—what she called the "straw that broke the camel's back." She said the "people of Illinois have put up with these scandals and corruption for far too long." In response, Madigan said he was focused on the upcoming November election, the coronavirus outbreak, and beating Republican President Donald Trump: "We are at a critical juncture in our country, and all of us should be focused on coming together to defeat Donald Trump and repair the hate and division he has sown in our communities. We have a lot of work to do."[11]

The work, though, kept getting harder for Illinois Democrats up and down the ticket as Madigan's increasingly troubled status cast a shadow on the party. After years of unsuccessfully trying to boost their own political fortunes by trashing Madigan, Republicans found that the speaker's ComEd woes, which followed the lingering resentment over the sexual harassment scandal, had begun resonating with voters. Making Madigan Public Official A raised his profile—and not in a favorable way.

Republicans remained bent on using Madigan to weigh down any issue or candidate he touched. Madigan's decades-long support for Illinois Supreme Court Justice Thomas Kilbride, a Democrat, became a rallying point for his foes as he sought a third ten-year term. Republicans sent numerous attack brochures to residents, including one depicting Madigan and Kilbride dressed as James Bond–style secret agents, with the justice carrying a bag of money adorned with a giant dollar sign that represented the millions of dollars the speaker had poured into supporting the justice over the years. In many ways the Kilbride fight rekindled the old battle lines between Madigan and his Democratic special interest allies versus the wealthy Republicans who supported former Governor Bruce Rauner's antiunion, probusiness agenda.[12] The total $10.249 million spent supporting and opposing Kilbride's retention shattered the prior record for even a two-candidate race by nearly $1 million.[13] Spending for Kilbride hit $5.565 million, including $550,000 from Madigan's state Democratic Party in the closing weeks of the campaign. Kilbride opponents spent $4.684 million, an amount driven by Chicago hedge-fund billionaire Ken Griffin and other Republican funders. Kilbride's defeat meant Republicans would have a shot at toppling the high court's decades-old Democratic majority in a 2022 race to replace him.[14]

Republicans used Madigan as a foil on Pritzker's proposed tax amendment that called on voters to approve a higher tax for people with the highest incomes. They urged voters to question whether they could trust Democrats like Madigan and Pritzker with more of their money. Griffin, the conservative billionaire, pumped millions of dollars into both defeating Pritzker's graduated income tax proposal and denying Kilbride another term. Pritzker, the billionaire governor, poured $58 million of the $62.01 million raised to support higher taxes on a small percentage of people earning the biggest paychecks. Griffin, in turn, contributed $53.75 million of the $62.81 million raised to drive an effective opposition campaign.[15] Griffin disparaged the proposed amendment as "Gov. Pritzker and Mike Madigan's tax increase" and pointed out that the ComEd case implicated the speaker.[16]

Pritzker, whose tax proposal went on the ballot during his midterm election rather than when he ran for governor, had counted on voters to help plug a multibillion-dollar budget hole. But when the Pritzker amendment fell short, he and other leading Democrats looked around for a common theme among their losses—and someone else to blame. And they turned on Madigan, who also lost one House seat from his all-time-high majority.

U.S. Senator Dick Durbin, the Illinois Democrat freshly elected to his fifth term, told WTTW-TV that Democrats "paid a heavy price for the speaker's chairmanship of the Democratic Party." Durbin said Madigan should step down as party chair, and Pritzker echoed that sentiment. Democratic U.S. Senator Tammy Duckworth went further, saying Madigan should resign from both the party chairmanship and the speakership. But Madigan held firm.[17]

Two weeks after the election, pressure on Madigan intensified. Lausch unveiled a sweeping federal corruption indictment against McClain, the speaker's friend and confidant. Pramaggiore, Hooker, and Doherty were also indicted in the alleged scheme to funnel contracts and little-work jobs to Madigan loyalists in exchange for his help with ComEd's legislative agenda. All pleaded not guilty. Patrick Cotter, McClain's lawyer, said the indictment was the product of a prosecutor's zeal to put "maximum pressure on Mike McClain" to get to Madigan. But Cotter contended that McClain "cannot agree to allegations that are untrue, even to escape the crippling weight of the government's attacks," an improper attempt to "criminalize long-recognized legitimate, common, and normal lobbying activity into some new form of crime."[18]

Backed into a corner politically by the faltering support of his own House Democrats and legally by federal prosecutors winning indictments against his associates, Madigan prepared to engage in one of the biggest battles of his career. If he secured one more term as speaker, Madigan would keep control of the House he had built. He could redraw the legislative district boundaries to ensure that Democrats controlled the General Assembly up through at least the 2032 election. Illinoisans, as usual, would have to wait to see what he was thinking. But not for long.

Madigan struck back at the heart of the indictment the day after it reverberated throughout the state, saying in a statement that he was unaware of any attempt to influence him and that such an effort "would have been profoundly unwelcome." In one of his strongest denials, the Madigan statement said:

> If there was credible evidence that I had engaged in criminal misconduct, which I most certainly did not, I would be charged with a crime. But I have not, and with good reason because there is nothing wrong or illegal about making job recommendations, regardless of what people inside ComEd may have hoped to achieve from hiring some of the people who were recommended.
>
> Nonetheless, even though I am not alleged to have done anything in my official capacity as Speaker of the House to assist ComEd and have not been accused of any wrongdoing, this investigation has been used as a political weapon by those who seek to have me step down. I anticipate some will be disappointed that I was not a party to this indictment and find it difficult to swallow the fact that I have not been accused of or charged with any wrongdoing. These same individuals will likely claim this indictment should end my tenure as a public official, even though it alleges no criminal conduct on my part, nor does it allege I had knowledge of any criminal conduct by others.
>
> Some individuals have spent millions of dollars and worked diligently to establish a false narrative that I am corrupt and unethical. I have publicly

ignored their antics because those who know me and work with me know that this rhetoric is simply untrue. The truth is that I have never engaged in any inappropriate or criminal conduct. Despite baseless speculation alluding to the contrary, I have always gone to great lengths to ensure my conduct is legal and ethical, and any claim to the contrary is patently false.[19]

Madigan kept moving forward with plans to seek his nineteenth term as speaker, making his usual postelection calls to House Democrats asking for their support. But his support suddenly began eroding faster. Just two days after the McClain indictments, ten rank-and-file Democrats joined Kifowit and seven other members in announcing they would not support Madigan for another term. That raised the total to eighteen. If the eighteen held fast, Madigan would not be able to acquire the sixty votes needed from the seventy-three-member caucus he would have starting in January 2021.[20]

The nineteenth defector to go public, Representative Kathleen Willis of Addison, stung Madigan even harder. Willis was part of Madigan's leadership team, the majority conference chairperson whom the speaker once had recruited to make inroads into the suburbs. She and Chicago Representative Ann Williams, another member of the nineteen, soon jumped into the race for speaker. This type of mutiny was unheard of in the heyday of Madigan rule. But when House Democrats all gathered behind closed doors in Springfield, Madigan could muster only fifty-one of the sixty votes he needed. Along with several white downstate and Chicago establishment Democrats, Madigan had the steadfast support of twenty-one of twenty-two members of the House Black Caucus and ten of fourteen in the Latino Caucus. Williams received eighteen votes, the highest tally any woman would get. Williams, Willis, and Kifowit eventually all dropped out of the running. But while Madigan insiders hoped the bloc of nineteen opponents would crumble, the defectors issued a statement saying they would not back down.[21]

Still short of votes, Madigan pulled a major surprise only two days before the new legislative term would begin. He made a calculation that hinged on whether other lawmakers would be able to round up enough votes to be speaker. He put his bid for speaker on hold on January 11, a Monday, but he left open the possibility of a comeback if no one else could put together sixty votes when the House started a new term on Wednesday. "This is not a withdrawal," he said. "I have suspended my campaign for speaker. As I have said many times in the past, I have always put the best interest of the House Democratic Caucus and our members first. The House Democratic Caucus can work to find someone, other than me, to get 60 votes for speaker." Two major contenders surfaced quickly: Representative Chris Welch, the eight-year Black Caucus member who had stymied Republicans as chair of the House special investigation into Madigan, and Representative Jay Hoffman of downstate Swansea, a white, twenty-seven-year veteran who was on the speaker's leadership team but years earlier had bucked Madigan and allied himself with Governor Rod Blagojevich against the speaker.[22]

Madigan wasn't finished with surprises. Welch maintained that Madigan had called him that Monday morning and asked a key question: "Chris, do you want to be speaker?" Welch, like all but one of the twenty-two members of the House Black Caucus, had voted for Madigan for another term, so he spoke carefully: "I said, 'Mr. Speaker, if there's an opening, I don't know who wouldn't want an opportunity to make history. I do believe I would do a good job with it.'" Welch recalled in an interview with statehouse reporter Brenden Moore of Lee Enterprises that Madigan offered advice: "'I think you need to call your Black Caucus into a meeting and see if you can get them to endorse you for speaker. If you can get the Black Caucus to unite behind your candidacy, you should then go to the Latino Caucus, and see if they will unite behind your candidacy.'" Welch said the speaker advised that the next step would be to talk to downstate Democrats and "talk about their issues and assure them that you'll be a speaker that'll listen to them and be able to help." But Welch also recalled one more all-important piece of advice from Madigan: "And he says, 'But before you do any of those three things, call your wife[,] because if she says no, none of this matters.'" Welch got approval from his wife, ShawnTe, in his next call and started to work the plan.[23] He won the backing of the House Black Caucus late Monday and later picked up momentum with support from the House Democrat Latino Caucus.

As Welch moved closer to victory, though, he needed to answer questions about his past treatment of women. Most pressing was a 2002 police report in which an ex-girlfriend said Welch had slammed her head into a kitchen countertop and a 2010 sexual harassment lawsuit that alleged a different woman had lost her job at Proviso Township High School District 209 because she broke up with him while he was president of the school board. Though the details popped up in routine background checks of a politician on the verge of rising into a prominent position, Welch issued a statement blaming Republicans for the matters surfacing: "At no other occasion have these events been brought up, and I firmly believe my Republican colleagues are threatened by the potential growth of my profile." The issue drew a poignant question from Alaina Hampton, the former Madigan campaign staffer who had called out one of his aides for sexual harassment: "How does our state go through a #MeToo scandal that lasted two years and the solution to replacing Michael Madigan" is with a lawmaker once cited in a police report over allegations of domestic violence?[24]

With Democrats racing the clock to find a speaker by the time they were sworn in at noon on Wednesday, January 13, Durkin disclosed that Welch had sent "emissaries" in hopes of gaining Republican crossover votes to get to sixty, but Durkin said none of his forty-five GOP lawmakers would break ranks. Durkin saw Welch, a Madigan ally, as an "extension of Mike Madigan."[25] By late Tuesday, Welch had fifty votes compared to Hoffman's fifteen. Eight representatives—including Madigan—voted present. On Wednesday morning, shortly before lawmakers were sworn in for a new term, Welch tallied fifty-five in a closed-door caucus ballot. On the brink of starting a new term without a speaker, Welch nailed down his final five votes to get to sixty when he reached an agreement to keep Hoffman on the House Democratic leadership team. The deal was cut with only about an hour to spare. When the House was sworn in, Welch had received seventy votes, ten more than necessary, including one vote from Madigan.[26]

Only two years earlier, Madigan had taken the oath as the all-powerful speaker, with his biggest majority ever, looking forward to a new Democratic governor and preparing to deliver on a blockbuster spring session he would judge to be "historic." He had survived a #MeToo scandal that weakened him along with relentless personal Republican attacks designed to tear him down. But time caught up with the then seventy-eight-year-old Madigan's once deft ability to change course when he was waylaid by negative headlines. Despite not being charged with a crime, Madigan could not overcome the political damage of the federal government's ComEd investigation—a last-straw moment for too many of his Democratic troops.

Madigan's persistent push for old-style patronage, his legendary ability to squeeze votes when he needed them most, his fierce politics, his unrelenting fund-raising, his laser-like focus, his redistricting mastery that kept Democrats in charge, and his support from lobbyists, lawyers, and labor—all were not enough. There would be no White Sox Miracle, no powerful declaration of "Banzaiiiii!"

What was the speaker thinking? On the day he lost the gavel, he calmly walked away, down a long hallway, all alone. "It is time for new leadership in the House," he said in a statement. "I wish all the best for Speaker-elect Welch as he begins a historic speakership. It is my sincere hope today that the caucus I leave to him, and to all who will serve alongside him, is stronger than when I began," said Madigan, who marked his fiftieth anniversary in the House when he was sworn in. "As I look at the large and diverse Democratic majority we have built—full of young leaders ready to continue moving our state forward, strong women and people of color, and members representing all parts of our state—I am confident Illinois remains in good hands."[27]

The future of the House that Madigan Built was now not up to him. The Velvet Hammer's record reign as speaker was over.[28]

EPILOGUE

"I leave office at peace with my decision
and proud of the many contributions I've
made to the state of Illinois, and I do so
knowing I've made a difference."
—Rep. Michael Madigan,
    February 18, 2021

When he returned home from Springfield, stymied in his quest for one
more term as head of the Illinois House, Representative Michael Madigan's position as a rank-and-file lawmaker didn't have the same cachet
as that of the all-powerful speaker and the nation's longest-tenured legislative leader. Within weeks, he gave up the House seat he'd held for
just over fifty years and set his sights on orchestrating the selection of
his successor. Naturally, Madigan controlled the process of picking the
person who would replace him. He held 56 percent of the weighted vote
among Democratic committeepersons who would choose the new state
legislator to fill the vacancy. Their support was based on the share of votes
coming from wards and townships overlapping parts of Madigan's House
District 22. Once Madigan and other politicians listened to the pitches of
ten people who applied for his job, he did what one might expect from a
politician who promotes people in his political orbit. He chose Edward
Guerra Kodatt, a twenty-six-year-old aide to Thirteenth Ward Alderman
Marty Quinn. Some old political habits die hard. After all, Chicago is
where future liberal icon Abner Mikva once tried to join up with fellow
Democrats as a young University of Chicago law student and a ward heeler
bluntly told him, "We don't want nobody nobody sent."[1] But this time
Madigan's ward-style strategy backfired.

Madigan would not break away from his Thirteenth Ward myopia despite warning signs that his old-school methodologies had grown out of fashion. The insular political atmosphere he had fostered contributed to the sexual harassment controversy, inspired the over-the-top strategy to knock a college kid off the aldermanic ballot, and prompted a federal judge to say a jury could view evidence in the sham candidate case as a deliberate effort to interfere with voters' decisions. Even though prosecutors had implicated him in the patronage-style ComEd scheme to put his political friends on the utility's payroll, Madigan clung to his insider traditions. After Kodatt skated through his question-and-answer session with generic answers, Madigan gave him cover. "I think Mr. Kodatt will stand on his own merits," Madigan said. "He has spoken to his background. He spoke to his aspirations for service in the General Assembly, and I'm sure he'll be judged on his actions." On the same day, Madigan said he did not "feel the need to step down" as the state Democratic Party's chairman. Madigan had confided to friends that he planned to give up the chairmanship soon, but he told reporters, "We haven't gotten to that bridge yet." He had held the position since 1998, and his term did not expire until March 2022.[2] He ended the speculation the next day, confirming he would resign the chairmanship too. But it was Madigan's next big announcement that signaled his command of details had begun to wane.

Almost immediately after Madigan picked Kodatt, the deposed speaker learned of "alleged questionable conduct" about his successor. What was so egregious was not immediately made public, of course. Some things never change when it comes to Madigan and secrecy. But Madigan and Marty Quinn issued a joint statement that they were "committed to a zero-tolerance policy in the workplace" and that Kodatt had been asked to resign. Three days after he was crowned Madigan's successor, Kodatt dutifully caved and quit.[3]

No one could have imagined that Madigan would have been publicly humiliated this way when he held the speakership. At the height of his power, Madigan could not only command minions to dig up dirt against opponents in leave-no-stone-unturned background checks, but he could also blow up the tiniest issues into brutal political attacks. Now he couldn't even pick a successor—one working with his trusted Thirteenth Ward alderman—without the decision imploding. Kodatt had been properly vetted, Madigan said, but he wouldn't get into whether Kodatt spoke truthfully.[4] To both loyalists and detractors, Madigan's uncharacteristic stumble was a shocker, a symbolic coda to a reign once thought to be infallible.

Eager to put the Kodatt catastrophe behind him, Madigan took the equivalent of a political mulligan. He quickly threw support to Angelica Guerrero-Cuellar. She had finished second in the balloting among Democratic officials when Madigan chose Kodatt. She had been backed by Alderwoman Silvana Tabares, a former state legislator and Madigan ally serving as ward committee chair of the neighboring Twenty-Third Ward. In a hastily called second meeting, Guerrero-Cuellar became the second new state representative to hold Madigan's long-held seat in four days.[5] Married to a Chicago police officer, the daughter of Mexican immigrants was the mother of two daughters. She had worked as a community outreach organizer helping to fight COVID-19 on Chicago's Southwest Side.[6] Adding a dollop of irony was that Guerrero-Cuellar had campaigned for unsuccessful 2018 Cook County Board candidate Angie Sandoval, the daughter of then Senator Martin Sandoval. Madigan, then at growing odds with Senator Sandoval, had opposed the senator's daughter and helped defeat her.[7]

In Springfield, Madigan's replacement as speaker, Emanuel "Chris" Welch, made inroads in the spring 2021 session with rank-and-file Democrats who had wondered for decades what it would be like to have more input. Under the Madigan regime, many lawmakers were called "mushrooms" for being kept in the dark. House Republicans, naturally, said Welch's leadership fell short of his promise of a "new day." They contended their rights had been trampled upon, echoing the annual complaints of minority parties, including those of a young Minority Leader Madigan back when he started out as a legislative leader in 1981. And Republicans groused at having a budget shoved down their throats with little time to study it before an end-of-session vote. They felt a degree of vindication when last-second changes made by House Democrats meant Pritzker needed to use his veto power to rewrite dozens of passages to ensure that the budgeted money could be spent in the appropriate fiscal year. Both chambers had to approve Pritzker's changes before the budget would become law, an awkward do-over that required the House to give lawmakers permission to vote online. That type of rookie mistake would not have happened under Madigan.

What Welch did not lose sight of was that 2021 was a redistricting year, the most partisan of all partisan battles. Democratic mapmakers crafted state legislative boundaries that stretched the once-a-decade ger-rymandering of statehouse districts to new lengths. Borrowing a technique that Madigan had mastered, they repeatedly packed multiple incumbent Republicans into one district in hopes of thinning their ranks in the House. Democrats showed no qualms about realigning the Illinois Su-preme Court districts that Madigan had let languish on his watch. Faced with Democratic Justice Thomas Kilbride's loss, Democrats redrew the court boundaries to enhance the chances that they would keep both the seat and their 4–3 majority on the high court.[8]

For the state legislative districts, Democrats needed to redraw the boundaries in order to beat a June 30 deadline to complete the process or face the constitution's quirky winner-take-all drawing that would give both parties a 50–50 chance of winning the right to craft the maps with their own partisan tilt. The trick was completing the maps in the 2021 spring session without the final population figures from the U.S. Census, which were late and ultimately required a late summer do-over. Without a similar deadline to redraw congressional district boundaries for the U.S. House, Springfield lawmakers waited until the fall to construct the district maps for the federal candidates. Illinois lost one congressional seat due to its population decline, dropping to seventeen the members of Congress who would be elected in 2022.[9]

Though a *Politico* writer declared that Madigan had "punched his ticket to the partisan hall of fame" with a 2012 map that eventually netted a 13–5 Democratic advantage for the Illinois delegation in Washington, the new Democratic leaders in Springfield pondered how to pick up even more ground in the 2022 election.[10] Republicans who control other states, of course, worked on boosting their own ranks in Washington. But with a nation so evenly divided, every district counts. The partisan victories won simply by congressional mapmakers making tweaks here and there on district boundaries can make a difference in which party controls the U.S. House.

Meanwhile, as the ComEd's admission of a bribes-for-favors effort to woo Madigan hovered over the spring session, state lawmakers found themselves under pressure to improve the state's weak ethics laws. They did act, but nobody's going to be hailing the changes as a national model. Even so, the changes did mark the first basic improvements in extremely porous financial disclosures since the era of Secretary of State Paul Powell, whose 1970 death came complete with the discovery of $750,000 in cash in his suite at Springfield's St. Nicholas Hotel in two leather briefcases, three steel strong boxes, and an infamous shoebox.[11] Finally, following generations of lawmakers rolling off the state payroll and into lucrative lobbyist jobs, the new law limits this revolving door. But lawmakers will have to wait no more than six months, unlike bans of one or two years in other states.[12] Numerous lawmakers, particularly Republicans, and good-government groups groaned that the ethics changes didn't go far enough. But lawmakers did add bans on fund-raisers on the days before legislative sessions, an attempt to further address the coziness of the Madigan-style Evening on the Lake at the Springfield yacht club. They also required disclosures of consultants who operated as "shadow lobbyists" acting very much like registered lobbyists, one of many issues that arose in the ComEd probe.

Perhaps it should be no surprise that one of the biggest uncompleted deals of the Madigan-less spring session dealt with power companies. Exelon, ComEd's parent, came back to Springfield once again asking for more subsidies to save more nuclear power plants. Pritzker wanted to phase out coal-using and carbon-producing plants and expand clean energy like wind and solar. Labor folks understandably wanted to protect the jobs of miners, power plant workers, and the welfare of their families. Veteran lawmakers quietly questioned whether Madigan could have brought the disparate parties together rather than leave Springfield without a deal: Was Madigan's way better? Or worse? Without Madigan's presence as the adult in the room, lawmakers, special interest groups, and even Exelon had to feel their way around the new political zeitgeist, sometimes pressing the limits of what could and could not be done. Negotiators failed to come up with a compromise before the session ended but finally got it done in September.

At the Dirksen U.S. Courthouse in Chicago, more developments steadily unfolded in the ComEd case. Madigan's associates sought to knock holes in their criminal charges, and a grand jury kept rolling out indictments. Lawyers for Madigan's lobbyist pal Mike McClain and his codefendants argued that the longtime speaker never engaged in a quid pro quo in the bribery case, that he never cut deals to favor ComEd in exchange for favors or jobs. They compared Madigan's alleged activities to the politics of Illinois' all-time favorite son, Abraham Lincoln, who in May 1863 asked the U.S. Trust Corporation to hire the nephew of a Union general killed in a Civil War battle: "Even Abraham Lincoln, renowned for his honesty, made job recommendations while serving as president."[13]

Defense attorneys pulled back the curtain on one big question hanging in the ComEd case. They had heard that prosecutors were on the brink of bringing a major superseding indictment, leading them to question how they could plan when the case might become exponentially bigger. The not-so-subtle references prompted federal courts reporter Jason Meisner to jumpstart our story with this lede: "Michael Madigan was the elephant in the courtroom Wednesday as lawyers for four people charged with conspiring to bribe the former speaker on behalf of utility giant Commonwealth Edison said they expect more charges are coming soon in the bombshell case." We also learned that federal grand jurors continued to show interest in the former speaker. In secret grand jury testimony, former House Democrats explained the full breadth of Madigan's control of the chamber while he was speaker.[14]

Prosecutors then delivered one more unambiguous signal that they were far from done. They announced the indictment of Madigan's once-ubiquitous gatekeeper and hatchet man: Tim Mapes, the ex-speaker's longtime chief of staff, House clerk, and Democratic Party executive director, dumped in 2018 over sexual harassment allegations. Mapes had cut a deal with federal authorities for immunity from prosecution if he told the truth to the grand jury, but prosecutors contended he failed to go along. Mapes allegedly lied to a federal grand jury on March 31, 2021, when asked about Madigan's relationship with McClain and also about McClain's communications with Democratic state representatives on Madigan's behalf. The grand jury, according to the charges, wanted to know whether Madigan ever directed McClain to interact with House members, or "perform sensitive tasks," or exercise Madigan's "power and authority." Mapes pleaded not guilty, and his lawyers maintained the federal interest in charging Mapes was to squeeze him to get to Madigan.[15]

And then we learned a deeper truth, one that underscored how seriously federal authorities had been after Madigan. Even though Fourteenth Ward Alderman Ed Burke had been indicted with great fanfare on extortion charges, federal authorities saw his case as a spin-off. Madigan was the bull's-eye all along. Sources spelled it out in one more front-page story. Alderman Danny Solis of the Twenty-Fifth Ward had done extensive taping of Burke, but it was Madigan—not Burke—the feds first had in their sights when they approached Solis. Solis had audio and video of Madigan. Solis had even taped during the 2016 Democratic National Convention (DNC) in Philadelphia, where Madigan, Burke, and other elite Democrats gathered to nominate Illinois native Hillary Clinton. Given that Solis is the brother of Clinton's onetime 2008 presidential campaign chief Patti Solis Doyle, the recordings needed to be done with the utmost care. If a story had broken during the convention that Danny Solis was secretly recording at the DNC, the nightly news shows would have had a field day. Five years later, the revelations that the FBI first went to Danny Solis about Madigan provided fresh insight—as well as more intrigue—into the breadth of the investigation.[16]

Anyone with a remote interest in Illinois politics wondered what would happen next. They wondered whether the legacy of the speaker who built the House into a powerful political machine would stand or crumble. They wondered whether the Madigan Mystique would prevail or fail. And, of course, they wondered: What does the ex-speaker think?

ACKNOWLEDGMENTS

I would be remiss if I started this any other way. For if it were not for Dr. Nidhi Kansal and Dr. Christopher Malaisrie, I might not have been around to write this book. She identified a need for me to do a battery of tests, and he fixed me up in a six-hour surgery. I'm thankful for their care.

Just as critical are the numerous folks who helped give this book life. First among those I want to thank is Daniel Nasset, the editor in chief at the University of Illinois Press. He sent an email many moons ago with an invitation to write this book, and I am grateful for his faith and trust. With a cool head, he gave me the freedom, flexibility, and guidance needed for this book to take shape.

Most important, my life partner, Peggy Boyer Long, the former executive editor of *Illinois Issues* magazine and former public radio statehouse bureau chief, deserves a huge amount of credit for her many valuable suggestions from the time we started brainstorming to the moment I punched in the last period.

Longtime friend and onetime colleague Charles N. Wheeler III, a former *Chicago Sun-Times* statehouse reporter and retired director of the Public Affairs Reporting Program at the University of Illinois Springfield, came through on many levels, helping with historical context and details, as well as writing a foreword offering his fifty-year perspective on Michael Madigan. Multiple Democrats, Republicans, and lobbyists helped out but wanted their participation kept on the down-low, much like their assistance on stories over the years. Mike Lawrence allowed me to tap his vast experience as a longtime statehouse reporter, press secretary for Republican Governor Jim Edgar, and director of the Paul Simon Public Policy Institute at Southern Illinois University. Dennis Conrad, my former colleague with the Associated Press in Springfield, provided first-rate suggestions and intrepid fact-finding skills. Colleen Kujawa, a longtime *Chicago Tribune* copyeditor, contributed her sharp eye on the book's early pages, and Jill R. Hughes added her own smooth hand throughout for the University of Illinois Press.

Two academic reviewers who provided heft to this project were Chris Mooney, the W. Russell Arrington Professor of State Politics at the University of Illinois Chicago, and Kent Redfield, professor emeritus of political science at the University of Illinois Springfield. Others at the University of Illinois Press who contributed are Mariah Schaefer, Tad Ringo, and Lisa Connery.

Virtually all of my journalism colleagues and competitors over the years have made me a better reporter. Special thanks go to Bruce Dold, Peter Kendall, George Papajohn, Colin McMahon, and Christine Wolfram Taylor, top *Chicago Tribune* news executives who gave me the support necessary to move this project forward. *Chicago Tribune* political reporter Rick Pearson's prolific work on Madigan buttressed the tales outlined in many pages of this book. Former statehouse bureau mate Christi Parsons's decade covering Madigan before she followed Barack Obama to Washington added more invaluable insights. And more praise goes to Jeff Zeleny, who parachuted in to add his muscle to the Capitol beat, and to former bureau mate Jeffrey Meitrodt, who covered some of the more bizarre events of the statehouse circus under Governor Rod Blagojevich. They all teamed up with me to help make the Illinois statehouse a great beat. My hat is off to John Byrne, John Chase, Jeff Coen, Hal Dardick, Lisa Donovan, Monique Garcia, Kim Geiger, Ray Gibson, Jason Grotto, Christy Gutowski, Douglas Holt, David Kidwell, Susan Kuczka, Todd Lighty, John McCormick, Jason Meisner, David Mendell, Dan Mihalopoulos, Jamie Munks, Dan Petrella, Gregory Pratt, Bill Ruthhart, Erika Slife, Stacy St. Clair, Annie Sweeney, Gary Washburn, Andrew Zajac, Hanke Gratteau, Kerry Luft, Bob Secter, Jim Webb, Kaarin Tisue, Eric Krol, Matt O'Connor, Trevor Jensen, Phil Jurik, and Joe Biesk, current and past *Chicago Tribune* reporters and editors who worked with me on Madigan stories. And thanks to the awesome photographers whose pictures in these pages and on the cover enhance this book: Chuck Berman, Zbigniew Bzdak, Terrence Antonio James, Alton Kaste, John Kim, Jose More, Charles Osgood, Antonio Perez, Michael Tercha, and Pulitzer Prize winner E. Jason Wambsgans. Many thanks go to my friends Greg Campos, Al Martinez, Dennis King, and Mary Wisniewski for encouragement as well as to Pulitzer Prize winner Chuck Neubauer and legendary City Hall political reporter Bill Cameron, who graciously invited me to be on his radio shows and podcasts for three decades—about half of that time as a regular weekly panelist. In my forty-plus years spent tracking Illinois government and politics, the work of my other colleagues at *The Telegraph* of Alton, the Peoria *Journal Star,* the *Chicago Sun-Times,* the Associated Press, and the *Chicago Tribune*—and my many competitors—fleshed out the Madigan story I've put together.

This book is the first draft of Madigan's highs and lows. There are more chapters to be written about the nation's longest-serving speaker. Any mistakes or mischaracterizations are on me.

NOTES

Introduction

Epigraph. 101st Illinois General Assembly, House of Representatives transcript, June 1, 2019, https://www.ilga.gov/house/transcripts/htrans101/10100063.pdf.

1. Bill Ruthhart and Rick Pearson, "In Visit to Springfield, Chicago Mayor-Elect Lori Lightfoot Preaches Statewide Unity," *Chicago Tribune*, April 10, 2019.

2. Neil McLaughlin, "Wizard Madigan in Power," Associated Press, via (Decatur) *Herald and Review*, January 24, 1983.

3. Mike Lawrence interview of Michael Madigan, "One on One—Part 1," Paul Simon Public Policy Institute, spring 2004, https://www.youtube.com/watch?v=_GWfcInoVL8.

4. Amanda Vinicky and Craig Dellimore, "Michael Madigan: A DNC Interview with the Chairman of the Democratic Party of Illinois," Illinois Public Radio, August 1, 2016, https://www.nprillinois.org/post/michael-madigan-dnc-interview-chairman-democratic-party-illinois.

5. Kristen McQueary, "Sore Spot Remains on Statewide Ticket," *Daily Southtown*, August 13, 2006.

6. Dave McKinney, "The Man behind the Fiscal Fiasco in Illinois," Reuters, February 8, 2017, https://www.reuters.com/investigates/special-report/usa-illinois-madigan/.

7. Kim Geiger, "Rauner: I'm 'not in charge,' Speaker Madigan is," *Chicago Tribune*, December 4, 2017.

8. Monique Garcia, Rick Pearson, and Kim Geiger, "Illinois House Overrides Rauner Vetoes of Income Tax Increase, Budget," *Chicago Tribune*, July 7, 2017.

9. Michael Madigan deposition, *Gonzales v. Madigan et al.*, 2016 C 7915, September 13, 2018.

10. Ray Long and Rick Pearson, "Impeachment Inquiry Launched," *Chicago Tribune*, December 16, 2008.

11. Madigan deposition, *Gonzales v. Madigan et al.*

12. Democratic Party of Illinois, Michael J. Madigan, Chairman, "Illinois Voters Roundly Reject Republican Attacks on Speaker Madigan," Illinois Democratic Party of Illinois press release, November 7, 2018. Copy in author's possession.

13. Ray Long, Dan Petrella, and Jamie Munks, "Inside Illinois Lawmakers' Pork-Barrel Frenzy: Pickleball Courts, Dog Parks and Clout," *Chicago Tribune*, June 7, 2019.

14. Michael Madigan floor speech, Illinois House transcript, June 1, 2019, https://www.ilga.gov/house/transcripts/htrans101/10100063.pdf.

15. Ray Long and Jason Meisner, "Feds Recorded Calls of Close Confidant of House Speaker Michael Madigan: Sources," *Chicago Tribune*, November 13, 2019; Ray Long and Jason Meisner, "FBI Agents Asking Questions about House Speaker Madigan and His Political Operation, Say Four People They've Interviewed," *Chicago Tribune*, December 5, 2019.

16. Dan Hinkel, Rick Pearson, Alice Yin, Megan Crepeau, and Annie Sweeney, "Federal Investigation Draws Closer to Madigan as ComEd Will Pay $200 Million Fine in Alleged Bribery Scheme; Pritzker Says Speaker 'Must Resign' if Allegations Are True," *Chicago Tribune*, July 18, 2020.

17. Rick Pearson, Dan Petrella, Jamie Munks, Ray Long, and Megan Crepeau, "Michael Madigan's Decadeslong Grip on Illinois Ends as House Democrats Make Rep. Emanuel 'Chris' Welch State's First Black Speaker," *Chicago Tribune*, January 13, 2021.

Chapter 1. Remap Victory

Epigraph. Illinois House transcript, June 23, 1981, p. 129, https://www.ilga.gov/house/transcripts/htrans82/HT062381.pdf.

1. United Press International, "Police Called as Democrats in Illinois Storm Podium," UPI, June 19, 1981.

2. The Associated Press, "Illinois House Erupts, Tempers Fly . . .," *The Southern Illinoisan*, June 19, 1981.

3. Charles N. Wheeler III email to Ray Long, December 3, 2020.

4. Illinois House transcript, June 18, 1981, p. 273, https://www.ilga.gov/house/transcripts/htrans82/HT061981.pdf.

5. Illinois House transcript, June 23, 1981, p. 95, https://www.ilga.gov/house/transcripts/htrans82/HT062381.pdf.

6. Daniel Egler, "Legislative Melee Erupts in Illinois." *Chicago Tribune*, June 20, 1981.

7. Illinois House Transcript, June 19, 1981, p. 16, https://www.ilga.gov/house/transcripts/htrans82/HT061981.pdf.

8. Illinois House transcript, June 19, 1981, p. 17, https://www.ilga.gov/house/transcripts/htrans82/HT061981.pdf.

9. Illinois House transcripts, June 23, 1981, p. 59, https://www.ilga.gov/house/transcripts/htrans82/HT062381.pdf.

10. Ibid.

11. Larry Sandler, "GOP Votes Congressional Remap," *Chicago Tribune*, June 24, 1981.

12. Illinois House transcript, June 23, 1981, https://www.ilga.gov/house/transcripts/htrans82/HT062381.pdf.

13. Ibid.

14. Ibid.

15. Ibid., 118.

16. Linnet Myers, "Remap Issue Explodes in House," *Chicago Tribune*, March 2, 1984.

17. Illinois House transcript, June 23, 1981, p. 126, https://www.ilga.gov/house/transcripts/htrans82/HT062381.pdf.

18. Ibid.

19. Ibid., 128–29.

20. Ibid., 129.

21. Charles N. Wheeler III, "A Democratic Decade?" *Illinois Issues*, April 1982, https://www.lib.niu.edu/1982/ii820410half.html.

22. Christi Parsons, James Oliphant, and Peter Nicholas, "'Time for Games Has Passed,'" *Chicago Tribune*, September 10, 2009.

23. Thomas Hardy, "Luck of the Draw to Settle Remap Fight," *Chicago Tribune*, September 5, 1991.

24. John Camper, "In Control: Everybody Listens to the Speaker," *Chicago Tribune*, July 5, 1988.

25. Wheeler, "Democratic Decade?"

26. Ray Long, "Lawmakers Brace for Rocky Ride on Remap, 3rd Airport and a Lot More," *Chicago Tribune*, January 11, 2001.

27. Richard E. Cohen, "Ill. Makes Redistricting Hall of Fame," *Politico*, June 3, 2011, https://www.politico.com/story/2011/06/ill-makes-redistricting-hall-of-fame-056225.

28. Katherine Skiba, "Illinois' Newer, Smaller Voice in D.C.," *Chicago Tribune*, January 2, 2013.

29. Rick Pearson, "Lawsuit Aims to Block Redistricting Reform," *Chicago Tribune*, May 13, 2016.

30. 2016 IL 121077, "*John Hooker et al., Appellees, v. Illinois State Board of Elections et al.* (Support Independent Maps, Appellant)," Illinois Supreme Court, August 25, 2016, https://www.chicagotribune.com/politics/ct-pdf-illinois-supreme-court-ruling-on-redistricting-ballot-question-20160825-htmlstory.html.

31. Ray Long, "Democrats Protect Their Own in State Legislative Remap," *Chicago Tribune*, August 9, 2011.

32. "Remarks by the President in Address to the Illinois General Assembly, February 10, 2016," White House transcript, https://obamawhitehouse.archives .gov/the-press-office/2016/02/10/remarks-president-address-illinois-general -assembly.

33. Adam Liptak, "Supreme Court Bars Challenges to Partisan Gerrymandering," *New York Times*, June 27, 2019.

34. U.S. Justice Elena Kagan, *Rucho v. Common Cause*, 588 U.S. (2019), Kagan J., dissenting, Nos. 18-422, 18-726, Supreme Court of the United States, June 27, 2019. https://www.supremecourt.gov/opinions/18pdf/18-422_9oll.pdf.

35. Author interview with Madeleine Doubek, executive director of CHANGE Illinois, by telephone, August 4, 2021.

36. Wheeler III, "Democratic Decade?"

Chapter 2. White Sox Miracle

1. Mark Brown, "Sox to City—We're Leaving—Addison 1st Choice, but Team May Leave State," *Chicago Sun-Times*, July 8, 1986.

2. Mark Brown, Charles N. Wheeler III, "Tax Boost Dead: Gov. Madigan Blamed," *Chicago Sun-Times*, June 29, 1988.

3. Illinois Senate transcripts, June 30, 1988, p. 168, https://www.ilga.gov/ senate/transcripts/strans85/ST063088.pdf.

4. Rick Pearson, "Miracle of '88 Led to This One," *Chicago Tribune*, October 26, 2006.

5. David Olinger, "Governor Calls His Feat a 'Baseball Resurrection,'" *St. Petersburg Times*, July 2, 1988.

6. Illinois Senate transcript, June 30, 1988, p. 169, https://www.ilga.gov/ senate/transcripts/strans85/ST063088.pdf.

7. Ibid., p. 172.

8. Ibid., pp. 175, 176.

9. Mark DePue, interview with James Thompson for oral history project of the Abraham Lincoln Presidential Library and Museum, October 27, 2015, https://www2.illinois.gov/alplm/library/collections/OralHistory/illinois statecraft/Thompson/Documents/ThompsonJam/Thompson_Jam_PFNL _Vol_V.pdf.

10. John Patterson, "How Thompson Kept the Sox in Chicago. Former Governor Came through to Preserve Deal," *Daily Herald*, October 15, 2005.

11. Charles McBarron, "White Sox Stadium Vote," June 30, 1988, https:// www.youtube.com/channel/UCyt8WunUxe6_gdNXemE5-_g.

12. Illinois House transcript, June 30, 1988, p. 199, https://www.ilga.gov/ house/transcripts/htrans85/HT063088.pdf.

13. Ibid.

14. John Kass and Daniel Egler, "Legislators Vote to Save Sox. Bipartisan Rally Pushes Deal Through," *Chicago Tribune*, July 1, 1988.

15. Illinois House transcript, June 30, 1988, p. 201, https://www.ilga.gov/ house/transcripts/htrans85/HT063088.pdf.

16. Ibid., p. 205.

17. McBarron, "White Sox Stadium Vote."

18. Ibid.

19. Ibid.

20. Ibid.

21. Illinois House transcript, June 30, 1988, p. 205, https://www.ilga.gov/house/transcripts/htrans85/HT063088.pdf.

22. Ibid.

23. McBarron, "White Sox Stadium Vote."

24. Ibid.

25. Mark Brown, "'Shot Clock' Saves the Sox," *Chicago Sun-Times,* July 3, 1988.

26. McBarron, "White Sox Stadium Vote."

27. Ibid.

28. Illinois House transcript, June 30, 1988, p. 205, https://www.ilga.gov/house/transcripts/htrans85/HT063088.pdf.

29. Rick Pearson, "Miracle of '88 Led to This One," *Chicago Tribune,* October 26, 2005.

30. Illinois House transcript, June 30, 1988, p. 205, https://www.ilga.gov/house/transcripts/htrans85/HT063088.pdf.

31. Ibid.

32. Ibid.

33. Olinger, "Governor Calls His Feat a 'Baseball Resurrection."

34. Kass and Egler, "Legislators Vote to Save Sox."

35. Pearson, "Miracle of '88 Led to This One."

36. Kass and Egler, "Legislators Vote to Save Sox."

37. McBarron, "White Sox Stadium Vote."

38. Olinger, "Governor Calls His Feat a 'Baseball Resurrection."

39. Pearson, "Miracle of '88 Led to This One."

40. Mark DePue, interview with James Thompson, October 27, 2015.

41. Ibid.

42. Kass and Egler, "Legislators Vote to Save Sox."

43. Bruce Rushton, "Steve Brown Has a Front-Row Seat to Illinois' Politicians. After 37 Years, He's Winding Down," *State Journal-Register,* July 2, 2021, https://www.sj-r.com/story/news/politics/2021/07/02/former-michael-madigan-spokesperson-speaks-up-career-winds-down/7834855002/.

44. Illinois House roll call, Senate Bill 2202, July 1, 1988.

45. Mark DePue, interview with Lee Daniels for oral history project of the Abraham Lincoln Presidential Library and Museum, February 8, 2012, https://presidentlincoln.illinois.gov/Resources/5aefa81a-0fbc-4535-a905-674f60dba093/Daniels_Lee_4FNL.pdf.

46. DePue, interview with James Thompson, October 27, 2015.

47. Pearson, "Miracle of '88 Led to This One."

Chapter 3. Operation Cobra

1. Daniel Egler and Rick Pearson, "State Income Tax Hike Gains," *Chicago Tribune,* May 18, 1989.

2. Ray Long, "Political Fear May Be Toughest Hurdle," Associated Press, April 9, 1997.

3. Joan A. Parker, "The Only Game in Town," *Illinois Issues*, August 1983, https://www.lib.niu.edu/1983/ii830804.html.

4. Illinois House transcript, May 17, 1989, p. 57, https://www.ilga.gov/house/transcripts/htrans86/HT051789.pdf.

5. Ibid., pp. 58, 59, 60, 61.

6. Ibid., p. 62.

7. Ibid., pp. 76, 77, 78.

8. Daniel Egler and R. Bruce Dold, "Madigan's Tax Flip-Flop Has Heads Spinning," *Chicago Tribune*, May 18, 1989.

9. Don Thompson, "Madigan Used 'Surprise Element,'" *The Pantagraph* (Bloomington), May 21, 1989, https://mail.google.com/mail/u/0/?tab=rm&ogbl#search/Don+Thompson/FMfcgxwJXVJCJgbHJJFStbJcZHNfjSnM?projector=1&messagePartId=0.1.

10. Kathleen Best, "Thompson Loses in Tax Fight," *St. Louis Post-Dispatch*, May 21, 1989.

11. Ray Long, "Senate Warfare May Doom Madigan's Income Tax Hike," *Crain's Chicago Business*, June 5, 1989.

12. Daniel Egler, "Madigan Tax Plan May Be It, Republicans Unable to Reach Compromise," *Chicago Tribune*, June 28, 1989.

13. Ibid.

14. Daniel Egler, "Democrats Sweeten Tax Plan," *Chicago Tribune*, June 30, 1989.

15. Illinois House transcript, June 30, 1989, p. 85, https://www.ilga.gov/house/transcripts/htrans86/HT063089.pdf.

16. Daniel Egler, "20% Income Tax Hike Passes," *Chicago Tribune*, July 1, 1989.

17. Ray Long, interview with Jim Edgar, February 3, 2021.

18. Rick Pearson, "House OKs Deal to End Budget Crisis Surcharge, Tax Cap Sent to Senate," *Chicago Tribune*, July 18, 1991.

19. Charles N. Wheeler III, "Edgar-Madigan Duel Drags On," *Chicago Sun-Times*, July 7, 1991.

20. Rick Pearson and Hugh Dellios, "McCormick Expansion Improved," *Chicago Tribune*, July 19, 1991.

21. Rick Pearson and Tim Jones, "Edgar, Top Legislators OK Deal," *Chicago Tribune*, June 30, 1993.

22. Rick Pearson and Tim Jones, "Legislature Wraps It All Up," *Chicago Tribune*, July 14, 1993.

23. Thomas Hardy and Susan Kuczka, "Democrats Left to Pick Up Pieces," *Chicago Tribune*, November 10, 1994.

24. Ray Long and Michael Gillis, "Pate's Declaration: Let's Swap Taxes; The Idea: Property Tax Down, Other Levies Up," *Chicago Sun-Times*, November 11, 1994.

25. Rick Pearson, "Edgar Readies Tax Bombshell," *Chicago Tribune*, March 21, 1996.

26. Rick Pearson, "GOP Kills Edgar's School Tax Plan," *Chicago Tribune*, March 28, 1996.

27. Ibid.

28. Ray Long, interview with Jim Edgar, February 3, 2021.

29. Rick Pearson and Courtney Challos, "Madigan Has His Side behind Edgar Tax Plan," *Chicago Tribune*, May 17, 1997.

30. Rick Pearson, "Edgar's School Bill Survives," *Chicago Tribune*, May 30, 1997.

31. Rick Pearson, "GOP Leaders Team Up against Edgar's School Plan," *Chicago Tribune*, May 28, 1997.

32. Molly Parker, "Former Gov. Edgar: Speaker Madigan Is 'Not the Big Problem' in Springfield Political Standoff," *Southern Illinoisan*, May 4, 2017, https://thesouthern.com/news/local/govt-and-politics/former-gov-edgar-speaker-madigan-is-not-the-big-problem-in-springfield-political-standoff/article_1c0f61ff-03fa-516e-b0a0-641c561debf3.html.

Chapter 4. Historic Impeachment

1. Rick Pearson and Jeff Coen, "U.S. Say Blagojevich, Crew Ran State as a Racket," *Chicago Tribune*, April 3, 2009.

2. Jeff Coen and Rick Pearson, "Blagojevich Arrested on Federal Charges," *Chicago Tribune*, December 9, 2008.

3. Jeff Coen, Rick Pearson, and David Kidwell, "Blagojevich Arrested; Fitzgerald Calls It a 'Political Corruption Crime Spree,'" *Chicago Tribune*, December 10, 2008.

4. Coen and Pearson, "Blagojevich Arrested on Federal Charges."

5. Illinois House Speaker Michael Madigan news conference at Illinois State Capitol, December 15, 2008.

6. Ray Long and Rick Pearson, "Impeachment Inquiry Launched," *Chicago Tribune*, December 16, 2009.

7. Ray Long and Jeff Coen, "We're Fighting Shadows," *Chicago Tribune*, December 30, 2008.

8. CNN, "Blago's Lead Defense Lawyer to Resign," *Political Ticker*, January 24, 2009, https://politicalticker.blogs.cnn.com/2009/01/24/blagos-lead-defense-lawyer-to-resign/.

9. Daniel W. Cain, FBI special agent, "*United States of America v. Rod R. Blagojevich and John Harris*," FBI Affidavit, December 7, 2008, https://www.justice.gov/archive/usao/iln/chicago/2008/pr1209_01a.pdf.

10. Ibid.

11. John Chase, "Old Allies Rahm Emanuel and Rod Blagojevich in Spotlight Again," *Chicago Tribune*, April 17, 2011.

12. Cain, "*United States of America v. Rod R. Blagojevich.*"

13. Jeff Coen, John Chase, and David Kidwell, "Feds Taped Blagojevich," *Chicago Tribune*, December 5, 2008.

14. Bob Secter and Jeff Coen, "Blagojevich Had Big Plans, Witness Says: White House Hopes Linked to Pay-to-Play, *Clout Street*, April 15, 2008, https://newsblogs.chicagotribune.com/clout_st/2008/04/witness-links-b.html.

15. House Speaker Michael Madigan press conference recording, "Madigan Announces Committee to Look into Impeachment," *Illinois Information Service*, December 15, 2008.

16. Ray Long and Monique Garcia, "Quinn Grabs at Reins, Wants Blagojevich Out," *Chicago Tribune*, December 12, 2008.

17. Illinois House transcript, December 15, 2008, https://www.ilga.gov/house/transcripts/htrans95/09500295.pdf.

18. Rick Pearson, "Tribune Poll: Blagojevich's Popularity at 13%," *Chicago Tribune*, October 23, 2008.

19. Jeff Coen and John Chase, *Golden: How Rod Blagojevich Talked Himself out of the Governor's Office and into Prison* (Chicago: Chicago Review Press, 2012), 256.

20. House Speaker Michael Madigan press conference at Illinois State Capitol, *Illinois Information Service*, December 15, 2008.

21. Ray Long, "Career of Contrasts," *Chicago Tribune*, December 9, 2008.

22. Ray Long and John Biemer, "Governor Defensive on Wife's Business; Questions Her Deals Called Sexist," *Chicago Tribune*, October 31, 2006.

23. House of Representatives, Final Report of the Special Investigative Committee, January 8, 2009, https://www.ilga.gov/house/committees/95Documents/Final%20Report%20of%20the%20Special%20Investigative%20Committee.pdf.

24. Ibid.

25. John Chase, Kim Barker, and David Kidwell, "How Illinois Flu Vaccine Vanished in Pakistan," *Chicago Tribune*, August 5, 2007.

26. Rick Pearson and Ray Long, "3 Kings' Egos Entangle Budget," *Chicago Tribune*, June 2, 2004.

27. Ray Long and Christi Parsons, "8 Weeks Late, Lawmakers OK $46 Billion Plan," *Chicago Tribune*, July 25, 2004.

28. Ray Long and Christi Parsons, "Democrats Try to Be Friends," *Chicago Tribune*, August 19, 2004.

29. Rick Pearson and John Chase, "Feds Hot on State Jobs Trail," *Chicago Tribune*, July 1, 2006.

30. Ray Long, Rick Pearson, and John Chase, "Watchdog Rips State Hiring," *Chicago Tribune*, July 2, 2006.

31. John Chase, "Governor Outspent Foe 3–1 Near End," *Chicago Tribune*, February 1, 2007.

32. Rick Pearson, "Judy Baar Topinka Remembered for Political Style," *Chicago Tribune*, December 10, 2014.

33. 2006 General Election Results, Illinois State Board of Elections records, https://www.elections.il.gov/ElectionOperations/ElectionVoteTotals.aspx?T=637404664074280659.

34. Rick Pearson, Ray Long, and David Mendell, "Charges against Tony Rezko, One of the Governor's Closet Fundraisers, Could Stir Firestorm on Eve of Election," *Chicago Tribune*, October 12, 2006.

35. Greg Hinz, "Blagojevich Plans New Payroll Tax," *Crain's Chicago Business*, March 2, 2007.

36. Ray Long and Jeffrey Meitrodt, "107–0," *Chicago Tribune*, May 11, 2007.

37. Ray Long and Jeffrey Meitrodt, "Budget Talks Hit Low Point." *Chicago Tribune*, July 8, 2007.

38. Ibid.

39. Ibid.

40. Ray Long and Jeffrey Meitrodt, "Despite Budget OK, Session Plods Along," *Chicago Tribune*, August 11, 2007.

41. Ray Long and Jeffrey Meitrodt, "Governor Picks and Chooses," *Chicago Tribune*, August 24, 2007.

42. Jeffrey Meitrodt and Ray Long, "Senate Won't Follow House on Override," *Chicago Tribune*, October 3, 2007.

43. Ray Long, author interview with confidential source in the days following Blagojevich veto of $463 million from budget on August 23, 2007.

44. Illinois House of Representatives, Final Report, January 8, 2009.

45. Jeffrey Meitrodt, Ray Long, and John Chase, "The Governor's $25,000 Club," *Chicago Tribune*, April 27, 2008.

46. Illinois General Assembly, House of Representatives, Final Report of the Special Investigative Committee, p. 29, https://www.ilga.gov/house/committees/95Documents/Final%20Report%20of%20the%20Special%20Investigative%20Committee.pdf.

47. Rick Pearson and Ray Long, "Gov. Rod Blagojevich Picks Former Attorney General to Replace Obama," *Chicago Tribune*, December 31, 2008.

48. Ibid.

49. Jill Zuckman and Rick Pearson, "It May Be the Time for Burris' Close-Up," *Chicago Tribune*, January 12, 2009.

50. Katherine Skiba, "Senate Ethics Panel Admonishes Burris," *Chicago Tribune*, November 21, 2009.

51. Rick Pearson and Ray Long, "House Panel Vote: Impeach Governor," *Chicago Tribune*, January 9, 2009.

52. Illinois House transcript, 300th Legislative Day, Illinois General Assembly, January 9, 2009, https://www.ilga.gov/House/transcripts/Htrans95/09500300.pdf.

53. Ray Long and Rick Pearson, "IMPEACHED, Blagojevich Vows to Fight," *Chicago Tribune*, January 10, 2009.

54. Ashley Rueff, "Deb Mell Refuses to Vote to Impeach Brother-In-Law Blagojevich," *Clout Street*, January 14, 2009, https://newsblogs.chicagotribune.com/clout_st/2009/01/deb-mell-refuse.html.

55. Illinois Senate transcript, "In re: Impeachment of Governor Rod R. Blagojevich," January 26, 2009, https://ilga.gov/senate/Impeachment/Transcripts/1-26-2009%20Transcript-FINAL.pdf.

56. Ray Long and Rick Pearson, "Blagojevich's 'Own Words' Merit Conviction," *Chicago Tribune,* January 27, 2009.

57. John Kass, "A Comedy for Some; For Us a Horror Show," *Chicago Tribune,* January 27, 2009.

58. Illinois Senate transcript, "In re: Impeachment of Governor Rod R. Blagojevich."

59. Ibid.

60. Ibid.

61. Ibid.

62. Ibid.

63. James Ylisela Jr., "Michael Madigan Is the King of Illinois," *Chicago,* November 20, 2012, https://www.chicagomag.com/Chicago-Magazine/December-2013/michael-madigan/.

64. Jason Meisner and Bob Secter, "Some Rod Blagojevich Convictions Tossed; Wife Tells Him Disappointing News," *Chicago Tribune,* July 21, 2015.

65. *United States of America vs. Rod Blagojevich,* Transcript of proceedings before the honorable James B. Zagel re-sentencing, Proceedings Before, In the United States District Court Northern District of Illinois Eastern Division, p. 49.

66. Ibid., p. 31, 32.

67. Stacy St. Clair, "Patti's Strategy: Fox News, Flattery and a Wife's Fervor," *Chicago Tribune,* February 19, 2020.

68. Jason Meisner, "Trump Floats Blago Clemency," *Chicago Tribune,* June 1, 2018.

69. Jason Meisner, Rick Pearson, and Erin Hooley, "Blagojevich Released from Prison," *Chicago Tribune,* February 19, 2020.

70. St. Clair, "Patti's Strategy."

71. Rod Blagojevich, "I'm in Prison for Practicing Politics," *Wall Street Journal,* May 28, 2018, https://www.wsj.com/articles/im-in-prison-for-practicing-politics-1527517322.

72. Rick Pearson and Jason Meisner, "Trump Considering Ending Rod Blagojevich's Prison Term, Citing 'Comey Gang and All These Sleazebags," *Chicago Tribune,* August 8, 2019.

73. Sophie Sherry and Stacy St. Clair, "Calling Himself a 'Freed Political Prisoner,' Rod Blagojevich Thanks Trump and Remains Unbowed," *Chicago Tribune,* February 20, 2020.

Chapter 5. Partisan Math

1. Ray Long and Ashley Rueff, "Quinn Faces 'Giant Hole,'" *Chicago Tribune,* February 5, 2009.

2. Ray Long and Ashley Rueff, "Big State Income Tax Hike?" *Chicago Tribune,* March 13, 2009.

3. Ray Long and John Chase, "Quinn Says Tax-Hike Plan Is about Reform," *Chicago Tribune,* March 14, 2009.

4. Rick Pearson and Ray Long, "Quinn Lets Tax Out of Bag," *Chicago Tribune,* March 19, 2009.

5. Rick Pearson and Ray Long, "Tax Hike Defeated; Budget Gap Remains," *Chicago Tribune*, June 1, 2009.

6. Ray Long, Monique Garcia, and Bob Secter, "Raise Taxes or Cut Education, Quinn Says," *Chicago Tribune*, March 10, 2010.

7. Ray Long and Monique Garcia, "Madigan Pulls Out All Stops," *Chicago Tribune*, January 6, 2011.

8. Ray Long and Monique Garcia, "On Deck: 75% Tax Hike," *Chicago Tribune*, January 7, 2011.

9. Ray Long, interview with Pat Quinn, February 5, 2021.

10. Ray Long, Rick Pearson, Monique Garcia, and Todd Wilson, "Democrats Rush for Tax Deal," *Chicago Tribune*, January 11, 2011.

11. Illinois General Assembly, House transcript, January 11, 2011, p. 113, https://www.ilga.gov/house/transcripts/htrans96/09600165.pdf.

12. Rick Pearson and Monique Garcia, "Dems Go Down to Wire on Tax Hike," *Chicago Tribune*, January 12, 2011.

13. Todd Wilson, "GOP Seeks Curbs on Lame-Duck Sessions," *Chicago Tribune*, March 13, 2011.

14. Illinois General Assembly, House transcript, January 11, 2011, p. 124, https://www.ilga.gov/house/transcripts/htrans96/09600165.pdf.

15. Pearson and Long, "Dems Go Down to Wire on Tax Hike."

16. Tribune Editorial Board, "All of These Quinncidences," *Chicago Tribune*, February 17, 2012.

17. Rick Pearson and Ray Long, "Democrats Dangled Deals to Bag Votes," *Chicago Tribune*, January 13, 2011.

18. Charles N. Wheeler III, "Democrat's Election Wins Make Illinois History," *Illinois Issues*, December 2012, https://www.nprillinois.org/post/democrats-election-wins-make-illinois-history#stream/0.

19. Ray Long and Monique Garcia, "Quinn Budget Keeps Tax Hike," *Chicago Tribune*, March 26, 2014.

20. Rick Pearson, Ray Long, and Monique Garcia, "Keep Tax Hike or Face Stark Cuts, Quinn Says," *Chicago Tribune*, March 27, 2014.

21. Ray Long, Monique Garcia, and Maura Zurick, "Madigan: Still 'Significantly' Short on Income Tax Vote," *Chicago Tribune*, May 20, 2014.

22. Charles N. Wheeler III, "End and Means: Budget Is Constitutionally Balanced but Full of Flaws," *Illinois Issues*, July/August 2014.

23. Ray Long, interview with Pat Quinn, February 5, 2021.

24. Monique Garcia and Rick Pearson, "Minimum Wage Hike Can Still Be Quinn Win," *Chicago Tribune*, November 17, 2014.

25. Bob Secter, Rick Pearson, and Monique Garcia, "Illinois Budget Big Challenge as Rauner Takes Over," *Chicago Tribune*, January 3, 2015.

26. Ray Long, notes from Rauner speech in Quincy, Illinois, November 1, 2014.

27. Ray Long, notes on Rauner at Pasfield House event, November 3, 2014.

28. Ray Long, "Gov. Quinn Says Post-Blagojevich Stability His Greatest Accomplishment," *Chicago Tribune*, January 6, 2015.

29. Ray Long, notes on question-and-answer session with reporters at Executive Mansion, January 2015.

30. Deposition of Michael J. Madigan on September 13, 2018. *Jason Gonzales v. Michael J. Madigan et al.*, 2014 C 7915.

31. Rick Pearson, Monique Garcia, and Ray Long, "Rauner's 'Turnaround Budget' Has Cuts Called 'Reckless,' 'Wrong Priorities,'" *Chicago Tribune*, February 19, 2015.

32. Molly Parker, "Former Gov. Edgar: Speaker Madigan Is 'Not the Big Problem' in Springfield Political Stand-Off," *Southern Illinoisan*, May 4, 2017, https://thesouthern.com/news/local/govt-and-politics/former-gov-edgar-speaker-madigan-is-not-the-big-problem-in-springfield-political-standoff/article_1c0f61ff-03fa-516e-b0a0-641c561debf3.html.

33. Kim Geiger and Monique Garcia, "Madigan Sends Rauner Message on Tax Hike Vote as Talks Break Down at Capitol," *Chicago Tribune*, July 1, 2017.

34. Dave McKinney and Karen Pierog, "Illinois House Passes $5 Billion Tax Package, Spending Plan," Reuters, July 2, 2017, https://fr.reuters.com/article/us-illinois-budget-idUSKBN19O020.

35. Monique Garcia, Rick Pearson, and Kim Geiger, "Illinois House Overrides Rauner Vetoes of Income Tax Increase, Budget," *Chicago Tribune*, July 7, 2017.

36. Illinois House transcript, July 6, 2017, p. 30, https://www.ilga.gov/house/transcripts/htrans100/10000075.pdf.

Chapter 6. The Art of Persuasion

1. Bob Crawford audio archive, University of Illinois at Chicago Library, September 14, 1988, http://findingaids.library.uic.edu/sc/MSCraw04.xml.

2. Monique Garcia, "Signed and Sealed: Illinois 16th State to Legalize Gay Marriage," *Chicago Tribune*'s blog *Clout Street*, November 21, 2013.

3. Monique Garcia, "Illinois Gay Marriage: How It Passed," *Chicago Tribune*, November 10, 2013.

4. Illinois House transcript, November 5, 2013, p. 71, https://www.ilga.gov/house/transcripts/htrans98/09800076.pdf.

5. Ibid.

6. Monique Garcia, "Quinn Signs Gay Marriage Bill into Law," *Chicago Tribune*, November 21, 2013.

7. Ray Long, "Illinois Gay Marriage Law Draws Exorcism in Springfield," *Chicago Tribune*, November 21, 2013.

8. Ibid.

9. Adam Liptak, "Supreme Court Ruling Makes Same-Sex Marriage a Right Nationwide," *New York Times*, June 26, 2015.

10. Dr. Robert V. Remini and Jason Marcus Waak, "Interview with Illinois House Speaker Michael J. Madigan," Richard J. Daley Oral History Collection at the Special Collections and University Archives Department at the University of Illinois at Chicago, August 10, 2009, https://blog.library.uic.edu/transcript_files/Madigan,%20Michael%2020090810.pdf.

11. In the United States Court of Appeals for the Seventh Circuit Nos. 12-1269, 12-1788, *Michael Moore, et al., and Mary E. Shepard, et al., Plaintiffs-Appellants, v.*

Lisa Madigan, Attorney General of Illinois, et al., Defendants-Appellees, https://cases
.justia.com/federal/appellate-courts/ca7/12-1269/12-1269-2012-12-11.pdf.

12. Ibid.

13. Ray Long, "Illinois Concealed Carry Ban Tossed by Federal Appeals Court," *Chicago Tribune,* December 12, 2012.

14. Ibid.

15. Ibid.

16. Illinois House transcript, May 24, 2013, p. 100, https://www.ilga.gov/house/transcripts/htrans98/09800062.pdf.

17. Ibid. pp. 100–101.

18. Ibid., pp. 35, 36.

19. Ray Long, Rick Pearson, and Monique Garcia, "Legislators' Time Running Out," *Chicago Tribune,* May 26, 2013.

20. Ray Long, "Illinois Senate Concealed Carry Showdown: One Up, One Down," *Chicago Tribune,* May 28, 2013.

21. Ray Long, telephone interview with Brandon Phelps, February 3, 2021.

22. Rick Pearson, Ray Long, Monique Garcia, "Hot-Button Issues Pile Up for Springfield Finale," *Chicago Tribune,* May 31, 2013.

23. Ray Long, telephone interview with Brandon Phelps, February 3, 2021.

24. Pearson, Long, and Garcia, "Hot-Button Issues Pile Up for Springfield Finale."

25. Illinois Senate transcript, May 31, 2013, p. 23, https://www.ilga.gov/senate/transcripts/strans98/09800062.pdf.

26. Ray Long, telephone interview with Bill Haine, April 22, 2021.

27. Ray Long, "Speaker Madigan Not Worried about Quinn on Gun Control Measure," *Chicago Tribune,* June 18, 2013.

28. Ibid.

29. Ray Long and Monique Garcia, "Quinn Writes Stricter Rules into Concealed Carry Bill," *Clout Street,* July 2, 2013, https://www.chicagotribune.com/politics/chi-quinn-writes-stricter-rules-into-concealed-carry-bill-20130702-story.html.

30. Ray Long, Monique Garcia, and Rick Pearson, "General Assembly Overrides Governor's Veto of Concealed Carry Bill," *Chicago Tribune,* July 9, 2013.

31. Neil McLaughlin, "Wizard Madigan in Power," Associated Press, Decatur *Herald and Review,* January 24, 1983.

32. Ibid.

33. Interview by Mike Lawrence, with Madigan on "One on One," 2004 SIU Public Policy Institute, https://www.youtube.com/watch?v=_GWfcInoVL8&list=UUCkGN04JBP0mw7JUWTDPJng&index=75&t=361s.

34. Response to question from audience at Elmhurst College forum, January 24, 2012, Elmhurst University, 5th Annual Elmhurst College Governmental Forum, https://www.youtube.com/watch?v=J8y3h_GqzJM.

35. Elmhurst College forum, January 24, 2012, Elmhurst University, 5th Annual Elmhurst College Governmental Forum, https://www.youtube.com/watch?v=J8y3h_GqzJM.

36. Ibid.

37. Justin Kaufmann, "Madigan Rule, Episode 2." Better Government Association podcast, October 2021.

38. Mark DePue, director of oral history, "Interview with Lee Daniels," Abraham Lincoln Presidential Library, February 8, 2012, https://www2.illinois.gov/alplm/library/collections/oralhistory/illinoisstatecraft/legislators/Documents/DanielsLee/Daniels_Lee_4FNL.pdf.

39. Ray Long and Monique Garcia, "Quinn Wants Lawmakers Back to Pass Minimum Wage Hike," *Chicago Tribune*, December 3, 2014.

40. Dan Petrella, "Gov. J. B. Pritzker Signs Law Raising Illinois' Minimum Wage to $15 an Hour by 2025," *Chicago Tribune*, February 19, 2019.

41. Ray Long, interview with Pat Quinn, February 5, 2021.

42. Amanda Vinicky and Craig Dellimore, "Michael Madigan: A DNC Interview with the Chairman of the Democratic Party of Illinois," Illinois Public Radio, August 1, 2016, https://www.nprillinois.org/post/michael-madigan-dnc-interview-chairman-democratic-party-illinois.

43. Ibid.

44. Ibid.

45. Ray Long, interview with Jim Edgar, February 3, 2021.

46. Ken Armstrong and Steve Mills, "Ryan Suspends Death Penalty," *Chicago Tribune*, January 31, 2000.

47. Ray Long, interview with Pat Quinn, February 6, 2021.

48. Ibid.

Chapter 7. Pension Failure

1. Ray Long and Monique Garcia, "Quinn: I Was 'Put on Earth' to Fix State Pension Mess," *Chicago Tribune*, April 20, 2012.

2. Doug Finke, "State-Funded Pensions Tapped," Peoria *Journal Star*, August 27, 2010, https://www.pjstar.com/article/20100827/NEWS/308279917.

3. State of Illinois Constitution, Article 13, General Provisions, Section 5, Pension and Retirement Rights, https://www.ilga.gov/commission/lrb/conent.htm.

4. Editorial, "Madigan Takes Charge," *Chicago Tribune*, May 1, 2013.

5. Kurt Erickson, "Madigan's Pension Plan Endorsed by Committee, Headed to House Vote," Decatur *Herald and Review*, May 2, 2013, https://herald-review.com/business/local/madigans-pension-plan-endorsed-by-committee-headed-to-house-vote/article_62690014-b2d9-11e2-aa49-001a4bcf887a.html.

6. Ray Long and Rafael Guerrero, "House Oks State Pension Fix," *Chicago Tribune*, May 3, 2013.

7. Ray Long, "Rival Pension Measures Could Force Showdown in Springfield," *Chicago Tribune*, May 7, 2013.

8. Ibid.

9. Charles N. Wheeler III, email exchange with author, January 9, 2021.

10. Ibid.

11. Ray Long, Monique Garcia, and Rafael Guerrero, "Senate Passes Pension Bill, Setting Up Showdown with House," *Chicago Tribune*, May 10, 2013.

12. Ray Long, "Illinois General Assembly; 1 Pension Shortfall, 2 Routes Out," *Chicago Tribune*, May 19, 2013.

13. Ray Long, Bob Secter, and Bill Ruthhart, "Illinois Lawmakers Strike Out on Pensions," *Chicago Tribune*, June 2, 2013.

14. Jamey Dunn and Meredith Colias, "Quinn Gives Committee Three Weeks for Pension Reform," *Illinois Issues* (blog), June 19, 2013, http://illinoisissues blog.blogspot.com/2013/06/quinn-gives-committee-three-weeks-for.html.

15. Monique Garcia, "Lawmakers Can't Agree on Pension Reform, Blame Quinn," *Chicago Tribune*, August 18, 2012.

16. Illinois House transcript, 98th General Assembly, House of Representatives, 1st Special Session, December 3, 2013, https://www.ilga.gov/house/transcripts/htrans98/09801003.pdf.

17. Ray Long and Monique Garcia, "Pension Deal Done," *Chicago Tribune*, December 4, 2013.

18. Dave McKinney, "What Went Wrong?," *Crain's Chicago Business*, August 10, 2015, https://www.chicagobusiness.com/static/section/pensions.html.

19. Long and Garcia, "Pension Deal Done."

20. Monique Garcia, Hal Dardick, and Rick Pearson, "Court Affirms Pension Rights," *Chicago Tribune*, July 4, 2014.

21. Ray Long and Hal Dardick, "Judge KOs Pension Law," *Chicago Tribune*, November 22, 2014.

22. Rick Pearson and Kim Geiger, "Court Strikes Pension Law," *Chicago Tribune*, May 9, 2015.

23. Illinois Official Reports, Supreme Court, "In re Pension Reform Litigation, 2015 IL 118585," May 8, 2015, https://www.illinoiscourts.gov/resources/53088c76-f22f-49db-9132-99d0fcb96235/file.

24. Bob Secter and Rick Pearson, "Pension Debate at 1970 Constitutional Convention Echoes in Today's Crisis," *Chicago Tribune*, September 23, 2013.

25. Justice Lloyd Karmeier, "In re Pension Reform Litigation," Illinois Supreme Court, May 8, 2015, https://courts.illinois.gov/Opinions/Supreme Court/2015/118585.pdf.

26. Eric Madiar, "Illinois Public Pension Reform: What's Past Is Prologue," *Illinois Public Employee Relations Report* 31, no. 3, p. 5, https://scholarship.kentlaw.iit.edu/iperr/94.

27. Ibid.

28. Ibid., 8.

29. Ibid., 11.

30. Ibid.

31. Ibid., 12.

32. Ibid., 13.

33. Ibid., 12.

34. Ibid., 13.

35. Ibid.

36. Ibid., 14.

37. Daniel Egler, "Thompson Signs Bills Altering Pension Plans," *Chicago Tribune*, August 24, 1989.

38. Madiar, "Illinois Public Pension Reform," 14.

39. Rick Pearson, "Edgar, Netsch Jostle on Pension Plans," *Chicago Tribune*, April 19, 1994.

40. Rick Pearson, "Compromise Bill Assures Cash for State Pensions," *Chicago Tribune*, August 23, 1994.

41. Illinois Commission on Government Forecasting and Accountability, *State of Illinois Budget Summary*, July 31, 2020, https://cgfa.ilga.gov/Upload/FY2021BudgetSummary.pdf.

42. Pearson, "Compromise Bill Assures Cash for State Pensions."

43. Ray Long, "Pension Rift Has Workers Retiring," *Chicago Tribune*, August 13, 2012.

44. Jason Grotto and Ray Long, "Digging a Pension Hole," *Chicago Tribune*, December 15, 2011.

45. Ibid.

46. Ray Long, "Pension Reforms on Fast Track," *Chicago Tribune*, March 25, 2010.

47. Grotto and Long, "Digging a Pension Hole."

48. Illinois Commission on Government Forecasting and Accountability, "Special Pension Briefing," November 2020, https://cgfa.ilga.gov/Upload/1120%20SPECIAL%20PENSION%20BRIEFING.pdf.

49. Bob Secter, "Brainstorming on Pension Fix Abounds after Illinois High Court Rejected Law," *Chicago Tribune*, May 16, 2015.

50. Ray Long, "Pension Reform Could Hit Oldest Retired Teachers the Hardest," *Chicago Tribune*, February 3, 2013.

51. Ray Long, "Court: Ill. Lobbyist Can Keep Public Pension Windfall," *Chicago Tribune*, April 5, 2019.

52. Jason Grotto, "How Daley Beefed Up His Pension Payouts," *Chicago Tribune*, May 2, 2012.

53. Dan Petrella, "Michael Madigan Resigns from Illinois House after Being Ousted as Speaker, Defends His Legacy in Face of 'Vicious Attacks,'" *Chicago Tribune*, February 18, 2021.

54. Jason Grotto and Ray Long, "Ex-Lawmaker Nearly Doubles His Pension with One Month of Work," *Chicago Tribune*, December 16, 2011.

Chapter 8. A Patronage Army

1. Robert V. Remini and Jason Marcus Waak, interview with Illinois House Speaker Michael J. Madigan, Richard J. Daley Oral History Collection, Special Collections and University Archives Department, University of Illinois at Chicago, August 10, 2009, https://blog.library.uic.edu/transcript_files/Madigan,%20Michael%2020090810.pdf.

2. Robert V. Remini and Jason Marcus Waak, interview with Illinois House Speaker Michael J. Madigan, Richard J. Daley Oral History Collection, Special Collections and University Archives Department, University of Illinois at Chicago, for online exhibit "Remembering Richard J. Daley," August 10, 2009, https://blog.library.uic.edu/transcript_files/Madigan,%20Michael%20 20090810.pdf.

3. Richard Wronski, "Metra Releases Names from Its 'Patronage Files,'" *Chicago Tribune*, April 16, 2014.

4. Ann L. Schneider and George Ranney Jr., "Transit for the 21st Century," Northeastern Illinois Public Transit Task Force Report, March 31, 2014, p. 53, available at https://www.chicagotribune.com/news/breaking/chi-transit-task -force-report-pdf-20140401-htmlstory.html.

5. Jeff Coen, Laurie Cohen, and Todd Lighty, "Official: Clout Got Rookie Job," *Chicago Tribune*, March 6, 2009.

6. Richard Wronski, "FBI File Sheds More Light on Disgraced Ex-Metra CEO," *Chicago Tribune*, April 3, 2014.

7. David Kidwell, John Chase, and Alex Richards, "How Madigan Builds His Patronage Army," *Chicago Tribune*, January 5, 2014.

8. Richard Wronski and Stacy St. Clair, "Metra CEO Memo Alleges More Madigan Influences," *Chicago Tribune*, July 12, 2013.

9. Ibid.

10. Ibid.

11. Ibid.

12. Paris Schutz, "Former Metra CEO's Memo Alleges Political Pressure," WTTW-TV, July 15, 2013, https://news.wttw.com/2013/07/15/former-metra -ceos-memo-alleges-political-pressure.

13. Rosalind Rossi, Art Golab, and Dave McKinney, "Metra Memo Blasts Madigan," *Chicago Sun-Times*, July 13, 2013, https://www.pressreader.com/usa/ chicago-sun-times/20130713/281479274014336.

14. Wronski and St. Clair, "Metra CEO Memo Alleges More Madigan Influences."

15. Stacy St. Clair and Richard Wronski, "Ousted Metra Chief Gives New Details on Patronage Allegations," *Chicago Tribune*, July 18, 2013.

16. Richard Wronski and Ray Long, "State IG: Madigan Did Not Break Ethics Rules on Metra Pressure Allegation," *Chicago Tribune*, April 9, 2014.

17. Kidwell, Chase, and Richards, "How Madigan Builds His Patronage Army."

18. Ray Long, "Madigan's Metra Influence Detailed in Report," *Chicago Tribune*, July 8, 2014.

19. Ibid.

20. Ibid.

21. Ibid.

22. Ibid.

23. Ibid.

24. Ibid.

25. Hal Dardick, Ray Long, and Gregory Pratt, "Toni Preckwinkle Hired the Children of Politicians, Former Aldermen, Daley and Madigan Workers—Despite Her Pledge to End Patronage," *Chicago Tribune*, March 27, 2019.

26. Ray Long, "Report Slams IDOT Political Hiring," *Chicago Tribune*, August 22, 2014.

27. Bill Cameron, "Shakman—Patronage Bad for 3 Reasons," WLS-AM 890, May 5, 2014.

28. Author interview with Attorney Mary Lee Leahy in 2000s.

29. Michael Madigan deposition, *Jason Gonzales vs. Michael Madigan et al.*, N. 2016 C 7915, Northern District of Illinois Eastern Division, September 13, 2018.

30. Jeff Coen and Todd Lighty, "Madigan Letters Offer Glimpse of Clout in Cook County Judge Selection," *Chicago Tribune*, April 15, 2011.

31. Ibid.

32. Ibid.

33. Remini and Waak, interview with Illinois House Speaker Michael J. Madigan, August 10, 2009.

34. John Camper, with Daniel Egler and Tim Franklin contributing, "In Control," *Chicago Tribune*, July 5, 1988.

35. Michael Madigan deposition, *Jason Gonzales v. Michael Madigan et al.*, September 18, 2018.

36. Ibid.

37. William Gaines and Bob Secter, "Job Fortunes Rose with Richard J.'s," *Chicago Tribune*, June 13, 1999.

38. Ray Long, "House Speaker Michael Madigan Says It's Not 'Ethically Improper' to Find Government Jobs for People. Here's What He's Failing to Mention," *Chicago Tribune*, October 2, 2020.

Chapter 9. Madigan and Madigan

1. Rick Pearson, "Big-Dollar Donors Favor Lisa Madigan in 1st Quarter," *Chicago Tribune*, April 5, 2013.

2. Rick Pearson, Ray Long, and Monique Garcia, "Lisa Madigan Takes Pass on Governor's Race," *Chicago Tribune*, July 15, 2013.

3. Ibid.

4. Monique Garcia, "Speaker Madigan: Daughter Knew I Wasn't Going to Retire," *Chicago Tribune*, August 7, 2013.

5. Ibid.

6. Christi Parsons and Ray Long, "Her Own Space," *Chicago Tribune*, September 11, 2005.

7. Rick Pearson, "Farley Cries Foul in Run for Second Senate Term," *Chicago Tribune*, October 28, 1997.

8. Parsons and Long, "Her Own Space."

9. Christi Parsons and Mike Cetera, "Star Is Rising for a 2nd Madigan," *Chicago Tribune*, March 18, 1998.

10. Rick Pearson, "Madigan's Muscle Lifts Daughter," *Chicago Tribune*, February 24, 2002.

11. Ibid.

12. John McCormick, "Famous Dad a Mixed Blessing for Madigan," *Chicago Tribune*, October 13, 2002.

13. John Kass, "Madigan Expects Daughter's Win and Last Laugh," *Chicago Tribune*, March 13, 2002.

14. Christi Parsons and Rudolph Bush, "Madigan Defeats Schmidt," *Chicago Tribune*, March 20, 2002.

15. Eric Zorn, "Ruling to Test Madigan's Talk of Truth, Justice," *Chicago Tribune*, June 24, 2003.

16. Ray Long, interview with Joe Birkett, February 5, 2021.

17. Dan Mihalopoulos, "For Ex-Boxer Birkett, It's Bout of His Life," *Chicago Tribune*, October 13, 2002.

18. Ray Long, "Birkett Defends $10,000 Loan from DuPage Judge," *Chicago Tribune*, September 26, 2002.

19. Ray Long and John McCormick, "Patronage Pays for Lisa Madigan," *Chicago Tribune*, September 22, 2002.

20. Ibid.

21. Andrew Zajac and John McCormick, "Judge Defends 2 Sons' $50,000 Donation," *Chicago Tribune*, September 6, 2002.

22. Illinois State Board of Elections, Election Results, 2002 General Election, https://www.elections.il.gov/ElectionOperations/ElectionVoteTotals.aspx.

23. Ray Long, "Lisa Madigan Denies Asking for Senate Seat," *Chicago Tribune*, December 23, 2006.

24. John Chase, Mike Dorning and Rick Pearson, "Madigan: Decision to Pass on Senate, Governor 'Agonizing' But Best for Family," *Clout Street*, July 8, 2009, https://newsblogs.chicagotribune.com/clout_st/2009/07/madigan-to-seek-reelection-as-attorney-general.html.

25. Ibid.

26. Kim Geiger, Rick Pearson, and John Byrne, "Attorney General Lisa Madigan Won't Seek Re-Election in 2018," *Chicago Tribune*, September 15, 2017.

27. Courtney Flynn and John Chase, "Madigan Links Mob to Rosemont Mayor," *Chicago Tribune*, March 26, 2004.

28. Rick Pearson and John Chase, "Feds Hot on State Jobs Trail," *Chicago Tribune*, July 1, 2006.

29. Ray Long, Monique Garcia, and James Janega, "Madigan: He's Unfit," *Chicago Tribune*, December 13, 2008.

30. Crystal Yednak and David Mendell, "Blagojevich Told to Yield Subpoenas," *Chicago Tribune*, October 27, 2006.

31. John Chase and Ray Long, "Subpoenas Add Details of Probe," *Chicago Tribune*, December 30, 2008.

32. Rachel Droze, "Illinois House of Representatives: 34 Years under Madigan's Rule," WICS-TV, January 10, 2019, https://newschannel20.com/news/

local/illinois-house-of-representatives-34-years-under-madigans-rule-01
-11-2019.

Chapter 10. The Politics of Money

1. Author interviews with anonymous sources who spoke to Madigan following his fund-raiser and others familiar with his fund-raising.

2. Ray Long, "Lobbyists Bearing Gifts," *Illinois Issues,* April 1996, https://www.lib.niu.edu/1996/ii960426.html.

3. Kent Redfield, telephone and written communication with author, March 26, 2021.

4. Kent Redfield, data analysis and communication with author, March 26, 2021.

5. Kent D. Redfield, "What Keeps the Four Tops on Top? Leadership Power in the Illinois General Assembly," in *Almanac of Illinois Politics—1998,* ed. Jack R. Van Der Silk (Springfield: Institute for Public Affairs, University of Illinois at Springfield, 1998).

6. Kent Redfield, interview, data analysis, and communication with author, March 26, 2021.

7. Sandy Bergo and Chuck Neubauer, "Top Legislators Blowing Past Limits in Illinois Campaign Finance Reform Law," Better Government Association, August 7, 2020, https://www.bettergov.org/news/top-legislators-blowing-past-limits-in-illinois-campaign-finance-reform-law/.

8. Ibid.

9. Ray Long and Alissa Groeninger, "The Year's Busiest Day of Campaign Fundraising Shows How Springfield Really Works," *Chicago Tribune,* March 12, 2012.

10. Author's interviews with anonymous sources with knowledge of the fundraisers.

11. Kent D. Redfield, professor emeritus, University of Illinois Institute of Government and Public Affairs, campaign fund data analysis communicated to author, August 27, 2019.

12. Kent D. Redfield, professor emeritus based at the University of Illinois' Institute of Government and Public Affairs, ComEd and Exelon data analysis communicated to author, August 27, 2019.

13. Ray Long and Jamie Munks, "Watchdog Group Says 2011 Smart Grid Legislation Cited in Federal Bribery Case Put ComEd Interests over Public Good," *Chicago Tribune,* December 1, 2020.

14. Kent D. Redfield, professor emeritus based at the University of Illinois Institute of Government and Public Affairs, ComEd and Exelon data analysis communicated to author in email and interview, April 28, 2021.

15. Rick Pearson, "Madigan Exerts Might," *Chicago Tribune,* March 3, 1998.

16. Ray Long and Rick Pearson, "Taxpayers Paid Rent for Democrats, Madigan Satellite State Site for His Colleagues," *Chicago Tribune,* August 11, 2002.

17. Pearson, "Top of Ticket Woes Put Speaker on Spot."

18. Matt O'Connor, "Witness Links Trucker to Bribe," *Chicago Tribune*, September 28, 1999.

19. Rick Pearson, "Edgar, Rock Slam TV Ad from Poshard," *Chicago Tribune*, October 4, 1998.

20. Matt O'Connor and Ray Long, "U.S. Says Ryan Fund Got Money in License Scam," *Chicago Tribune*, October 7, 1998.

21. Rick Pearson, "Wary Democrats Brace for November," *Chicago Tribune*, October 18, 1998.

22. Less than a year into Ryan's tenure as governor, the Willis family secured a $100 million settlement for the deaths of their six children. Julie Deardorff, "$100 Million Settlement in Van Horror," *Chicago Tribune*, August 27, 1999. Ryan himself was indicted after leaving office in 2003 on sweeping corruption charges, found guilty, and sentenced to six and a half years in prison. Matt O'Connor, "Ryan Gets 6 ½ Years," *Chicago Tribune*, September 7, 2006.

23. Ray Long, Andrew Zajac, and Ray Gibson, "$1.5 Billion Pot Brims with Secretive Pork," *Chicago Tribune*, February 3, 2002; Ray Long, "Pork on the Burner While Budget Melts," *Chicago Tribune*, April 23, 2002.

24. Ray Long and Andrew Zajac, "Call It Pork-Barrel Halo Effect," *Chicago Tribune*, March 18, 2002.

25. Ray Long, interview with Jim Edgar, February 3, 2021.

26. Kurt Erickson, "It's No Wonder Madigan Loves That Pork Cologne," *The Pantagraph* (Bloomington), June 9, 2002.

27. Ray Long, "Money Flows to Madigan District While State Dollars Tight," *Chicago Tribune*, July 17, 2015.

28. Ibid.

29. Ibid.

30. Ray Long, "For First Time in 107 Years, Illinois House Prepares to Expel a Lawmaker," *Chicago Tribune*, August 16, 2012.

31. Ibid.

32. Ray Long, Maura Zurick, and John Chase, "Madigan Backs Lawmaker Two Years after Expelling Him," *Chicago Tribune*, March 16, 2014.

33. Jason Meisner, "Former State Rep. Derrick Smith Gets 5 Months in Prison for Bribery, Corruption Charges," *Chicago Tribune*, April 24, 2015.

34. Email and interview with Kent Redfield, May 2, 2021.

35. Ibid.

Chapter 11. Turning Point

Epigraph. Ray Long, "Speaker Madigan Cuts Political Worker Loose over Inappropriate Advances to Campaign Worker," *Chicago Tribune*, February 13, 2018.

1. The Women Who Make Illinois Run, "#MeToo? It's Time to Demand #NoMore in Illinois," open letter, October 22, 2017, https://drive.google.com/file/d/0B2l4co-dU1JJekJ0MG5mLTlEWE0/view.

2. Kim Geiger, "Madigan Bill Urges Lessons to Curb Sexual Harassment," *Chicago Tribune*, October 27, 2017.

3. Kim Geiger and Monique Garcia, "Victim Rights Advocate Says State Lawmakers Sexually Harassed Her, Complaint Went Nowhere at Capitol," *Chicago Tribune*, November 1, 2107.

4. Ibid.

5. Monique Garcia and Kim Geiger, "Amid Harassment Allegation, Illinois Senator Loses Leadership Spot and a Scramble to Investigator's Job," *Chicago Tribune*, November 2, 2017.

6. Monique Garcia and Kim Geiger, "Watchdog: Silverstein's Conduct 'Unbecoming of a Legislator,' but Not Sexual Harassment," *Chicago Tribune*, January 26, 2018.

7. Ray Long, interview with Alaina Hampton; Stacey Wescott video, "Texts Filed as Evidence of Sexual Harassment," *Chicago Tribune*, February 13, 2018.

8. Ibid.

9. Wescott, "Texts Filed as Evidence of Sexual Harassment."

10. Long interview with Alaina Hampton; Wescott video, "Texts Filed as Evidence of Sexual Harassment."

11. Long, "Speaker Madigan Cuts Political Worker Loose."

12. Ray Long, Stacy St. Clair, and Christy Gutowski, "Madigan's Lawyer Defends How He Handled Harassment Complaints as Major Case Snares Spotlight," *Chicago Tribune*, February 23, 2018.

13. Long, "Speaker Madigan Cuts Political Worker Loose."

14. Long, St. Clair, and Gutowski, "Madigan's Lawyer Defends How He Handled Harassment Complaints."

15. Ibid.

16. Long, "Speaker Madigan Cuts Political Worker Loose."

17. Long, St. Clair, and Gutowski, "Madigan's Lawyer Defends How He Handled Harassment Complaints."

18. Long, "Speaker Madigan Cuts Political Worker Loose."

19. Ibid.

20. Ibid.

21. Ibid.

22. Rick Pearson, Ray Long, and Bill Lukitsch, "Speaker Madigan Takes Heat over Handling of Sexual Harassment Complaint against Now-Fired Political Aide," *Chicago Tribune*, February 14, 2018.

23. Ibid.

24. Monique Garcia and Bill Lukitsch, "Speaker Madigan: 'I Take Responsibility' for Not Doing Enough on Sexual Harassment Issue," *Chicago Tribune*, February 17, 2018.

25. Michael Madigan, "Michael Madigan Letter to Lawmakers on Sexual Harassment," *Chicago Tribune*, January 25, 2018.

26. Michael Madigan, "Michael Madigan Letter to Lawmakers on Sexual Harassment," *Chicago Tribune*, February 16, 2018.

27. Monique Garcia, Ray Long, and Christy Gutowski, "Madigan Releases List of 9 Misconduct Complaints, but Number Could Be Higher," *Chicago Tribune,* February 28, 2018.

28. Ray Long and Monique Garcia, "Madigan Parts Ways with Second Operative after Female Lawmaker Alleges 'Abuse of Power,'" *Chicago Tribune,* February 20, 2018.

29. Trevor Jensen, "Thomas J. Hanahan: 1934–2009," *Chicago Tribune,* April 9, 2009; Peggy Boyer, "Illinois House Defeats ERA in Raucous Session," *Washington Post,* June 23, 1978, https://www.washingtonpost.com/archive/politics/1978/06/23/illinois-house-defeats-era-in-raucous-session/16ad7161-281e-43ee-bf19-b80b311e9645/; Wanda Brandstetter case documents, https://casetext.com/case/people-v-brandstetter; Rick Pearson, "Equal Rights Amendment Approval Comes 36 Years after Raucous Capitol Protests," *Chicago Tribune,* June 1, 2018; Ray Long, "ERA Sees Old Critic Resurface at Debate," *Chicago Tribune,* May 30, 2003.

30. Illinois House transcript, 100th General Assembly, June 30, 2018, p. 287, http://www.ilga.gov/house/transcripts/htrans100/10000141.pdf.

31. Gregory S. Schneider and Laura Vozzella, "Virginia Finalizes Passage of Equal Rights Amendment, Setting Stage for Legal Fight," *Washington Post,* January 27, 2020, https://www.washingtonpost.com/local/virginia-politics/virginia-expected-to-finalize-passage-of-era-monday-setting-stage-for-legal-fight/2020/01/27/b178265c-4121-11ea-b503-2b077c436617_story.html.

32. Ray Long, interview with Rep. Lou Lang, May 30, 2018.

33. Monique Garcia, Ray Long, and Kim Geiger, "Lawmaker Resigns from Madigan's Leadership Team Following Allegations of Retaliation, Verbal Abuse," *Chicago Tribune,* May 31, 2018.

34. Ibid.

35. WLS-TV, "Lang Announces Resignation as House Deputy Majority Leader after Harassment Allegations," WLS-TV, May 31, 2018, https://abc7chicago.com/3545128/.

36. Illinois House transcript, "142nd Legislative Day," House of Representatives, May 31, 2018, p. 194, https://www.ilga.gov/house/transcripts/htrans100/10000142.pdf.

37. Garcia, Long, and Geiger, "Lawmaker Resigns from Madigan's Leadership Team."

38. Mike Riopell, "Misconduct Inquiry Closed against Illinois State Rep. Lou Lang: 'Evidence Does Not Support Complaints,'" *Chicago Tribune,* September 6, 2018.

39. Mike Riopell, "Illinois Rep. Lou Lang Leaves House for Lobbying 2 Days before Being Sworn In for New Term," *Chicago Tribune,* January 7, 2019.

40. Kim Geiger, Ray Long, and Monique Garcia, "Speaker Madigan's Chief of Staff Resigns Hours after Aide Accused Him of Repeated Sexually Inappropriate Comments," *Chicago Tribune,* June 7, 2018.

41. Ibid.

42. Ibid.

43. Ibid.

44. Illinois House of Representatives, Office of the Speaker, "Investigations, Analysis & Recommendations Regarding Workplace Culture," *Chicago Tribune*, August 20, 2019.

45. Ibid.

46. Ibid.

47. Ibid.

48. Carol Pope, "LIG Summary Report—Case No. 18-017," Office of Legislative Inspector General, August 5, 2019, https://www.ilga.gov/commission/lig/CasesDocuments/LIG%20Founded%20Report%20-%20Case%20No.%2018-017%20Redacted.pdf.

49. Alaina Hampton, letter to Office of the Legislative Inspector General Carol Pope, September 25, 2019, https://www.ilga.gov/commission/lig/Cases-Documents/Complainant%20Response%20Letter%20-%20Case%20No.%2018-017.pdf.

50. Kevin Quinn, letter to Office of Legislative Inspector General Carol Pope, September 27, 2019, https://www.ilga.gov/commission/lig/CasesDocuments/Respondent%20Reponse%20Letter%20-%20Case%2018-017.pdf.

51. Carol Pope, "LIG Summary Report—Case No. 18-021," Office of Legislative Inspector General, August 29, 2019, https://www.ilga.gov/commission/lig/CasesDocuments/LIG%20Summary%20Report%20-%20Case%20No.%2018-021.pdf.

52. James C. Pullos, "Re: Timothy Mapes, Case 18-021," letter from Clifford law offices to Laurie Eby, executive director, Legislative Ethics Commission, https://www.ilga.gov/commission/lig/CasesDocuments/Respondent's%20Letter%20-%20Case%20No.%2018-021.pdf.

53. Ray Long, Dan Petrella, and Jamie Munks, "Women Describe Trauma, Panic Attacks in Madigan Aides' #MeToo Scandal as Watchdog Cracks Down," *Chicago Tribune*, October 2, 2019.

Chapter 12. Ups and Downs

1. Mike Riopell, "After 4-Year Political War, House Speaker Michael Madigan Calls Gov. Bruce Rauner's Term an 'EPIC Struggle,'" *Chicago Tribune*, January 8, 2019.

2. Mike Riopell and Juan Perez Jr., "Madigan Vilifies Rauner as Dems Bolster Numbers in Springfield," *Chicago Tribune*, January 9, 2019.

3. Ibid.

4. Ray Long, Dan Petrella, and Jamie Munks, "Inside Illinois Lawmakers' Pork-Barrel Frenzy: Pickleball Courts, Dog Parks and Clout," *Chicago Tribune*, June 7, 2019.

5. Bill Ruthhart and Jason Meisner, "Campaign Money Tied to Ald. Edward Burke's Alleged Extortion Scheme Was Intended for County Board President Toni Preckwinkle, Sources Say," *Chicago Tribune*, January 3, 2019.

6. Bill Ruthhart, John Byrne, and Jason Meisner, "Federal Agents Raid Powerful Chicago Ald. Ed Burke's City Hall and Ward Offices," *Chicago Tribune*, November 29, 2018.

7. Bill Ruthhart and Jason Meisner, "Cash Allegedly Pushed to Preckwinkle Camp," *Chicago Tribune*, January 3, 2019.

8. Ibid.

9. Gregory Pratt, "In About-Face, Toni Preckwinkle Says She'll Return $116K from Fundraiser Held at Ald. Edward Burke's Home," *Chicago Tribune*, January 7, 2019.

10. Gregory Pratt, "Ald. Edward Burke's Son Was Under Investigation for Misconduct Allegations When Toni Preckwinkle's Administration Hired Him," *Chicago Tribune*, January 23, 2019.

11. Jon Seidel, Fran Spielman, Mark Brown, and Tim Novak, "Viagra, Sex Acts, Use of Luxury Farm: Feds Detail Investigation of Ald. Solis," *Chicago Sun-Times*, January 29, 2019.

12. Ibid.

13. FBI Special Agent Steven D. Nolin, "Application and Affidavit for a Search Warrant," Federal Bureau of Investigation, filed May 27, 2016, https://www.scribd.com/document/401798808/Part-1-of-the-Ald-Danny-Solis-investigation#fullscreen&from_embed.

14. Jason Meisner, "Chinatown Developer Who Wore Wire on Ald. Daniel Solis Charged with Fraud," *Chicago Tribune*, March 11, 2020.

15. Ibid.

16. Nolin, "Application and Affidavit for a Search Warrant."

17. Jon Seidel, Tina Sfondeles, and Fran Spielman, "FBI Secretly Recorded Mike Madigan at His Law Office Pitching Firm's Services," *Chicago Sun-Times*, January 29, 2019, https://chicago.suntimes.com/2019/1/29/18413125/fbi-secretly-recorded-mike-madigan-at-his-law-office-pitching-firm-s-services.

18. Jeff Coen and Matt O'Connor, "Daniels Aide Going to Prison," *Chicago Tribune*, July 13, 2006.

19. National Weather Service, "Lowest Temp & Wind Chill—Morning of 1/31/19," https://www.weather.gov/lot/RecordColdJan2019.

Chapter 13. Shams?

1. Ray Long, "Illinois House Speaker Michael Madigan Gave His First-Ever Deposition. Here's What He Said," *Chicago Tribune*, January 31, 2019.

2. Ray Long, "Secret Depositions in Madigan Lawsuit Show Ties between Illinois House Speaker's Operatives, Alleged Sham Candidates," *Chicago Tribune*, February 1, 2019.

3. Michael Madigan deposition, *Jason Gonzales v. Michael Madigan et al.*, September 18, 2018.

4. Jason Gonzales deposition, *Jason Gonzales v. Michael Madigan et al.* August 31, 2018.

5. Kent Redfield, interview with author, spring 2021.

6. Ibid.

7. Kim Geiger, Rick Pearson, and Monique Garcia, "Rauner 'Turnaround' Tour Not Producing Results So Far," *Chicago Tribune*, May 21, 2015.

8. Monique Garcia, "AG Madigan Says No to Rauner Right-to-Work Zones," *Chicago Tribune*, March 20, 2015.

9. Geiger, Pearson, and Garcia, "Rauner 'Turnaround' Tour Not Producing Results So Far."

10. Michael Madigan deposition, *Jason Gonzales v. Michael Madigan et al.*, transcript in 2016 C 7915, Northern District of Illinois Eastern Division, September 18, 2018.

11. Ibid.

12. Jason Gonzales deposition, *Jason Gonzales v. Michael Madigan et al.*, transcript in 2016 C 7915, Northern District of Illinois Eastern Division, August 31, 2018.

13. Michael Madigan deposition, *Jason Gonzales v. Michael Madigan et al.*, September 18, 2018.

14. Jason Gonzales deposition, *Jason Gonzales v. Michael Madigan et al.*, August 31, 2018.

15. Ibid.

16. Ibid.

17. Ibid.

18. Jason Meisner and Kim Geiger, "Former Madigan Challenger's Suit OK'd to Proceed," *Chicago Tribune*, September 14, 2017.

19. Long, "Secret Depositions in Madigan Lawsuit."

20. Michael Madigan deposition, *Jason Gonzales v. Michael Madigan et al.*, September 18, 2018.

21. John Chase, "Madigan Primary Foe Denies She's a GOP Plant," *Chicago Tribune*, February 11, 2012.

22. Ray Long, Monique Garcia, and Alissa Groeninger, "State Lawmaker Charged with Bribery Cruises to Primary Victory," *Chicago Tribune*, March 21, 2012.

23. Chase, "Madigan Primary Foe Denies She's GOP Plant."

24. Yasmin Rammohan, "Michele Piszczor vs. Mike Madigan," WTTW-TV, February 28, 2012, https://news.wttw.com/2012/02/28/michele-piszczor-vs-mike-madigan.

25. Michael Madigan deposition, *Jason Gonzales v. Michael Madigan et al.*, September 18, 2018.

26. Grasiela Rodriguez deposition, *Jason Gonzales v. Michael Madigan et al.*, transcript in 2016 C 7915, Northern District of Illinois Eastern Division, June 13, 2018.

27. Jennifer Solski deposition, *Jason Gonzales v. Michael Madigan et al.*, transcript in 2016 C 7915, Northern District of Illinois Eastern Division, August 7, 2018.

28. Grasiela Rodriguez deposition, *Jason Gonzales v. Michael Madigan et al.*, June 13, 2018.

29. Ray Long, "New Depositions Reveal Team Madigan's 'Strange' Request: Help a Candidate Run against the Speaker," *Chicago Tribune*, July 1, 2019.

30. Michael Madigan deposition, *Jason Gonzales v. Michael Madigan et al.*, September 18, 2018.

31. Long, "New Depositions Reveal Team Madigan's 'Strange' Request."

32. Ibid.

33. Ibid.

34. Long, "Secret Depositions in Madigan Lawsuit."

35. Ibid.

36. Kim Geiger and Monique Garcia, "Speaker Madigan Gets a Challenge, for a Change," *Chicago Tribune*, March 11, 2016.

37. Jason Gonzales deposition, *Jason Gonzales v. Michael Madigan et al.*, August 31, 2018.

38. Michael Madigan deposition, *Jason Gonzales v. Michael Madigan et al.*, September 18, 2018.

39. Jason Gonzales deposition, *Jason Gonzales v. Michael Madigan et al.*, August 31, 2018.

40. Michael Madigan deposition, *Jason Gonzales v. Michael Madigan et al.*, September 18, 2018.

41. *Jason Gonzales v. Michael J. Madigan et al.*, "Defendants' Joint Response to Plaintiffs' Motions to Strike Defendants' First and Second Affirmative Defenses," July 8, 2019, https://jnswire.s3.amazonaws.com/jns-media/ef/ca/1456319/Gonzalez_v_Madigan_oppo_motion_to_strike.pdf.

42. Ray Long, "Judge Dismisses Lawsuit Alleging House Speaker Michael Madigan's Political Operation Put 'Sham' Candidates on Ballot in 2016," *Chicago Tribune*, August 23, 2019.

43. U.S. District Judge Matthew F. Kennelly, Memorandum Opinion and Order, *Jason Gonzales v. Michael Madigan et al.*, 2016 C 7915, Northern District of Illinois Eastern Division, August 23, 2019.

44. Ray Long, "Illinois House Speaker Michael Madigan Wins Latest Round in Suit Alleging Sham Candidates," *Chicago Tribune*, May 23, 2020.

45. Ray Long, "Madigan Wins Legal Battle Centered on Dirty Tricks Allegation," *Chicago Tribune*, March 8, 2021; Ray Long, "Supreme Court declines to take up Madigan opponent's appeal," *Chicago Tribune*, November 5, 2021.

Chapter 14. Marty's Campaign

1. Ray Long and Gregory Pratt, "Relentless Visits, Repeated Voicemails and Yelling: Inside Madigan's Ward's Push to Keep a College Student from Running for Alderman," *Chicago Tribune*, October 10, 2019.

2. Ibid.

3. Bay Area News Group, "What Happened to the Top 10 Finishers in California's 2003 Recall Election?" *Los Angeles Daily News*, October 7, 2013, https://www.dailynews.com/2013/10/07/what-happened-to-the-top-10-finishers-in-californias-2003-recall-election/.

4. David Jackson and Ray Long, "From 2007: Showing His Bare Knuckles," *Chicago Tribune*, April 4, 2007.

5. Long and Pratt, "Relentless Visits, Repeated Voicemails and Yelling."

6. Ibid.

7. Ibid.

8. Ibid.

9. Ibid.

10. Ibid.

11. Ibid.

12. Ibid.

13. Ibid.

14. Ibid.

15. Ibid.

16. Ibid.

17. Ibid.

Chapter 15. Himself

Epigraph. Dan Petrella and Jamie Munks, "Lawmakers Call for Tougher Ethics Rules and Begin Process to Remove State Rep. Luis Arroyo Following Bribery Charge," *Chicago Tribune*, October 29, 2019.

1. Steve Daniels, "It's Sweet to Be a Utility Company in Illinois," *Crain's Chicago Business*, April 23, 2021, https://www.chicagobusiness.com/utilities/its-sweet -be-utility-company-illinois.

2. Doug Wilson, "McClain Retires from Long, Successful Career as Lobbyist," *Quincy Herald-Whig*, October 30, 2016, https://www.whig.com/archive/article/ mcclain-retires-from-long-successful-career-as-lobbyist/article_69c8c3f0-91a2 -5176-a1f5-8a50b26cd0bb.html.

3. Bernard Schoenburg, "Retiring Lobbyist McClain Criticizes Rauner's Strategy," Springfield *State Journal-Register*, December 24, 2016, https://www.sj-r.com/ opinion/20161224/bernard-schoenburg-retiring-lobbyist-mcclain-criticizes -rauners-strategy.

4. David Kidwell of the Better Government Association and Dan Mihalopoulos of WBEZ-FM, "Sources: Feds Search for Michael Madigan Records at Home of Retired Alderman," WBEZ-FM, July 12, 2019, https://www.wbez.org/ stories/feds-search-for-michael-madigan-records-at-home-of-retired-alderman/ dbf601da-9cc7-4856-8cdc-b9147d00e273.

5. Ray Long and Jason Meisner, "Feds Investigating $10,000 in Checks from ComEd Lobbyists to Ousted Madigan Operative," *Chicago Tribune*, July 24, 2019.

6. Ibid.

7. Ray Long and Jason Meisner, "ComEd Discloses Feds Subpoenaed Its 'Communication' with State Sen. Martin Sandoval," *Chicago Tribune*, October 10, 2019.

8. U.S. District Court, Norther District of Illinois (Chicago), Criminal Docket

for Case #1:20-cr-00056, *United States v. Martin Sandoval,* "Unopposed Motion to Dismiss," United States Attorney John Lausch, March 31, 2021.

9. Ray Long and Jason Meisner, "Exelon Utilities CEO Anne Pramaggiore Abruptly Retires amid Federal Probe into Illinois Lobbying," *Chicago Tribune,* October 16, 2019.

10. Jason Meisner, Jamie Munks, and Dan Petrella, "Feds Allege State Rep. Luis Arroyo Caught on Undercover Recording Paying $2,500 Bribe. 'This Is the Jackpot,'" *Chicago Tribune,* October 29, 2019.

11. Associated Press, "Illinois Lawmaker Charged with Bribery Resigns," Willradio.tv.online, November 1, 2019, https://will.illinois.edu/news/story/illinois-lawmaker-charged-with-bribery-resigns.

12. Ray Long and Jason Meisner, "Feds Recorded Calls of Close Confidant of House Speaker Michael Madigan: Sources," *Chicago Tribune,* November 12, 2019.

13. Ray Long and Jason Meisner, "'Keep All of This Confidential': How a Powerful ComEd Lobbyist Lined Up Contracts for a Disgraced Ex-Aide to Speaker Michael Madigan and Why Federal Authorities Are Interested," *Chicago Tribune,* November 21, 2019.

14. Ibid.

15. Ibid.

16. "State Senator Iris Y. Martinez Calls on Democratic Party Chairman/ Speaker Madigan to Explain His Cronies Secret Payments to His Disgraced Former Aide/Sexual Harasser," Martinez press release, November 22, 2019, https://www.politico.com/f/?id=0000016e-a0fb-dc5f-a9ef-a2fbbbbc0000.

17. Ray Long, "Senator to Speaker Madigan: Explain Payments to Accused Sexual Harasser or Resign as Democratic Chairman," *Chicago Tribune,* November 22, 2019.

18. Ray Long, "Ex-Campaign Worker Settles Federal Lawsuit with House Speaker Michael Madigan's Political Committees over Sexual Harassment Claims against Top Staffer," *Chicago Tribune,* November 29, 2019.

19. Ray Long and Jason Meisner, "FBI Agents Asking Questions about House Speaker Madigan and His Political Operation, Say Four People They've Interviewed," *Chicago Tribune,* December 5, 2019.

Chapter 16. Public Official A

1. Dan Hinkel, Rick Pearson, Alice Yin, Megan Crepeau, and Annie Sweeney, "Federal Investigation Draws Closer to Madigan as ComEd Will Pay $200 Million Fine in Alleged Bribery Scheme; Pritzker Says Speaker 'Must Resign' if Allegations True," *Chicago Tribune,* July 18, 2020.

2. Ibid.

3. Ibid.

4. Dan Petrella, Jamie Munks, and Ray Long, "New Cache of ComEd Documents Shows Indicted Madigan Confidant Pressing Utility for Jobs and Contracts," *Chicago Tribune,* November 25, 2020.

5. Ray Long, "House Speaker Michael Madigan Says It's Not 'Ethically Im-

proper' to Find Government Jobs for People. Here's What He's Failing to Mention," *Chicago Tribune*, October 2, 2020.

6. Ibid.

7. Dan Petrella, "Illinois House Speaker Michael Madigan Declines to Testify before Special Committee Investigating His Conduct in Alleged ComEd Bribery Scheme," *Chicago Tribune*, September 25, 2020.

8. Long, "House Speaker Michael Madigan Says It's Not 'Ethically Improper.'"

9. Petrella, "Illinois House Speaker Michael Madigan Declines to Testify."

10. Jason Meisner, "Former ComEd VP Pleads Guilty, Agrees to Cooperate with Feds in Bribery Case Orbiting House Speaker Michael Madigan," *Chicago Tribune*, September 29, 2020.

11. Dan Petrella and Rick Pearson, "Under Fire amid Federal Corruption Probe, Illinois House Speaker Michael Madigan Faces a New Challenge from a Fellow Democrat," *Chicago Tribune*, October 1, 2020.

12. Ray Long, "Shadow of Madigan Hangs Over Campaign," *Chicago Tribune*, October 26, 2020.

13. Kent Redfield, data analysis, email, and interview with author, May 3, 2021.

14. Ray Long, "Madigan, Billionaires Clash in Record-Shattering $10.7 Million Illinois Supreme Court Contest That Threatens Court's Democratic Majority," *Chicago Tribune*, October 23, 2020.

15. Kent Redfield, written communication by Redfield, March 26, 2012.

16. Rick Pearson, "Billionaire Ken Griffin Drops Extra $26.7M against Pritzker's Graduated-Rate Income Tax Amendment Proposal. His Total Stands at More Than $46.7M," *Chicago Tribune*, October 2, 2020.

17. Rick Pearson, "Still out of Power, Illinois Republicans Ride Voter Dissatisfaction with State Government to Deal Pritzker, Madigan Defeats," *Chicago Tribune*, November 4, 2020.

18. Jason Meisner and Ray Long, "Madigan Confidant, Three Others Indicted in ComEd Bribery Scheme Allegedly Aimed at Influencing Speaker," *Chicago Tribune*, November 19, 2020.

19. Michael Madigan, "Statement from Speaker Madigan," Illinois Speaker of the House, November 19, 2020.

20. Ray Long and Rick Pearson, "Embattled House Speaker Michael Madigan Says He'll Be a Candidate for Re-Election in January, Claiming 'Significant Support," *Chicago Tribune*, November 20, 2020.

21. Jamie Munks and Dan Petrella, "Illinois House Democrats Wrangle over Madigan's Future behind Closed Doors as Criminal Justice Overhaul Dominates Public Debate," *Chicago Tribune*, January 11, 2021.

22. Dan Petrella, Rick Pearson, and Jamie Munks, "In Politically Calculated Move, Illinois House Speaker Michael Madigan Suspends Bid for Another Term but Doesn't Bow Out," *Chicago Tribune*, January 11, 2021.

23. Brenden Moore, "Meet the New Boss: Speaker Emanuel 'Chris' Welch

Seeks to Put His Stamp on Illinois House," *The Pantagraph* (Bloomington), January 31, 2021, https://www.pantagraph.com/news/state-and-regional/govt-and-politics/meet-the-new-boss-speaker-emanuel-chris-welch-seeks-to-put-his-stamp-on-illinois/article_2ba94b84-aae9-576d-932b-77c1ae77f895.html.

24. Ray Long and Megan Crepeau, "Rep. Emanuel 'Chris' Welch, Madigan's Successor as Illinois House Speaker, Faces Questions about His Treatment of Women," *Chicago Tribune*, January 13, 2021.

25. Dan Petrella, Rick Pearson, and Jamie Munks, "With New General Assembly about to Be Inaugurated, House Democrats Continue Scramble to Elect Speaker," *Chicago Tribune*, January 13, 2021.

26. Rick Pearson, Dan Petrella, Jamie Munks, Ray Long, and Megan Crepeau, "Michael Madigan's Decadeslong Grip on Illinois Ends as House Democrats Make Rep. Emanuel 'Chris' Welch State's First Black Speaker," *Chicago Tribune*, January 13, 2021.

27. Ibid.

28. Jason Meisner and Ray Long, "Michael Madigan May No Longer Be 'Mr. Speaker,' but Federal Corruption Probe Still Looms Despite His Sidelining," *Chicago Tribune*, January 22, 2021.

Epilogue

1. Milton L. Rakove, *We Don't Want Nobody Nobody Sent* (Bloomington: Indiana University Press, 1979).

2. Rick Pearson, "Former Speaker Michael Madigan Unsure How Long He'll Remain State Democratic Chair as He Picks 26-Year-Old Successor," *Chicago Tribune*, February 21, 2021.

3. Dan Petrella and Rick Pearson, "Michael Madigan's Hand-Picked Successor in State House Resigns Just Three Days after Being Installed," *Chicago Tribune*, February 24, 2021.

4. Rick Pearson, "Madigan Picks Another House Successor after Quickly Forcing Out His First Choices over 'Alleged Questionable Conduct,'" *Chicago Tribune*, February 25, 2021.

5. Petrella and Pearson, "Michael Madigan's Hand-Picked Successor in State House Resigns."

6. Illinois General Assembly, "Representative Angelica Guerrero-Cuellar (D) 22nd District," ILGA.gov, biography, February 2021, https://www.ilga.gov/house/Rep.asp?GA=102&MemberID=3011.

7. Pearson, "Madigan Picks Another House Successor."

8. Rick Pearson, Dan Petrella, and Bill Ruthhart, "With Madigan Gone, Democrats Roll Republicans in Springfield to Keep Control, Reward Allies," *Chicago Tribune*, May 29, 2021.

9. Rick Pearson, "Mexican American Civil Rights Group Sues to Block Illinois Democratic-Drawn Legislative Maps," *Chicago Tribune*, June 11, 2021.

10. Richard E. Cohen, "Ill. Makes Redistricting Hall of Fame," *Politico*, June

3, 2011, https://www.politico.com/story/2011/06/ill-makes-redistricting-hall-of-fame-056225.

11. Ron Grossman, "From Hero to Bum in a Flash," *Chicago Tribune*, February 24, 2013.

12. Rick Pearson, Dan Petrella, and Bill Ruthhart, "Illinois Lawmakers Go into Overtime, Approve $42 Billion Budget, Elections Changes and an Ethics Package," *Chicago Tribune*, June 1, 2021.

13. Jason Meisner and Ray Long, "Lawyers for 4 Charged in ComEd Bribery Case Say No Quid Pro Quo with Madigan, Ask for Charges to Be Dismissed," *Chicago Tribune*, June 1, 2021.

14. Jason Meisner and Ray Long, "Michael Madigan Is Elephant in Courtroom as Lawyers in ComEd Bribery Case Hint More Charges Are Coming, Former Lawmakers Appear before Grand Jury," *Chicago Tribune*, May 5, 2021.

15. Jason Meisner and Ray Long, "Former Chief of Staff to House Speaker Michael Madigan Charged with Lying to Federal Grand Jury in ComEd Probe," *Chicago Tribune*, May 26, 2021.

16. Jason Meisner and Ray Long, "Former Chicago Alderman Aiding Corruption Probe Made Audio and Video Recordings of then-Speaker Michael Madigan on Multiple Topics, Sources Say," *Chicago Tribune*, June 9, 2021.

INDEX

Note: *Italicized* page numbers indicate material in photo captions.

abortion rights, xv, 4
Academy for Global Leadership, 182
Acevedo, Eddie, 88
Adam, Sam, Jr., 57–58
Allen, Jim, 206
Alvarez, Mike, 214–15
amendatory veto (AV), xiii, 91
Ameren, 152
American Federation of State, County, and Municipal Employees (AFSCME), 80, 100
Annunzio, Frank, 19
Arlington International Racecourse, 34
Arroyo, Luis, 216
AT&T, 152, 221

Baise, Gregory, 63
Bangser, Henry, 110
"Banzaiiiii!" 41, 42, 74, 230
Barboza, Joe, 193–94, 197, 199
Barker, Kim, 61
Beavers, William, 84
Behar, Joy, 68
Belz, John, 103

Bergo, Sandy, 150–51
Berrios, Joe, 9, *116*
Best, Kathleen, 46
Better Government Association, 93, 145, 150–51, 214
Biden, Joe, 26
Bilandic, Michael, 133
Birkett, Joe, 141–43
Biss, Daniel, 101–2, 171
Black, Bill, 64
Black Democratic Caucus, 20–21, 88, 158, 227–28
Blagojevich, Patricia "Patti," 58, 60, 71, 72
Blagojevich, Rod, 55–72; budgeting under, 61–65, 68–70, 108; campaign finance and, 62–63, 65–67, 68, 70–71, 148; as Democratic Governor, 55–72, *113*; election as Democratic governor (2002), xv, 56, 61; FBI investigation and arrest, 5, 8, 55–59, 66–69, 72, 143–44; health-care programs, xii, 8, 60–61, 63–65, 68–69; impeachment probe and removal from office (2009), xii, 5, 8, 57–58, 60, 63, 65–71, 73–75, 143–44; Lisa Madigan and, 62, 64, 143–44, 145; MJM support for, 5, 8, 61–62, 66, 108, 228;

Blagojevich, Rod (*continued*): Obama U.S. Senate seat and, xii, 56–59, 65–66, 143, 145; patronage and, 62, 63, 66–67, 69; pay-to-play politics of, xii, 56–59, 62, 65, 148–50; pension plans under, 8, 62, 108; in prison, 70, 71–72, 181; Quinn as replacement for governor, 70, 73, 144; reelection as governor (2006), 8, 61–63, 66; as son-in-law of Richard Mell, 60, 67, 141; Special Investigative Committee findings and, 57–58, 60, 65–67; tax policy under, 83; Trump and, 71–72
Bost, Mike, 63–64
Boulton, Stephen, 196–97, 200
Boyce, Eileen, 217
Boyer, Peggy, 41
Bradley, John, 214–15
Brady, Bill, 75, 76
Brandstetter, Wanda, 173
Braun, Carol Moseley, 20, 21
Bray, Jim, 41
Breslin, Peg, 33–34
Brookins, Howard, 88
Brown, Mark, 184
Brown, Steve, 39, 140, 157, 158
budgets and budgeting: under Blagojevich, 61–65, 68–70, 108; under Edgar, 48–52, 155–56; health care in (*see* health care); Operation Cobra (1989) and, 7, 41–48, 73–74, 82; pension plans in (*see* pension plans); under Pritzker, 9–10, 225, 233; under Quinn, 73–79, 156–57; under Rauner, 6, 79–83, 156–58, 180–81, 191; under Ryan, 73, 155–56; school financing in (*see* school financing). *See also* tax policy
Burke, Anne, 70, 103, 132, 182
Burke, Dan, 157, 182
Burke, Edward M.: federal investigation and extortion charges, 182–84, 236–37; as Fourteenth Ward Alderman, xi, 70, 111, 132, 182, 184, 236; Illinois judicial appointments and, 132, 184; Bob Molaro pension benefits and, 111
Burris, Roland, x, 65–66, 143, 144
Bush, George H. W., 79
Bush, George W., 64

Byrne, Jane, 47, 133
Byrnes, Pat, *114*

Cain, Daniel, 67
Cameron, Bill, 131
campaign finance, 147–59; Blagojevich and, 62–63, 65–67, 68, 70–71, 148, 149–50; ComEd and, 152–53, 217–18; federal investigation of the Democratic primary (2016), 189–90; increased regulation of, 234–35; loophole in state law, 150–52; machine politics and, 148–49; Michael McClain/ComEd involvement with MJM, 217–18; MJM "Evening on the Lake," 147, 148, 151, 235; MJM in the 2020 election cycle, 149–52, 223; MJM support for Derrick Smith, 158–59; quartet of Democratic legislative leaders and, 149, 150, 155–56; recent spending growth, 149–50, 152; George Ryan licenses-for-bribes scandal, 8, 148, 154–55; Super Tuesdays, 151
Camper, John, 133
Canary, Cynthia, 65
Capitol Fax, 216
Carey, Bernard, 207
Carey, Mary, 204
Carrigan, Michael, 100
casino gambling, 2, 9, 56, 145, 181–82
Cassidy, Kelly, 172, 176
Catania, Susan, 20
Center for Tax and Budget Accountability, 109
CHANGE Illinois, 28
Chase, John, 61, 127
Chicago Board of Elections Commissioners, 205–9
Chicago City Council: "Council Wars" under Washington, xi; Thirteenth Ward City Council campaign (2019), 201, 202–9
Chicago Cubs, 56, 158
Chicago Streets and Sanitation Department Bureau of Electricity ("Madigan Electric"), 123, 195
Children's Memorial Hospital (Chicago), 56

Clifford, Alex, 123–27, 129, 138
Clinton, Bill, 25, 51–52
Clinton, Hillary, 236–37
Coen, Jeff, 132
Coleman, Gary, 204
Comey, James, 72
Commission on Government Forecasting and Accountability, 107, 108–9
Commonwealth Edison (ComEd): bribery scheme, 10–11, 134–35, 213–27, 234–36; federal grand jury investigation of lobbying activities, 153, 214–19, 220–27, 235–36; Lisa Madigan and, 145; Michael McClain and (see McClain, Michael); MJM as "Public Official A," 10, 221, 224; nuclear power plants and, 152–53, 214, 220, 235; smart-grid modernization law and, 213–14, 220
Cotter, Patrick, 226
Cousineau, Will, 214–15
COVID-19 pandemic, 28, *118*, 215, 220, 233
credit ratings of Illinois, 82, 104–6
Cross, Tom, 59, 61, 64, 67, 74
Cruz, Rolando, 142
Cullen, Tom, 124, 127–29, 214, 215
Cullerton, John: Blagojevich investigation and, 67–68; as Democratic Senate President, xii, 94–95, 97–105, *114, 116,* 181–82; gay marriage legislation, 85–87; gun rights and, 89–90; Illinois House cutback amendment (1980) and, 19–20; #MeToo controversy and, 165–66; pension plan reform proposals, 97–103, 108; tax policy and, 74–78
Cupich, Blase, xv
Currie, Barbara Flynn: as Illinois House Majority Leader, 57–58, 60, 65–67, 77, 108, 157, 174–75; redistricting and, 19–20; Special Investigative Committee, 57–58, 60, 65–67

Daley, Bill, 91
Daley, Eleanor "Sis," 87
Daley, John, 34
Daley, Richard J.: as the "American Pharaoh," ix, x–xi; as chairman of the Cook County Democratic Party (1953–1976), x–xi; Chicago machine politics and, 2, 3–4, 15; coalition-building by, 92; death (1976), x–xi; Eleventh Ward and, 31; as mentor to MJM, 2–4, 15–16, 87, 92, 121–22, 129, 133; patronage and, 121–23, 125, 129, 130, 133–35, 188; redistricting and, 28; sons, 31, 34, 45, 91; statue unveiling (1981), 15–16, 20–23; Thirteenth Ward and, 121–23, 125
Daley, Richard M.: as Cook County State's Attorney, 31; Eleventh Ward and, 31; as Mayor of Chicago, 45, 46, 110, *113,* 130; patronage and, 123, 129, 130; pension benefits, 110–11; support for Michael Howlett, 137
Daniels, Lee: as Illinois House Minority Leader, 39, 42–45, 93–94, 149, 156, 186; as Illinois House Speaker, 51, 149, 154; Operation Cobra income tax increase (1989) and, 42, 44–45
Dart, Tom, 130, 184
Davis, Corneal, 173
death penalty, 95–96
Decremer, Shaw, 172, 193–94
Degnan, Tim, 31, 32
Dellimore, Craig, 94
Democratic National Convention (1968, Chicago), 122
Democratic National Convention (1996, Chicago), 84
Democratic National Convention (2004, Boston), 61
Democratic National Convention (2016, Philadelphia), 4, 236–37
Democratic Party leadership in Illinois: Democratic Party chairman for Cook County, x–xi; MJM as Committeeman for the 13th Ward, 4, *112,* 122–23 (see also Thirteenth Ward Democratic Organization); MJM as Democratic Party Chairman of Illinois, 1–2, 8, 153, 188, 218–19, 221, 225, 232; MJM as Speaker of the Illinois House (see Speaker of the Illinois House of Representatives); redistricting and (see redistricting)
Dixon, Alan, 48

Doherty, Jay, 223–24, 225–26
Dorf, Michael, 205–9
Doris, Carole, 129
Doyle, Patti Solis, 237
Duckworth, Tammy, 225
Dunkin, Ken, 159, 167, 176
Dunn, John, 33, 37
Dunn, Ralph, 47
Durbin, Dick, 225
Durkin, Jim, 66, 149–51, 223, 229

Easterbrook, Frank, 200
Ebbesen, Joseph, 17
Edgar, Jim: budgeting under, 48–52, 155–56; pension plan "Edgar ramp," 106–7, 109; as Republican Governor, 7, 25, 80, 95, 106–7, 155–56; as Republican Secretary of State, 25, 48, 155; tax policy under, xi–xii, 7, 48–52
Einhorn, Eddie, 29
Elder, Larry, 204
Ellis, David, 67–68, 69
Emanuel, Rahm: as Mayor of Chicago, 58, 89, 101, *115*, 130, 134, 208; as Obama chief of staff, 58, 208; Shakman (patronage) cases and, 130, 134; in the U.S. House of Representatives, 58, 68–69
Equal Rights Amendment (ERA), 22, 172–73
"Evening on the Lake," Island Bay Yacht Club, 147, 148, 151, 235
Exelon Utilities: as parent company of Commonwealth Edison (ComEd), 152–53, 213, 235; Anne Pramaggiore as CEO, 215–16, 222, 225–26. *See also* Commonwealth Edison (ComEd)

Farley, Bruce, 139
Federal Bureau of Investigation (FBI): Blagojevich investigation and arrest (2008), 5, 8, 55–59, 66–69, 72, 143–44; Ed Burke investigation on extortion charges, 182–84, 236–37; MJM recorded by feds, 184–86, 236–37; raids and investigation of MJM colleagues in ComEd investigation, 10–11, 214–19, 221–22, 225–27, 235–36

Fitzgerald, Patrick, 56, 62, 63, 123, 145
Fitzgerald, Thomas, 67
Flynn, Michael, 122
Flynt, Larry, 204
Forby, Gary, 151
Fowler, Carol, 37
Foxx, Kim, 208
Francis, Pope, 85
Franks, Jack, 66
Friedrich, Dwight, 17–18

Gagliardo, Joseph, 125
gambling: casino, 2, 9, 56, 145, 181–82; Illinois lottery, 44; sweepstakes, 216
Garcia, Monique, 78, 138
Garrett, Sherri, 175–79, 236
Gawel, Mike, 17–18
gay marriage legalization (2013), 84–87
Gedge, Lindsay, 17–18
Genson, Ed, 57–58
Geo-Karis, Adeline, 32
gerrymandering. *See* redistricting
Gingrich, Newt, 4, 25
Giorgi, E. J. "Zeke," 44
Gonzales, Jason, 188, 191–201, 208
Goodman, Leonard, 70
Grant, Robert, 56, 72
Great Recession, 73, 104, 145
Greiman, Alan, 25
Griffin, Ken, 225
gross receipts tax, 63
Guerrero-Cuellar, Angelica, 233
Guidice, Richard, 151
gun laws, 87–91

Haine, Bill, 90–91
Hampton, Alaina: #MeToo sexual harassment controversy and, 163, 166–71, 174, 176, 178, 203, 217, 218–19; retaliation claims and legal settlement, 178, 179, 218–19; Chris Welch candidacy as Speaker and, 229
Hannig, Gary, 21–22
Hanrahan, Thomas "Terrible Tommy," 173
Harold, Erika, 144
Harris, David, 82
Harris, Greg, 85

Harris, Sheldon, 143
Harry, Jim, xv
Hartigan, Neil, 48
health care: Blagojevich programs, xii, 8, 60–61, 63–65, 68–69; medical malpractice lawsuit cap, xiii–xiv
Heiple, James, 57
Hernandez, Charlie, 197
Hickey, Maggie, 176–77
Hillman, G. Robert, xx, 18
Hispanic Democratic Organization, 123, 195
Hoffman, Jay, 228, 229
Holland, William, 60–61
Holmes, Linda, 102
Homer, Thomas, 126–30, 166
Hooker, John T., 26, 222, 225–26
Howlett, Michael, 137
Huggins, Larry, 124
Hull, Blair, 189–90
Hynes, Dan, 60, 73, 75, 141
Hynes, Thomas, 141

Ikenberry, Stanley, 51
Illinois Arts Council, 182
Illinois Constitution: House cutback amendment (1980), 16–23, 70, 213; Illinois Supreme Court role as redistricting tiebreaker, 24–27, 234; pension plan requirements and, 98–102; Sixth Constitutional Convention (Con-Con), ix–x, xx, 18, 24, 45, 104; tax code and, 81; terms of governor and General Assembly under, 76–78
Illinois Department of Central Management Services, 129
Illinois Department of Transportation, 131
Illinois Economic and Fiscal Commission, 106
Illinois Education Association, 100
Illinois Federation of Teachers, 100, 110
Illinois House of Representatives: campaign contributions (see campaign finance); Jason Gonzalez candidacy and federal lawsuit, 188, 191–201, 208; House cutback amendment (1980), 16–23, 70, 213; Metra patronage scandal and investigation, 121, 123–30; MJM first joins (1971), ix; MJM replacements in, 231–33; Operation Cobra income tax increase (1989), 7, 41–48, 73–74, 82; Paprocki eucharist decree, 86; patronage and House committee chairs, 3, 131–32; redistricting (see redistricting); Speaker (see Speaker of the Illinois House of Representatives); tax policy (see tax policy); White Sox Midnight Miracle (1988), 7, 33–40. See also Speaker of the Illinois House of Representatives
Illinois lottery, 44
Illinois Manufacturers' Association, 63
Illinois Senate: Blagojevich impeachment and, 67–70; Lisa Madigan in, 139, 144; Barack Obama in, 61, 144, 189, 204; White Sox Midnight Miracle (1988), 7, 31–32
Illinois Solidarity Party, 43
Illinois Supreme Court: Blagejovich and, 145; election challenges and, 43; patronage and, 132; pension plan reform and, 98–99, 101, 102–4, 110, 111; redistricting tiebreaker procedures and, 3, 24–27, 234
Illinois United for Change, 189–90
I-Save-Rx, 60

Jackson, Jesse, Jr., 20, 70
Jacobs, Mike, 64
Jarrett, Valerie, 58
Jenner, Caitlyn, 204
Jones, Emil: as Democratic Senate President, 19–20, 61, 62, 64–65, 108; as Illinois Senate Minority Leader, 149
Julka, Anjali, 129

Kagan, Elena, 28
Karmeier, Lloyd, 103–4, 109
Kasper, Michael, 26, 67, 192, 197–99, 208
Kass, John, 141
Kaufmann, Justin, 93
Kelly, Christopher, 58
Kelly, Richard, 32
Kennedy, Anthony M., 86
Kennedy, Chris, 171

Kennedy, Edward, 68–69
Kennelly, Matthew, 199–200
Kidwell, David, 61, 127
Kiernicki, Nikki, 207
Kifowit, Stephanie, 224, 227
Kilbride, Thomas, 26, 224–25, 234
King, Larry, 68
Kodatt, Edward Guerra, 231–33
Krupa, David, 203, 205–9
Kuba, Michael, 196–97
Kustra, Bob, 51

Lake Shore Club, 122
Lang, Lou, 35, 173–76
LaRouche, Lyndon, 43
Lassar, Scott, 155
Latino Democratic Caucus, 227–28
Lausch, John, 220–21
Leahy, Mary Lee, 131
legislative inspector general: #MeToo
    sexual harassment controversy and,
    165–66, 174–78; Metra patronage hir-
    ing scandal and, 126–30, 138, 166, 186
Leone, Tony, 21
Lightfoot, Lori, 2, 183–84, 205
Lighty, Todd, 132
Lincoln, Abraham: as Illinois' all-time fa-
    vorite son, 5, 29, 56, 71, 139, 163, 235;
    Lincoln-Douglas debate (1858), 16, 80
Link, Terry, 216
Lipinski, Dan, 168
Lipinski, William, 214
Loncar, Maryann, 174, 176
Lubet, Steven, 142
Lyons, Joe, 64, 76

Madiar, Eric, 104–5
Madigan, Lisa (daughter), 136–46;
    Blagojevich administration and, 62, 64,
    143–44, 145; campaign for Illinois At-
    torney General, 125, 139–43; ComEd
    and, 145; education, 139; election as
    Illinois Attorney General (2002), 114,
    142–46; family background, 138–39; in
    the Illinois Senate, 139, 144; pension
    reform and, 103; as potential challeng-
    er to Pat Quinn for governor (2010),
    91, 136–38, 144; as potential U.S. Sena-
    tor, 143, 144; unions and, 190

Madigan, Michael J. (MJM): campaign
    finance and (see campaign finance);
    Chicago machine politics and, 2–11;
    coalition building skills, 85–86, 88–96;
    and the ComEd bribery scheme,
    10–11, 134–35, 213–27, 232; daughter,
    Lisa, 138–39 (see also Madigan, Lisa);
    as Democratic Committeeman, 4, 112,
    121–23 (see also Thirteenth Ward Dem-
    ocratic Organization); as Democratic
    Party Chairman of Illinois, 1–2, 8, 153,
    188, 218–19, 221, 225, 232; education,
    5, 121–22; FBI secret recordings of,
    184–86, 236–37; federal investigation
    of the Democratic primary (2016), 179,
    186, 188–201; as hearing examiner at
    the Illinois Commerce Commission,
    122; and the Illinois Constitutional
    Convention, ix–x, xx, 18, 24, 45, 104; as
    Illinois House Minority Leader, 15–25,
    51, 154, 213, 233; joins Illinois House
    of Representatives (1971), ix, 5 (see also
    Illinois House of Representatives); and
    judges in Cook County courts / "Ma-
    digan's List," 132–33; as the longest-
    serving legislator in U.S. history, ix, 17,
    230; "Madigan Mystique" and, 2–11,
    61, 86, 164, 184, 237; Metra patronage
    scandal and investigation, 121, 123–30,
    138; patronage and (see patronage);
    pension benefits of, 110–11; pension
    plan reform proposals, 98–103, 108;
    property tax law practice, 9, 132–33,
    164, 184–86, 221–22, 223; as protégé
    of Richard J. Daley, 2–4, 15–16, 87, 92,
    121–22, 129, 133; public policy agenda
    of Democratic control, x, xi, 3–4, 47–
    48; redistricting and (see redistricting);
    sexual harassment accusations among
    aides (see #MeToo sexual harassment
    controversy); as Speaker (1983–1994,
    1997–2021), ix, x, 2, 4, 25, 112–18, 213
    (see also Speaker of the Illinois House
    of Representatives); as "the Sphinx
    from Pulaski Road," ix, 96; support
    for Blagojevich, 5, 8, 61–62, 66, 108,
    228; ties to Michael McClain, 213–19,
    222, 225–26, 236; White Sox Midnight
    Miracle (1988) and, 33–40

Madigan, Shirley (wife), 64, *114,* 138, 182

"Madigan Electric" (Chicago Streets and Sanitation Department Bureau of Electricity), 123, 195

Madrzyk, John S., xi

Mapes, Timothy, 175–79, 236

marijuana, recreational, 9, 181–82

Marquez, Fidel, 223–24

Martinez, Iris, 218

Martire, Ralph, 109

Matijevich, John, 17

Mautino, Dick, 21

Mautino, Frank, 157

McAuliffe, Roger, 34

McBarron, Charlie, 33–36, 38

McCain, John, 68–69

McClain, Michael: as ComEd contract lobbyist, 10–11, 171, 213–14, 216, 222, 223, 226, 235–36; FBI investigation and indictments, 10–11, 214–19, 225–27, 235–36; in the Illinois House of Representatives, 20, 21, 28; #MeToo reckoning and, 171, 214–15, 217, 218; payments to Kevin Quinn, 214–15, 217, 218; redistricting and, 20, 21, 28; ties to MJM, 213–19, 222, 225–26, 236

McPike, Jim, 18, 34–37

Means, Richard, 207

Meeks, James, 69–70

Meisner, Jason, 214, 216–17, 236

Mell, Deb, 67, 125–26

Mell, Richard "Dick," 125; Blagojevich as son-in-law, 60, 67, 141

Mendoza, Susana, 66

#MeToo sexual harassment controversy, 5, 10, 163–79; Shaw Decremer ousted from political operations, 172; Sherri Garrett / Timothy Mapes accusations, 175–79, 236; Alaina Hampton / Kevin Quinn accusations, 163, 166–71, 174, 176, 178, 203, 217, 218–19; Illinois House passes the Equal Rights Amendment, 172–73; legislative inspector general and, 165–66, 174–78; Maryann Loncar / Lou Lang accusations, 174, 176; "Madigan letter," 171–72; MJM op-ed and, 215; MJM orders outside investigation, 176–78; open letter from

"The Women Who Make Illinois Run" (2017), 165; Denise Rotheimer / Ira Silverstein accusations, 165–66, 174; sexual harassment training and, 165, 166, 179

Metra patronage hiring scandal: accusations, 121, 123–26; legislative inspector general and, 126–30, 138, 166, 186

Meza, Ricardo, 131

Michel, Bob, 105

Midway Airport: Chicago city control of, xii; sexual harassment allegations, 164–65

Mikva, Abner, 231

Mikva, Mary, 26

Miller, Rich, 216

minimum wage, 94–95, 181–82

MJM. *See* Madigan, Michael J.

Molaro, Bob, 61, 111

Moody, Ed, 222

Moore, Brenden, 228

Murphy, Matt, 157

Nasella, Joseph, 195–96

National Rifle Association (NRA), 89, 91

Nekritz, Elaine, 101

Netsch, Dawn Clark, 24, 50–51, 106, 107

Neubauer, Chuck, 150–51

Newman, Marie, 168

Nicarico, Jeanine, 142

Nixon, Richard M., 5, 57, 68, 69

Noldin, Steven D., 184–86

Novak, Tim, 184

Obama, Barack: address at Democratic National Convention (2004, Boston), 61; address to the Illinois House and Senate (2016), 5, 27, *116;* address to the nation (2009), 24; Blagojevich as Governor and, 66; in the Illinois Senate, 61, 144, 189, 204; as "The Messiah," 4; presidential campaign and election (2008), 4–5, 56–59, 66, 143; presidential center in Chicago, 5; presidential reelection (2012), 158; support for Julianna Stratton, 159; U.S. Senate seat for Illinois and, xii, 56–59, 65–66, 143, 145, 189

Ochoa, Juan, 222

O'Connell, Bill, 41
Ogilvie, Richard, 25
O'Halloran, Brad, 124, 126
O'Hare Airport: Chicago city control of, xii; sexual harassment allegations, 164–65
Olivo, Frank, 202, 222
Operation Cobra income tax increase (1989), 7, 41–48, 73–74, 82
Operation PUSH, 20
"Operation Safe Road" scandal, 8, 148, 154–55
Ortiz, Aaron, 182

Pagano, Phil, 123, 124
Pagois, Eugene, 196–97
Palmer, Alice, 204
Paprocki, Thomas, 86
Parke, Terry, 35
patronage, 121–35; antipatronage court orders / "Shakman decrees," 130–31; Blagojevich and, 62, 63, 66–67, 69; and the Chicago Streets and Sanitation Department Bureau of Electricity ("Madigan Electric"), 123, 195; Clifford memo, 123–27, 129, 138; ComEd federal investigation and, 10–11, 134–35, 213–27, 232; Richard J. Daley and, 121–23, 125, 129, 130, 133–35, 188; Richard M. Daley and, 123, 129, 130; employee types and, 131; House committee chairs and, 3, 131–32; Metra patronage scandal and investigation, 121, 123–30, 166, 186; precinct workers and (see Thirteenth Ward Democratic Organization); Kevin Quinn and, 164, 170, 195–96, 197; U.S. Supreme Court Rutan decision, 131
Pearson, Rick, 38, 51, 140, 153
Pelosi, Nancy, 26
pension plans, 97–111; under Blagojevich, 8, 62, 108; cost-of-living increases, 98, 100, 102, 106, 110–11; Cullerton reform proposals, 97–103, 108; under Edgar, 106–7, 109; fairness questions for lawmakers, 109–11; five state retirement systems in Illinois, 97, 105; Illinois Constitution requirements for, 98–102; Illinois credit ratings and, 82,

106; Illinois history of underfunding, 97–98, 104–6, 108–9; Illinois Supreme Court and reforms in, 98–99, 101, 102–4, 110, 111; increase in benefits, 47; MJM reform proposals, 98–103, 108; under Quinn, 97–103, 108; reamortization proposal, 109; revision of benefits for new employees, 108, 109; under Ryan, 107–8; under Thompson, 105–6
Peraica, Tony, 189, 193–97, 200–201, 208
petition challenges, 203–9
Phelan, Richard, 50
Phelps, Brandon, 88, 89–90
Philip, James "Pate": Operation Cobra income tax increase (1989), 46, 50; as Republican Senate President, xv, 25, 46, 50–52, 93, 149; as Senate Minority Leader, 31–32; tax-swap effort under Edgar, 50–52; White Sox Midnight Miracle (1988) and, 31–32
Piszczor, Michele, 194
Pope, Carol, 178
Porter, Julie, 166, 175
Poshard, Glenn, 153–54
Posner, Richard, 87
Powell, Paul, 234–35
Power, Joseph, Jr., 155
Pramaggiore, Anne, 215–16, 222, 225–26
Pratt, Gregory, 207
Preckwinkle, Toni, 130, 183–84
Pritzker, J. B.: budgeting under, 9–10, 225, 233; casino gambling and, 9, 181–82; ComEd and, 221, 235; COVID-19 pandemic and, 220; as Democratic governor, 2, 9–11, 94, 159, 189, 214; election as Democratic governor (2018), 9, 180; #MeToo sexual harassment controversy and, 171; minimum wage and, 94, 181–82; recreational marijuana and, 9, 181–82; tax policy under, 182, 221, 225
public employee pension plans. See pension plans
Pullos, James C., 178

Quinn, Kevin: ComEd lobbyist payments to, 214–15, 217, 218; and the Democratic primary (2016), 195–97; Alaina

Hampton #MeToo sexual harassment controversy and, 163, 166–71, 174, 176, 178, 203, 217, 218–19; patronage and, 164, 170, 195–96, 197

Quinn, Marty: Alaina Hampton / Kevin Quinn #MeToo sexual harassment controversy and, 163, 166–71, 203; as Thirteenth Ward Alderman, 128–29, 163, 166–69, 170, 197, 201–9, 221, 231, 232; and the Thirteenth Ward City Council campaign (2019), 201, 202–9

Quinn, Pat: budgeting under, 73–79, 156–57; death penalty and, 95–96; as Democratic Governor, 26, 71, 82, 181; election as Democratic governor (2010), 8, 75–76; exit interview with the *Tribune*, 80; gay marriage legalization (2013), 84–87; as governor replacement for Blagojevich (2009), 70, 73, 144; gun laws and, 87–91; Illinois House cutback amendment (1980) and, 16, 70, 213; as Lieutenant Governor, 8, 70; Lisa Madigan as potential challenger (2010), 91, 136–38, 144; minimum wage and, 94; pension reform legislation, 97–103, 108; reelection campaign for governor (2014), 78–79; school financing under, 156–57; temporary income tax increase, 8, 73–79

Radogno, Christine, 74–75
Raoul, Kwame, 90, 101
Rauner, Bruce: attacks on MJM, xiv–xv, 6, 8–9, 144, 159, 167, 180–81, 189–91, 198; budgeting under, 6, 79–83, 156–58, 180–81, 191; election as Republican Governor (2014), 8, 79; minimum wage and, 94–95; as Republican Governor, *114*, 150, 163–64; tax policy under, 79–83, 103–4, 180; "Turnaround Agenda" (pro-business), 9, 80, 81–82, 94–95, 181, 190–91, 224
Rea, Jim, 36
Reagan, Ronald, 44, 87, 105
Redfield, Kent, 148–49, 153, 189–90
redistricting, 15–28; in 1971, 24; in 1981, x, 15–25, 28; in 1991, x, 49–50; in 2001, 26, 154; in 2011, x, 26, 75, 151, 191–92, 234; in 2021, 11, 28, 180, 226, 233–34;

Illinois citizen initiatives, 26–27; Illinois House cutback amendment (1980) and, 16–23, 70, 213; Illinois Supreme Court and tiebreaker procedures, 24–27, 234; U.S. Supreme Court and, 28

Regional Transportation Authority, 124, 126. *See also* Metra patronage hiring scandal

Reilly, Jim, 43
Reinsdorf, Jerry, 29
Reis, David, 77
Rexing, Louis, 209
Rezko, Antoin "Tony," 58, 63
Rhoads, Mark, 23–24
Richards, Alex, 127
Righter, Dale, 69
Rittgers, Daisy, 109–10
Roberts, John, 28
Rock, Philip J.: as Democratic Senate President, ix, xi–xii, xx, 23–24, 31, 46–47, 49, 155; Operation Cobra income tax increase (1989), 46–47; as U.S. Senate candidate (1984), x; White Sox Midnight Miracle (1988) and, 31
Rodriguez, Grasiela, 193–96, 199
Rodriguez, Mike, 194
Roeser, Jack, 194
Roman Catholic Church: abortion rights and, xv, 4; gay marriage legislation (2013) and, 85–86
Ronan, Al, 44
Rostenkowski, Dan, 19
Rotheimer, Denise, 165–66, 174
"round-tabling," 203
Rueff, Ashley, 74
Rush University Medical Center, 221
Rutan, Cynthia, 131
Ryan, George: budgeting under, 73, 155–56; campaign finance / licenses-for-bribes scandal, 8, 148, 154–55; death penalty and, 95–96; election as Republican governor (1998), 154–56; as Illinois House Speaker, xv, 3, 15–25, 18; as Illinois Secretary of State, 8, 148, 154–55; as Lieutenant Governor, 33; pension reform, 107–8; pork-barrel projects, 155–56; in prison, 56, 57, 74–75, 148; problem-solving style of, 92–93; redistricting (1981), 15–25

Saltsman, Don, 36
Salvi, Al, 51
same-sex marriage legalization (2013), 84–87
Sanchez, Al, 123
Sandburg, Carl, 30–31
Sandoval, Angie, 233
Sandoval, Martin, 215–16, 233
Savickas, Frank, 196
Sawyer, Eugene, 47
Schaffer, Jack, 32, 125
Schlafly, Phyllis, 173
Schmidt, John, 141
Schoenberg, Jeff, 107–8
school financing: under Blagojevich, 61, 63, 69–70; Operation Cobra income tax increase (1989) and, 43–48; under Quinn, 156–57; under Rauner, 157–58; tax-swap effort under Edgar, 50–52. *See also* pension plans
Schwarzenegger, Arnold, 204
Scott, Zaldwaynaka "Z," 62
Seidel, Jon, 184
Seith, Alex, x
Senger, Darlene, 101
Service Employees International Union, 100
sexual harassment accusations. *See* #MeToo sexual harassment controversy
Shakman, Michael, 130–31
Shapiro, Sam, 25
Shilts, Gary, 143
shot clock, 36
Silverstein, Deb, 166
Silverstein, Ira, 165–66
Simon, Paul, x, 139, 148, 155
Simon, Seymour, 43
Sixth Illinois Constitutional Convention (1969), ix–x, xx
Smith, Derrick, 158–59
Sneed, Michael, 41
Solis, Danny, 184–86, 222, 236–37
Solski, Jennifer, 195
Speaker of the Illinois House of Representatives: amendatory veto (AV) and, xiii, 91; budgets and (*see* budgets and budgeting); Lee Daniels as (1995–1997), 51, 149, 154; death penalty and,

95–96; federal investigation of the Democratic primary (2016), 179, 186, 188–201; gay marriage legalization in Illinois, 85–87; gun laws in Illinois, 88–91; "Madigan Mystique" and, 2–11, 61, 86, 164, 184, 237; minimum wage and, 94; MJM as House Minority Leader vs., 15–25, 51, 154, 213, 233; MJM as the "Velvet Hammer," 3, 230; MJM loses speakership (1995–97, 2020), xiv, 11, 50–52, 94, 154, 229–30; MJM reelection campaign (2020), 223–30; MJM years as (1983–1994, 1997–2021, ix, x, 2, 4, 25, *112–18*, 213; Operation Cobra income tax increase (1989), 41–48, 73–74; pork-barrel spending and, 155–56, 164, 182; redistricting (*see* redistricting); George Ryan as, xv, 3, 15–25, 18; sexual harassment controversy (*see* #MeToo sexual harassment controversy); shot clock and, 36; tax policy (*see* tax policy); Chris Welch as (2021-), x, 11, 151, 229–30, 233–34; White Sox Midnight Miracle (1988), xiii, 7, 33–40
Spielman, Fran, 184
Stange, Jim, 37, 39
St. Clair, Stacy, 123–24
Steans, Heather, 101
Stephens, Donald, 145
Stevenson, Adlai, III, 43, 105
Stratton, Julianna, 159, 167, 171
Super Tuesdays, 151
sweepstakes gambling, 216

Tabares, Silvana, 134, 166, 233
tax policy: under Blagojevich, 63; under Edgar, xi–xii, 7, 48–52; MJM property tax law practice, 9, 132–33, 164, 184–86, 221–22, 223; Operation Cobra income tax increase (1989), 7, 41–48, 73–74, 82; under Pritzker, 182, 221, 225; property tax cap proposal (1991), xi–xii, 49; under Quinn, 8, 73–79; under Rauner, 79–83, 103–4, 180; under Thompson, 7, 30, 41–48, 73–74, 82, 106
Telcser, Art, 17, 19
Thirteenth Ward Democratic Organization: City Council seat campaign

(2019), 201, 202–9 (*see also* Quinn, Marty); ComEd federal investigation and, 10–11, 134–35, 213–27, 232; fake candidates in primary election (2016), 186–87, 193–97; Jason Gonzalez House candidacy and federal lawsuit, 188, 191–201, 208; Angelica Guerrero-Cuellar as House replacement for MJM, 233; Edward Kodatt as House replacement for MJM, 231–33; David Krupa campaign for City Council seat (2019) and fraud allegations, 203, 205–9; Lisa Madigan campaign for Illinois Attorney General and (2002), 125, 139–43; MJM as Committeeman for the 13th Ward, 4, *112*, 121–23; Marty Quinn as Alderman, 128–29, 163, 166–69, 170, 197, 201–9, 221, 231, 232; Kevin Quinn / Alaina Hampton #MeToo sexual harassment controversy, 163, 166–71, 174, 176, 178, 203, 217, 218–19

Thomas, Robert, 26–27

Thompson, James "Big Jim": election as Republican governor (1976), 137–38; Equal Rights Amendment (ERA) and, 173; Illinois House cutback amendment (1980) and, 16–23, 70, 213; Operation Cobra income tax increase (1989) and, 41–48, 73, 82; pension reform, 105–6; as Republican Governor, xiii, xv, xx, 30–48, 95, 105–6, *112*, 131; tax policy under, 7, 30, 41–48, 73–74, 82, 106; White Sox Midnight Miracle (1988) and, xiii, 7, 29–40

Topinka, Judy Baar, 62–63

Tracy, Jil, 101

Trejo, Olivia, 194

Tristano, Mike, 186

Trump, Donald, 9, 10, 71–72, 149, 224

Trump International Hotel and Tower Chicago, 145

Tuerk, Fred, 36, 37

Turnaround Illinois, 150

Turner, Art, 20, 21

unions: Rauner "Turnaround Agenda" (probusiness) and, 9, 80, 81–82, 94–95, 181, 190, 224. *See also* pension plans

U.S. Equal Employment Opportunity Commission (EEOC), 170

U.S. Equal Rights Amendment, 172–73

U.S. Food and Drug Administration (FDA), 60, 68–69

U.S. Senate: Lisa Madigan as potential candidate, 143, 144; Obama and, xii, 56–59, 65–66, 143, 145, 189; Philip Rock as candidate (1984), x

U.S. Supreme Court: antipatronage case / Rutan decision, 131; Blagojevich appeal and, 71; Illinois redistricting and, 28; misconduct in primary election (2016) and, 200–201; same-sex marriage legalization, 86–87; Second Amendment and, 87

Vadalabene, Sam, 24

Vallas, Paul, 66

Vaught, Adam, 192, 196–97, 199, 208

"Velvet Hammer," MJM as, 3, 230

Vinicky, Amanda, 81, 94

Viverito, Lou, 76

Vrdolyak, Edward, xi

Walgreens, 221

Walker, Dan: as Democratic Governor, 137, 181; in prison, 181

Walker, David Seth, 39–40

Walters, Barbara, 68

Ward, Patrick, 124–26, 128–29

Washington, Harold, xi, xx, 43, 47, 207

Watson, Frank, 61, 64

Welch, Emanuel "Chris": as Illinois Democratic Representative, 223, 228–30; as Illinois House Speaker, x, 11, 151, 228–30, 233–34

Welch, ShawnTe, 228

Wescott, Stacy, 166, 169–71

Wheeler, Charles N., III, ix–xv, xx, 18, 41, 100–101

White, Jesse, 130, 141, 157–58, 196

White Sox Midnight Miracle (1988), xiii, 7, 29–40; Illinois Senate Bill 2202 passage process, 31–40; St. Petersburg, Florida relocation offer, 29–30, 32–34

Whitney, Rich, 63

Wier Vaught, Heather, 67, 168–72, 185, 192

Williams, Ann, 87–88, 227
Willis, Duane "Scott," 155
Willis, Janet, 155
Willis, Kathleen, 227
Wilson, Joe, 24
Wolf, Sam, 36–37
Wong, See Y., 185
Wronski, Richard, 123–24

Wyma, John, 58

Ylisela, James, Jr., 70
Younge, Wyvetter, 39

Zagel, James, 70–71
Zalewski, Mike, 134, 214, 222
Zell, Sam, 150

RAY LONG is a *Chicago Tribune* investigative reporter and a two-time finalist for the Pulitzer Prize. He has covered Michael Madigan and Illinois politics for more than forty years as a journalist writing for the *Chicago Tribune,* Associated Press, *Chicago Sun-Times,* and Peoria *Journal Star* and *The Telegraph* of Alton.

The University of Illinois Press
is a founding member of the
Association of University Presses.

———————————————

Composed in 10.25/14 ITC New Baskerville
with Avenir display
by Lisa Connery
at the University of Illinois Press
Manufactured by Sheridan Books, Inc.

University of Illinois Press
1325 South Oak Street
Champaign, IL 61820-6903
www.press.uillinois.edu